Design
Transactions

Rethinking Information Modelling for a New Material Age

Design Transactions

Rethinking Information Modelling
for a New Material Age

Contents

INTRODUCTIONS

8   **1.1**
Design Transactions
Mette Ramsgaard Thomsen and Martin Tamke

14   **1.2**
Innochain: A Template for Innovative Collaboration
Jan Knippers, Bob Sheil and Mette Ramsgaard Thomsen

22   **1.3**
Design Methodologies: Rethinking Transactions Between the Drawn and the Made
Bob Sheil, Mathilde Marengo and Ulrika Karlsson

30   **1.4**
Perspectives: Transactions and Trajectories
Bob Sheil and Mette Ramsgaard Thomsen

MODELLING STRATEGIES AND NEW WORKFLOWS

42   **2.1**
New Paradigms for Digital Prefabrication in Architecture
Fabian Scheurer and Hanno Stehling

50   **2.2**
Information-Rich Exploration in the Early Design Phase
Zeynep Aksöz

56   **2.3**
Computational Extensibility and Mass Participation in Design
Paul Poinet and Al Fisher

62   **2.4**
Alternative Means of Digital Design Communication
Dimitrie Stefanescu

68   **2.5**
Negotiating Structured Building Information Data
Nathan Miller and David Stasiuk

74   **Research Summary**
Multiple Criteria Design Exploration in the Early Design Phase
Zeynep Aksöz

76   **Research Summary**
Morphogenetic Fluid Dynamics
Angelos Chronis

78   **Research Summary**
Multiple States of Equilibrium for Bending-Active Tensile Structures
Evy L. M. Slabbinck

80   **Research Summary**
Alternative Methods for Data Transaction
Dimitrie Stefanescu

82   **Research Summary**
Integrated Material Practice in Freeform Timber Structures
Tom Svilans

84   **Further Perspectives**
New Workflows and Collaborations
Kenn Clausen, Sean Lineham, Morten Norman Lund, Line Rahbek and Kåre Stokholm Poulsgaard

DESIGN INTEGRATION

92   **3.1**
Design Integration: Global Technological Advancement and Local Culture
In dialogue: Areti Markopoulou and Philip F. Yuan

98   **3.2**
Agency of Material Production Feedback in Architectural Practice
Tom Svilans, Jonas Runberger and Kai Strehlke

106   **3.3**
Acoustic Wall: Computational and Robotic Design Integration of Four Primary Generators
Isak Worre Foged, Anke Pasold and Mads Brath Jensen

114   **3.4**
Coreless Filament Winding: From Academia to Practice
James Solly, Jan Knippers and Moritz Dörstelmann

122 **3.5**
All That Is Porous: Practising
Cross-Disciplinary Design Thinking
Vasily Sitnikov

128 **Research Summary**
Bend&Block: A Passive Form-Giving Strategy
Efilena Baseta

130 **Research Summary**
Adaptive Robotic Carving
Giulio Brugnaro

132 **Research Summary**
How to Effectively Collaborate at Scale
in a Connected Digital Environment
Paul Poinet

134 **Research Summary**
Ice Formwork: Challenging the Sustainable
Production of Non-Regular Geometry
in Concrete
Vasily Sitnikov

136 **Research Summary**
Virtual Prototyping Tools for a Winding-Based
Composite Fabrication Technique
James Solly

138 **Further Perspectives**
Data in Design Practice
Sean Hanna

NOVEL STRATEGIES FOR MATERIALISATION

144 **4.1**
Rewired Engineering: The Impact of
Customisation and Interoperability on Design
Edoardo Tibuzzi

150 **4.2**
Drone Spraying on Light Formwork for Mud Shells
Stephanie Chaltiel, Maite Bravo,
Diederik Veenendaal and Gavin Sayers

158 **4.3**
Industrialising Concrete 3D Printing:
Three Case Studies
Nadja Gaudillière, Justin Dirrenberger,
Romain Duballet, Charles Bouyssou,
Alban Mallet, Philippe Roux and Mahriz Zakeri

166 **4.4**
Integration of Material and Fabrication
Affordances within the Design Workflow
Giulio Brugnaro, Silvan Oesterle, Sean Hanna,
Peter Scully and Bob Sheil

174 **4.5**
Making Timberdome
Christopher Robeller and Valentin Viezens

180 **4.6**
Robots for Skill Digitisation
Johannes Braumann

188 **Research Summary**
Building with Earth and Drones
Stephanie Chaltiel

190 **Research Summary**
Information Modelling for Assembly Planning,
Sequencing and Optimisation
Ayoub Lharchi

192 **Research Summary**
Digital Clay: Hybrid Manufacturing
for Automotive Design
Arthur Prior

194 **Research Summary**
Flectofold: From Academic Research
to Architectural Application
Saman Saffarian

196 **Research Summary**
Concrete Deposition: Choreographing Flow
Helena Westerlind

198 **Further Perspectives**
Performative Materials and Systems,
and Additive Manufacturing Futures
Johannes Braumann and Isak Worre Foged

REFLECTIONS

206 **5.1**
Innochain: External Perspectives
Mark Burry and Christoph Gengnagel
in conversation with Anja Jonkhans

212 **BIOGRAPHIES**

223 **ACKNOWLEDGEMENTS**

224 **COLOPHON**

Introductions

1.1 INTRODUCTIONS

Design Transactions

Mette Ramsgaard Thomsen and Martin Tamke
Centre for Information Technology and Architecture (CITA), the Royal Danish Academy of Fine Arts, Schools of Architecture, Design and Conservation

Design Transactions asks what the future of building culture will be. It asks how new, shared computational platforms are changing our disciplines, examining how the digitisation of tools affects the way architecture is conceived designed and made. Questions arise as we enter a new era of advanced modelling, informed by new concepts of Big Data computing, cloud-based collaboration and steered robotic fabrication: What might collaboration look like in the future? How can knowledge across the design change be interfaced and fed back for a more informed and materially-sensitive practice? What is the future for automation in architecture?

Today, computational design is ubiquitous in building practice; the tools of design, analysis, specification and manufacture are now primarily digital. While tools vary in sophistication and programmability, they share a common digital foundation. This makes them fundamentally open to interfacing, which, in turn, has led to the conception of a digital chain via which information is communicated, connected and extended across industry partnerships. This highly interdisciplinary vision has framed building practice for the last 15 years (Kolarevic, 2003).

Yet, despite this, the building industry remains unable to reap the benefits of technological progress. Practice remains fractured, and issues of ownership, discipline-based silo-thinking and legal proprietary boundaries continue to obstruct meaningful sharing and innovation. This paralysis has significant consequences, including the inability to effect the urgently-needed restructuring of building culture, which has contributed to a profound loss of productivity. The construction industry is, famously, one of the least efficient industries, having hit a plateau in production growth over the last 20 years. Where construction-related spending accounts for 13%

1 & 2. *Practice Futures – Building Design for a new Material Age* Innochain exhibition showcasing research by the programme's 15 Early-Stage Researchers, Meldahl Smedie Exhibition Hall, KADK, 2018. Photos: Anders Ingvartsen.

1
2

3. Prototype Canopy Component. Elytra Filament Pavilion. Exhibited by James Solly, ITKE. Photo: Anders Ingvartsen.

of the world's GDP, the sector's annual growth has increased by only 1% over the past 20 years (Barbosa et al., 2017). As we encounter new contexts of environmental crisis, resource scarcity and climate change, these consequences expand beyond the economic realm and into the ethical. It is therefore imperative that we find our way across the constraints that limit the potential of the digital chain, to deepen its positive impact and extend its disciplinary reach. The urgent call for innovation is trifold: to identify new methods to optimise our building practices and enable us to rethink the resources, energy consumption and climate adaptation of our buildings; to challenge the way knowledge is produced, shared and realised in design; and to profoundly rethink the technologies of fabrication, moving us from essentially subtractive practices to additive ones.

Computational design is continually evolving, and new tools present new opportunities. Digitisation and the creation of new methods to optimise construction processes and material performance remain key to benefitting from the innovation taking place (Ramsgaard Thomsen, 2019). The first generation of computation focused on developing shared industry standards, such as the Building Information Modelling (BIM) paradigm and the IFC standards, as well as maturing design-to-fabrication protocols that enabled individualised and mass-customised fabrication (Klinger, 2008). Knowledge transfer across the fields of Big Data, advanced sensing and robotic steering is challenging how we understand these models. Contemporary practice is reassessing what kind of information the model should contain, how it is shared and how it interfaces and back-propagates or 'handshakes' with other models, thus refining and reshaping the digital chain.

This fundamental re-examination of what advanced computation affords is also apparent in the continuous rethinking of fabrication. If the first generation of digitisation mainly focused on known material systems, contextualised by existing industrial processes, then a new generation of computational design research understands fabrication as a means of challenging the material practices of building cultures. The interfacing of a host of new and old materials, such as high-performance fibres (Ramsgaard Thomsen, 2015; Menges, 2015), metal plates (Nicholas, 2016), concrete (Sitnikov, 2014) and earthen materials (Šamec, et al., 2019), presents new alternatives to how we understand building systems.

Design Perspectives

Design Transactions captures the cutting edge of these innovations. Connecting research in academia and in practice, the book presents case studies examining the future methodologies and underlying paradigms of an information-rich design practice.

The projects showcased here challenge our thinking of how the practices of design, analysis and fabrication can intersect, and the perspective is purposefully wide. By engaging the breadth of the design chain and its disciplines, we ask how opportunities for advanced computation, integrated simulation and performance evaluation, human–computer interaction and robotic fabrication can create tangible differences in the way we build. What is at stake here is, on the one hand, the future of the design model and the collaborative nature of building practice, and, on the other, the way we understand our fabrication culture and the material systems with which we build. By expanding the simple BIM approach with more complex requirements – to engage and capitalise on analysis, to prototype new cloud-based communication platforms and to interface automation and robotic fabrication – we explore the nature of a new design practice that can handle data-rich design inquiries, enable collaboration and manage the complex and cyclical nature of feedback.

Foundations

Design Transactions takes its point of departure from the cross-disciplinary research network Innochain. Innochain is a European Union Horizon 2020 Innovation Training Network that brings together six internationally recognised academic research facilities (with a focus on computational design in architecture and engineering)
and 14 pioneering industry partners from architecture, engineering, design software development and fabrication. The aim of Innochain is to train a new generation of interdisciplinary practitioners with special inter-sector knowledge that traverses academia and industry on the specifics of the expanded digital design chain. With a focus on new computational design strategies, advanced design-integrated analysis and robotic fabrication systems, Innochain has established 15 new research collaborations across multiple disciplines and practices. The research horizon of these projects is intentionally wide, spanning from the applied and industry-ready context to the speculative. All projects have a foothold in academia and engage with different industry partners, creating novel relationships across the value chain. Some employ industry-based case studies for research investigation; some use industry partners' design information as empirical data; and others retain a speculative stance, asking 'blue sky' questions on how practices might change when engaging new technologies.

As a result, the work produced via the Innochain network is extremely diverse. The projects ask what new computational methods there are, from the examination of design interfaces for interdisciplinary collaboration to open cloud-based communication platforms, and novel means of integrating computational fluid dynamics (CFD) simulation to the Big Data strategies of machine learning for design investigation. The work presented here also explores the materialisation of architecture, developing novel ways of casting concrete with ice formwork, large-scale additive manufacture with concrete, clay, and drone-spraying mud structures. From their respective vantage points, the authors ask how advanced computational technologies can enable sustainable, informed and materially-smart design solutions.

What the projects have in common is an experimental design-led research method focused on the development of either prototypical applications – demonstrating new computational paradigms – or full-scale material prototypes testing advanced fabrication systems. With its emphasis on prototyping, whether digital or physical, Innochain engages directly with the investigated methods and technologies, positioning the research inquiries within a network of interconnected realms of expertise that make up architectural and engineering design practice. The experiments generate shared empirical data that can be tested, analysed and evaluated by the different research teams across the network, producing results that, in turn, can be appropriated and implemented within the industrial partnership.

Expanding Information Modelling

Design Transactions shares some of the primary research findings of Innochain, while presenting the wider context of these inquiries. It also brings together the most prolific keynote presentations and peer-reviewed papers from the Innochain conference 'Expanding Information Modelling' (November 2018, Danish Architecture Centre, Copenhagen). With three core themes providing the structure for the book – 'Advanced Modelling Strategies and New Workflows', 'Design Integration' and 'Material Strategies' – the key propositions emerging within the field are presented. 'Advanced Modelling Strategies and New Workflows' collects case studies that focus on the analysis, synthesis and communication of data in design thinking, and it discusses how new flows of information can be established and integrated with design practice. 'Design Integration' focuses on the emergence of hybrid practices in the building industry and discusses how this digital chain can be structured, how collaboration between partners at different ends of the design chain can be productive and how early design thinking with structural and material information can lead to smarter design solutions. 'Material Strategies', meanwhile, questions the potential of computer-controlled design-to-fabrication strategies to effect efficient, environmentally safe and sustainable building practices. The chapter discusses how these new workflows can be structured and how they present a rethinking of the relationship between man and machine, radically questioning established processes.

Each chapter is framed by an introductory keynote piece. Here, reflections are brought together to explore design futures. Fabian Scheurer and Hanno Stehling of Design-to-Production discuss the design and manufacture of the Headquarters for Swatch. They reflect on their work on complex-form solid timberframe buildings and how feedback between the design phase and fabrication led to new design opportunities. Philip F. Yuan, Professor of Tongji University in Shanghai and principal of Archi-Union, and Areti Markopoulou, Academic Director at the Institute for Advanced Architecture of Catalonia (IAAC), discuss how computationally-steered design and manufacturing technologies impact on local resources, culture and crafts. And Edoardo Tibuzzi from AKT II examines how computational design is challenging and changing engineering practices.

The keynotes are followed by contributions from practice and project presentations, ranging from consolidated large-scale design offices with dedicated research groups to comparatively young, small-scale practices with a high risk–high gain research investment. With a strong collaborative perspective, these presentations ask profound questions regarding how we understand collaboration, what infrastructures are needed to support real design feedback and how formalised material understanding can support robotic fabrication systems.

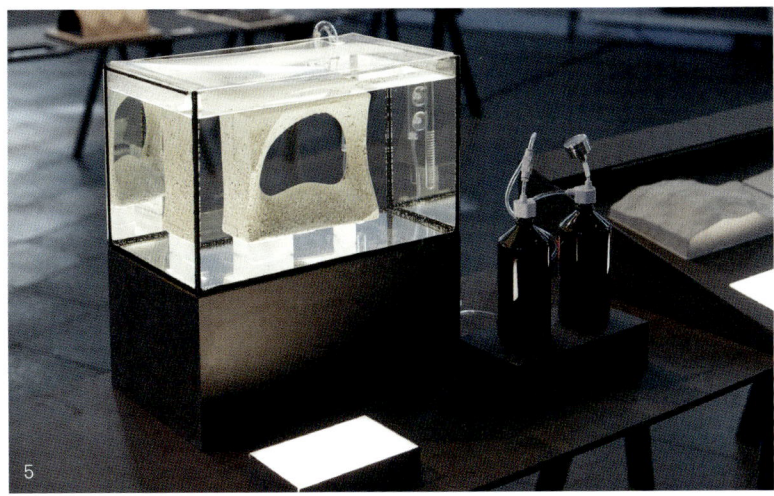

5

Conclusion

Design Transactions is intended to offer readers a sense of the future direction of computational design across building practice, with case studies of new collaborative practice enabled by computational advances that radically rethinks what the digital chain can be. While the array of examples presented here remain prototypical, they are actively building the kind of foundational methods and technologies that are needed for a sector-wide change, reshaping how partnerships within building practice can work together.

This volume has been made possible thanks to the many contributions from the various networks it brings together. We are thankful for the collaborative effort and generous knowledge-sharing of all the contributors, as well as the invaluable input of the wider Innochain network. These include industry partners: Foster + Partners; White; BIG; Henn; ROK; Cloud 9; BuroHappold; str.ucture; Design-to-Production; Smith Innovation; Blumer-Lehmann; S-Form; Robert McNeel & Associates; and FIBR, as well as the associated partnership, Robots. IO; and the academic partnerships: CITA, KADK; The Bartlett School of Architecture, UCL; ITKE, University of Stuttgart; the Institute of Architecture (IoA), School of Architecture, KTH; and IAAC. We are also grateful for the facilitation provided by EU Horizon 2020 Marie Skłodowska-Curie actions, together with various industry partnerships and institutions, all of which have helped to make *Design Transactions* a reality. Finally, we thank BLOXHUB Science Forum for its collaboration on the Innochain Conference.

References

Barbosa, F., Woetzel, J., Mischke, J., Ribeirinho, M.J., Sridhar, M., Parsons, M., Bertram, N. and Brown, S., 2017, *Reinventing Construction: A Route to Higher Productivity*, Washington DC, McKinsey Global Institute.

Klinger, K.R., 2008, 'Relations: Information Exchange in Designing and Making Architecture' in Kolarevic, B. and Klinger, K. (eds.), 2016, *Manufacturing Material Effects: Rethinking Design and Making in Architecture*, London, Routledge, p.25–36.

Kolarevic, B., 2003, 'Digital Morphogenesis' in *Architecture in the Digital Age: Design and Manufacture*, London, Spon Press, p.13.

Menges, A. and Knippers, J., 2015, 'Fibrous Tectonics' in *Architectural Design*, Vol. 85, No. 5, p.40–47.

Nicholas, P., Zwierzycki, M., Stasiuk, D., Nørgaard, E.C., Leinweber, S. and Ramsgaard Thomsen, M., 2016, 'Adaptive Meshing for Bi-directional Information Flows: A Multi-Scale Approach to Integrating Feedback between Design, Simulation, and Fabrication' in Adriaenssens, S., Gramazio, F., Kohler, M., Menges, A. and Pauly, M. (eds.), *Advances in Architectural Geometry 2016*, Zürich, vdf Hochschulverlag AG an der ETH Zürich, p.260–273.

Ramsgaard Thomsen, M., 2019, 'Radical Cross-Disciplinarity: Laying the Foundations for New Material Practices' in *Construction Robotics*. https://doi.org/10.1007/s41693-019-00023-7 (accessed 16 December 2019).

Ramsgaard Thomsen, M., Tamke, M., Holden Deleuran, A., Friis Tinning, I., Evers, H.L., Gengnagel, C. and Schmeck, M., 2015, 'Hybrid Tower, Designing Soft Structures' in Thomsen, M.R., Tamke, M., Gengnagel, C., Faircloth, B. and Scheurer, F. (eds.), *Modelling Behaviour: Design Modelling Symposium 2015*, Berlin, Springer, p.87–99.

Šamec, E., Srivastava, A. and Chaltiel, S., 2019, 'Light Formwork for Earthen Monolithic Shells' in *Proceedings of the International Conference on Sustainable Materials, Systems and Structures (SMSS2019): Challenges in Design and Management of Structures* (conference paper), Rovinj, Croatia.

Sitnikov, V., 2014, 'Monolith Translucent Lattice' in *Proceedings of ACADIA 14: Design Agency, Projects of the 34th Annual Conference of the Association for Computer Aided Design in Architecture*, Los Angeles, p.263–264.

4. Innochain conference 'Expanding Information Modelling', Danish Architecture Centre, 2018. Photo: Philip Ørneborg.

5. Ice Formwork de-moulding process demonstrator, Vasily Sitnikov, KTH. Photo: Anders Ingvartsen.

1.2 INTRODUCTIONS

Innochain: A Template for Innovative Collaboration

Jan Knippers
Institute of Building Structures and Structural Design (ITKE) at the University of Stuttgart
Bob Sheil
The Bartlett School of Architecture, UCL
Mette Ramsgaard Thomsen
Centre for Information Technology and Architecture (CITA), the Royal Danish Academy of Fine Arts, Schools of Architecture, Design and Conservation

Education, research and practice have evolved cyclically within the disciplines of architecture and engineering. Visions are in continual dialogue with challenges, experiments with experiences, plans with projects, prototypes with constructs, and theories with practicalities. Connecting each of these cycles is a constellation of nodes and flows, with centres of excellence and concentrations of activity. Intellectual and physical mobility across this matrix is oscillating, and the resulting consequences are played out in the perpetual adaptation of our built environment – in cities, villages, ports and infrastructures – every minute, every day, in actuality and simulation. Here, the scene is set for how conventional research exchange between academia and industry has been challenged by the Innochain project. We depict the fundamental role that the seamless relationship between new forms of practice, innovative academic laboratories and pioneering new industries plays in tackling the built environment's greatest challenges.

Innochain: Building Innovation in the Extended Digital Chain

Starting in late 2015, Innochain established a unique international research environment examining how advances in digital design tools challenge building culture, enabling more sustainable, informed and materially-smart design solutions. As a network of six academic institutions, 14 industry partners, and 15 early-stage researchers (ESRs), it created a structured training programme focused on the supervision of individual research projects, an inter-sector secondment programme and collective research events including workshop-seminars, colloquia, summer schools and

1. The new digital chain in an extended material practice, Innochain. Image: CITA.

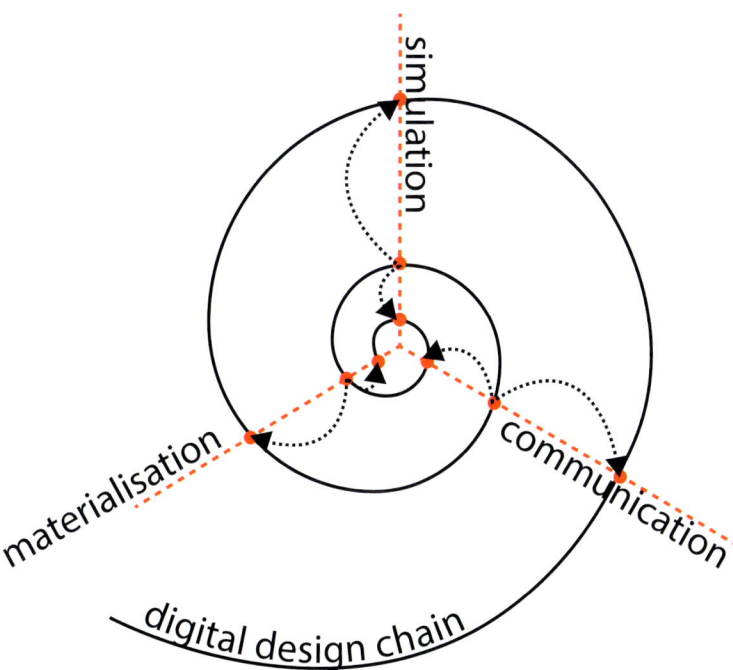

1

research courses for the ESRs to share knowledge and learn new skills. With each researcher positioned between strong innovative research practice and influential industrial impact, a new generation of interdisciplinary researchers has emerged, effecting change in the way that we consider, design and build our physical environment.

Innochain's philosophy can be understood as a field of an infinite spiral intersected by lines of concentration that cut square to the spiral field, generating recurrent intersections that revolve and evolve knowledge and its trajectory. Defining the spiral as the chain from design to construction, Innochain identified three intersecting axes of research enquiry and disruption that underpin its mission: communicating, simulating and materialising design. On this basis, these axes and spirals have stimulated feedback between processes to develop holistic and integrated design methods that interface advanced modelling and fabrication technologies.

A Matter of Urgency

The scientifically-informed goals of the United Nations Framework Convention on Climate Change demand that we drastically reduce the consumption of finite – especially fossil – resources for building construction and operations and thus fundamentally rethink the way we design and build architecture. Current rates of world population growth require that we build approximately the same living space over the next 30 years as we have to date, which will require a doubling of the entire building stock that currently exists. To do this, we must significantly increase the productivity of our construction processes and devise new methods and processes that reconcile architectural diversity and quality with automated prefabrication, while not repeating the failings of past attempts at prefabrication from 50 or 60 years ago.

It is a paradoxical challenge to build twice as much living space, using far fewer resources, in a way that is cleaner than ever before and in less time. If this is to be achieved, the productivity and ecological efficiency of building systems must be optimised in a parallel and mutually influential process, and this is only half the task. Necessary measures can only be successful if they are in line with culturally adapted and socially accepted designs for our buildings and environments. It is for this reason that solutions for a scientifically identified crisis cannot be solely addressed through science. It requires integrated solutions that are jointly rooted in science and design and also relate to culture, politics and economics.

An Unprecedented Challenge

The climate crisis penetrates every facet of the built environment, from its modes of experience to its mechanisms of education; from its lines of enquiry to its pace of development and delivery; and from the needs of initial occupancy to the uncertainty of its use beyond initial occupancy. Underpinning these considerations is a profound shortage of operational skill in the construction sector, where an abundance of advanced tooling and computational capability outweighs the workforce's ability to deliver. In parallel, there is an equal demand for a post-disciplinary matrix of cooperative and integrated expertise that operates in a realm of heightened knowledge exchange and holistic research.

At a global scale, conventional research culture is struggling to cope with these pressures. Aside from prominent exceptions, to which we will turn later, much of today's research is predominantly organised within disciplinary silos. Building sciences have a tendency to limit themselves to measuring incremental change – improvement – among existing planning methods, manufacturing processes and building systems in 'tested', often neat, conditions. Success criteria are logic-based and recognised or accepted by means of peer review in established journals and esteemed scientific awards, where discourse on social or historical relevance rarely takes place. On the other hand, design research is often misunderstood as being non-scientific and 'weak', and is dismissed as playing a negligible role in innovation and advancement. Here, it is argued that research developed within a single discipline will

2. La Seine Musicale, Paris. Architects, Shigeru Ban and Jean de Gastines. Fabrication: Design-to-Production. Photo: Design-to-Production.

3. Bespoke Workstation by Arthur Prior, The Bartlett School of Architecture, UCL.

inevitably be limited and incapable of fully addressing multifaceted problems that are not only technical, but social, cultural and economic.

Furthermore, if climate change is teaching us anything, it is that its cause – and, more so, its consequences – are not yet entirely understood. It is a deeply complex set of conditions, rooted in global human behaviours that are far from simple to 'solve'. This crisis emanates as much from cultural and political values as it does from industrial or agricultural processes. In this regard, design research as transdisciplinary, open to contribution, collaboration, context and wide-ranging scrutiny by multiple communities of practice, is a vital strength. *Design Transactions: Rethinking Information Modelling for a New Material Age* is thus shared on the premise that radical innovations are needed in all areas of technology and society, not only in the practice of planning and building but also in how we exchange and develop ideas and infrastructure for sustainable and resilient environments.

A Change in Approach

In response to these matters and more, new approaches to teaching and research are required that place collaborative working and hybrid expertise at the centre of knowledge acquisition and transferability. Innovation through research and education cannot happen solely within singular disciplines or institutions, but will emerge at the interfaces where different cultures, interests and perspectives are directly confronted with each other. Such new approaches require us to cross boundaries between academic disciplines in physical and social sciences and in humanities, while also bridging the gap between basic and applied research. Only approaches such as these will lead to discourse that questions established methods and enables radically new outcomes to emerge.

Architecture and engineering are uniquely placed to face and coordinate this challenge together, with both disciplines underpinning each Innochain project so that boundaries between them are erased. Their shared domain is design research, and its core competence lies in the synthesis and integration of the most diverse and often divergent requirements in the built environment. Design research has the power to transfer scientific, historical and cultural knowledge into artefacts that can be experienced, thus simultaneously initiating expert and public discourse on innovation and its trajectory. Design research is precisely the core competence and potential that is needed by science and industry to resolve future built-environment problems, offering

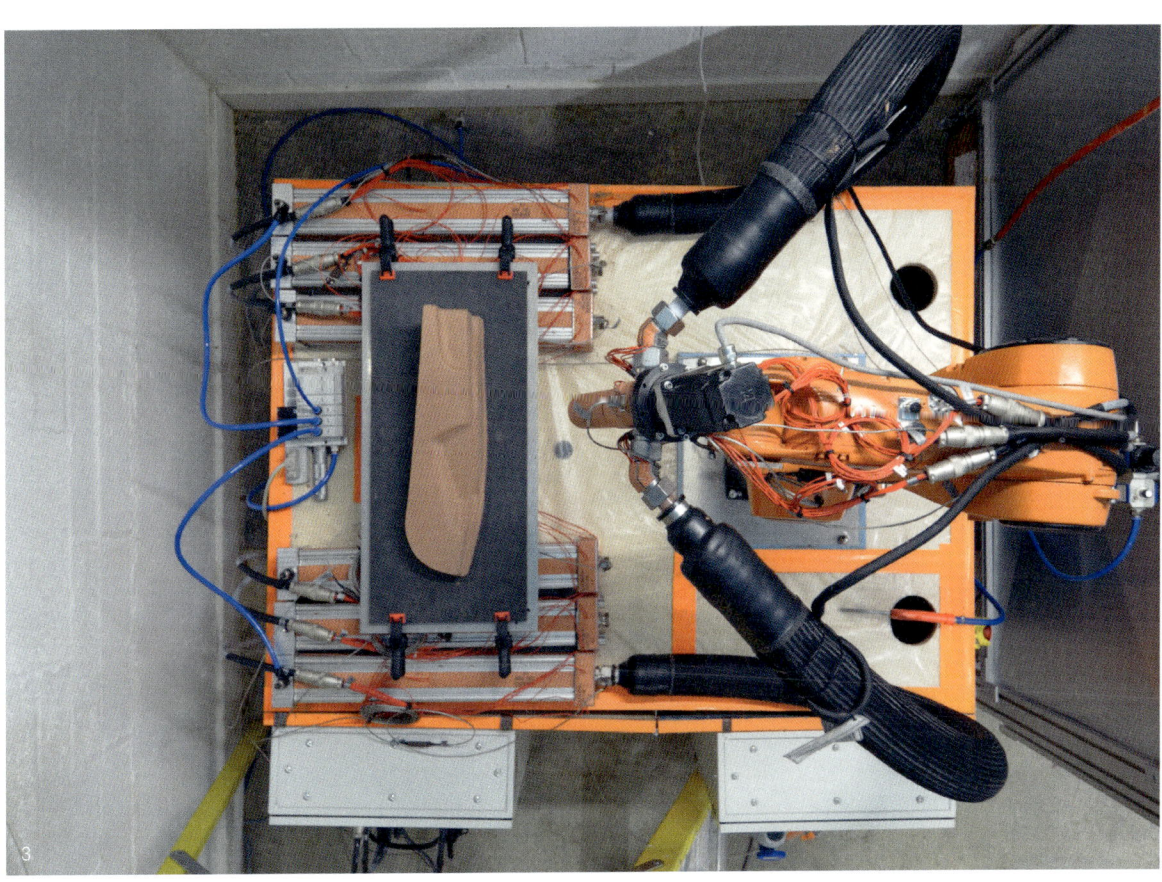

orientation in terms of content and organisation in terms of structure. In this sense, the Innochain network becomes a template for transnational research, industry and practice partnership.

A Collaborative Consortium

All of the six academic partners from six European countries not only have different professional and cultural backgrounds in the realm of architecture and engineering, but they also represent different modes, scales and outlooks on research, education and engagement with industry. From independent academies of experimental design in culturally-charged cities such as Barcelona's IAAC, to large, technically-orientated public universities in national industrial heartlands, such as the University of Stuttgart; and from internationally-renowned labs within national centres of excellence such as CITA at the Royal Danish Academy of Fine Arts, Copenhagen, to acclaimed departments within large multidisciplinary universities, such as The Bartlett School of Architecture, UCL, the Innochain network enjoys a vast array of parallel networks at its disposal. This framework is a backdrop that merges artistic creativity with engineering and manufacturing analysis.

In both architecture and engineering, established national and international funding is characterised by a strict separation between academic and industrial applied research. As a result, dynamic and everyday exchange is challenging, and it is often left to the market to decide on the viability of new propositions. This vulnerability risks the promising results of basic research not succeeding – even if successfully tested in an academic context – as there is no corresponding support for the transfer to practice. In this regard, Innochain has offered a new model by involving partners from industry in scientific development from the outset, each investing in research time as a necessary risk as basic as investment in capital and human resources. Each of the 14 industrial partners involved in Innochain has a very distinct background. But, together, their expertise covers the entire spectrum of architectural production, from internationally-operating architectural firms, such as Foster + Partners, BIG, BuroHappold and Henn, to medium-scale experimental architectural or engineering offices, such as ROK and Cloud 9, specialised construction companies, such as Design-to-Production and Blumer-Lehmann, and specialised services, such as McNeel, str.ucture and S-Form. Innochain's projects are thus based on the parallel and mutually influential development of design methods and manufacturing processes. This approach contradicts the strict separation of planning and execution, which is the basis of today's mainstream construction practice. Tendering processes, allocation of tasks and warranty are strictly organised along this dividing line. Innochain defined three fundamental research strands as intersections to the spiral (fig.1) to tackle these obstacles from the outset.

Intersection 1: Communicating Design

Current methods for communicating domain-specific knowledge in building practice assume disciplinary separation and discretisation of design control. In recent years, state-of-the-art research has questioned these professional boundaries by creating shared methods that integrate design and simulation. These methods either remain data-heavy – and, therefore, unintuitive and at odds with design creativity – or they borrow from unrelated fields such as the film industry. Such methods

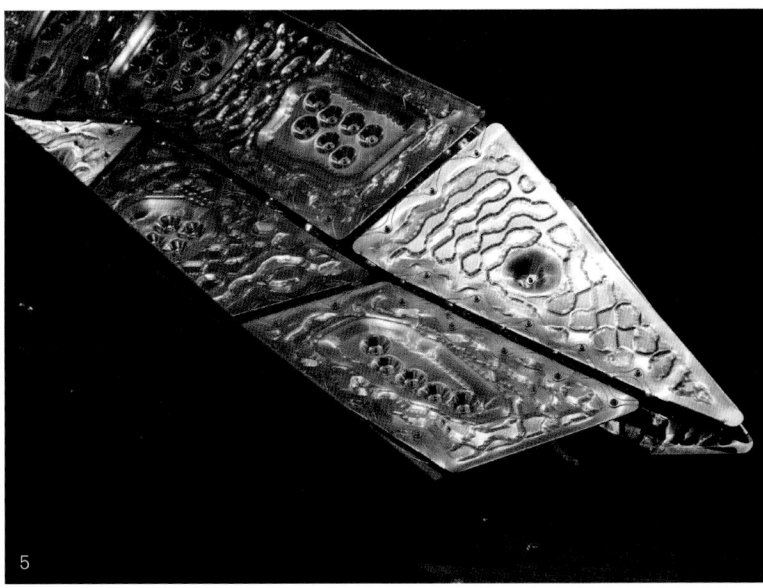

4. ICD/ITKE BUGA Wood Pavilion.
© ICD/ITKE, University of Stuttgart.

5. A Bridge Too Far by CITA at the Royal Danish Academy of Fine Art. Photo: Anders Ingvartsen

offer potential for innovative links between structural simulation, material development and design modelling. Integrating isogeometric analysis, for example, allows us to address issues of disciplinary collaboration by enabling interfacing of verified high-end Finite Element Analysis (FEA) with standard CAD design tools. Integrating material simulation allows us to address issues of design-phase integration by interfacing early-stage design development with material analysis and the activation of material performance, while integrating building physics for performance control enables us to extend the simulation and activation of material performance into the control of adaptable structures in real time. Innochain was thus charged with developing alternative means to communicate, measure and examine how complex design solutions with multiple criteria could be managed and communicated with non-expert stakeholders across the design chain. Tasks carried out at this intersection included:

- **Integrating isogeometric analysis.** Academic Lead: Institute for Building Structures and Structural Design (ITKE) at the University of Stuttgart. Industry Partners: BIG, McNeel.
- **Integrating material performance.** Academic Lead: Centre for Information Technology in Architecture (CITA), Royal Danish Academy of Fine Arts. Industry Partners: Blumer-Lehmann, White Arkitekter.
- **Integrating building physics for performance control.** Academic Lead: Institute for Advanced Architecture of Catalonia (IAAC). Industry Partners: McNeel, Foster + Partners.
- **Multi-criteria optimisation in early design phase.** Academic Lead: University of Applied Arts Vienna. Industry Partners: str.ucture, BIG.
- **Alternative means to communicate measure.** Academic Lead: The Bartlett School of Architecture, UCL. Industry Partner: HENN.

Intersection 2: Simulation for Design

Simulation for design has significant implications for the pace and effectiveness of iterative information as well as fabrication outcomes. Virtual Common methods for simulation in the built environment assume single-scale engagement across separate phases and exclude the simulation of material and fabrication processes. Recent research identifies new opportunities for simulation to link the design of material with the design of structures. This creates new implications for material deployment that necessitate new methods for analysing, specifying and controlling fabrication.

Following this path, a number of Innochain projects examine how simulation can be used as a means to cross between scales and synthesise material performances with machine-driven processes. Multi-scalar modelling and the simulation of anisotropic material performance, for instance, offer a design framework for the innovative use of known materials. Simulation can also be used as a tool for understanding production processes for the purpose of trialling innovative material configuration, such as fibre-reinforced polymers. Simulating concrete formwork offers the potential to examine the interdependencies in casting processes between the hydraulic forces of the liquid material and the formwork that counterbalances them, while innovative simulation of robotic feedback reveals novel digital fabrication strategies that may incorporate real-time feedback and mechanical or compositional changes in the material. Tasks carried out in this intersection included:

- **Multi-scalar modelling for building design.** Academic Lead: Centre for Information Technology in Architecture (CITA), Danish Royal Academy of Fine Arts. Industry Partners: BuroHappold.
- **Simulating anisotropic material.** Academic Lead: University of Applied Arts Vienna. Industry Partners: Cloud 9, Blumer-Lehmann.
- **Virtual prototyping, fibre-reinforced polymers.** Academic Lead: ITKE at the University of Stuttgart. Industry partners: S-Form.
- **Simulating concrete formwork.** Academic Lead: KTH Royal Institute of Technology. Industry Partners: BuroHappold, White Arkitekter.
- **Simulating robotic feedback.** Academic Lead: The Bartlett School of Architecture, UCL. Industry partners: ROK, Foster + Partners.

Intersection 3: Materialising Design

Current methods for materialisation within the building industry are overwhelmingly based on mass production. They rely on the standardisation of material and fabrication to afford control and optimise material use. With digitisation, these methods have become outdated and new models for material optimisation have emerged. Where subtractive digital fabrication techniques have matured and been applied to realise complex buildings, recent research efforts utilise bespoke machines or industrial robots as general fabrication tools for additive fabrication to innovate mass-customised materials with designed performances.

Innochain's focus in this domain focuses on trialling fabrication and planning methods for new designed materials that embed material optimisation within their composition. Concrete printing investigates how printing technology eliminates the need for formwork to create a more variable and precise concrete tectonic. Material gradient fibre-reinforced polymer (FRP) and applied robot-controlled material deposition investigates how fabrication processes grade material deployment for the purpose of varying structural and environmental properties. Design for manufacture and assembly (DfMA) develops innovative planning processes that interface new material practises with the requirements of industrial fabrication, transferring material and planning processes from the factory to onsite production. Tasks carried out at this intersection included:

- **Concrete printing.** Academic Lead: KTH Royal Institute of Technology. Industry Partners: Foster + Partners.
- **Material gradient FRP.** Academic Lead: ITKE at the University of Stuttgart. Industry Partners: str.ucture and S-Form.
- **Applied robot-controlled material deposition.** Academic Lead: The Bartlett School of Architecture, UCL. Industry Partners: Foster + Partners, BuroHappold.
- **Design for manufacture and assembly.**

Academic Lead: CITA, Danish Royal Academy of Fine Arts. Industry Partners: Design-to-Production, Blumer-Lehmann.
- **Small-scale robotic manufacturing for large-scale buildings.** Academic Lead: IAAC. Industry Partners: Cloud 9, ROK.

Innochain: A Template for Research and Practice Collaboration

All Innochain participants, including academics, industry partners, research fellows and their respective project associates, have been engaged in the project's fundamental aim of contributing to interdisciplinary and multi-sector operations across the digital chain. Focusing on innovation in practice has meant that research has not been limited to technological innovation but has also explored the potential of novel implementation of known tools and processes to create new products and solutions offering capability to address the sector's primary challenges. In this regard, the means through which we mutually transact our information and share our expertise – be it the adaptability of modelling information, the analysis of material performance or the integration of *as-built* with *as-designed* data – are fundamental to building an environment for the future that is sustainable, resilient, culturally enriching and diverse in its experience.

Bibliography

Knippers, J., 2013, 'From Model Thinking to Process Design' in *Architectural Design*, Vol. 83, No. 2, p.74–81.

Knippers, J., 2017, 'The Limits of Simulation: Towards a New Culture of Architectural Engineering' in *Technology, Architecture + Design*, Vol. 1, No. 2, p.155–162.

Knippers, J. and Speck, T., 2012, 'Design and Construction Principles in Nature and Architecture' in *Bioinspiration & Biomimetics*, Vol. 7, No. 1.

Menges, A. and Knippers, J., 2015, 'Fibrous Tectonics' in *Architectural Design*, Vol. 85, No. 5, p.40–47.

Sheil, R., 2005, 'Transgression from Drawing to Making' in *Architectural Research Quarterly*, Vol. 9, No. 1, p.20–32.

Sheil, R. (ed.), 2012, *Manufacturing the Bespoke: Making and Prototyping Architecture*, London, Wiley.

Sheil, R., Glynn, R., Menges, A. and Skavara, M. (eds.). 2017, *Fabricate 2017: Rethinking Design and Construction*, London, UCL Press.

6. Bespoke Workstation for Roboforming by Cristina Garza, Design for Manufacture student, The Bartlett School of Architecture, UCL.

1.3 INTRODUCTIONS

Design Methodologies: Rethinking Transactions Between the Drawn and the Made

Bob Sheil
The Bartlett School of Architecture, UCL
Mathilde Marengo
Institute for Advanced Architecture of Catalonia (IAAC), Universitat Politècnica de Catalunya
Ulrika Karlsson
KTH Royal Institute of Technology, Stockholm

Introduction

Bob Sheil
The Bartlett School of Architecture, UCL

Neither architects nor engineers tend to make buildings, instead they make information that is used by others in the production of buildings and the built environment. As an instruction to make, design data differs in its intent, accuracy, and role in the process of making, and systems tasked with the challenge of making will remake design data as a rehearsal for manufacture and as a means to verify what was made and what instructions it followed. Rather than act in partnership and union, the construction industry is fraught with obstacles and barriers that prevent the evolutionary flow of data, instead imposing a stop and start and highly inefficient rhythm.

Design Transactions: Rethinking Information Modelling for a New Material Age gathers projects that seek to intervene, challenge and innovate in this trade. They share an experimental research-by-design methodology focussing on design-led physical experimentation and full-scale prototyping. This emphasis allows the researcher to engage directly with the investigated techniques and technologies moving along the digital chain from design and analysis to specification and fabrication. Such an integrated approach positions each research enquiry within a network of interconnected expertise and practice that collaborates between academic, industry, and practice, providing the opportunity for research teams across the network to share tested, analysed and evaluated results.

Design as a method of enquiry is a reflective practice in which the researcher engages in a dual mode of reflecting on action and through action (Schön, 1983).

Scientifically, each physical experiment acts as a material research enquiry (Duits, 2003) by which the concepts and technologies of the research enquiries are evaluated. Moving between the exterior and the interior of making, design creates a conversation between the dissective action of analysis and critical assessment and the creative action of proposition and result. The method is relevant for design-led research in architecture and engineering as it ties design creativity to research investigation. Building practice has been described as a wicked problem, in which the 'information needed to understand the problem depends on one's idea for solving it' (Beim and Ramsgaard Thomsen, 2011). Design is therefore an active process by which the designer develops the dimensionality of solution in context of a given problem. Solutions are assessed not absolutely as true or false, but rather qualitatively as better or worse. To employ a research-by-design methodology therefore allows the individual research projects to engage with the solution-led processes of creative trouble-shooting that characterise the design process. From here, the discussion is taken up by Mathilde Marengo from the Institute for Advanced Architecture of Catalonia (IAAC), Universitat Politècnica de Catalunya, and Ulrika Karlsson of The Royal Institute of Technology (KTH), Stockholm.

1. Robotic fabrication and assembly of the Digital Urban Orchard that combines solar/wind shape optimisation, structural logics, the robotic fabrication constraints, together with in-situ manual assembly. Developed in IAAC's Open Thesis Fabrication Programme 2015-16.

Situated and Experimental Research Protocols Integrating Academia and Industry within the Construction Sector

Mathilde Marengo
Institute for Advanced Architecture of Catalonia (IAAC), Universitat Politècnica de Catalunya

Today, development and innovation in technology are taking place at an unprecedented pace and are drastically changing the way we live, by introducing augmented design solutions and applications. Across social habitats and habits, political decisions and many market sectors, the impact of technological development is undeniable. Yet, within this context, the construction sector lags behind in its evolution. Recent research underlines this, stating that it is among the least digitised sectors worldwide (Barbosa et al., 2017). It is estimated that the integration of digital technologies, including advanced automation, data optimisation, onsite execution and the upskilling of the workforce has the potential to 'boost productivity in construction by some 50 to 60 percent' (Barbosa et al., 2017).

In response, new research foreseeing technological trends and their transformative potential are being produced and developed in academia, practice and related startups. Fundamental to their success is their integration with the construction industry, as *'no matter how hard scientists work, our impact will almost always be limited to our immediate academic circles if our results never catch the attention of those who have the power to act on them'* (Safford and Brown, 2019). Although many such enterprises are already under way, connecting new tools through multidisciplinary

frameworks and approaches, their practical impact is yet to be seen on a wider scale in the construction industry. Nonetheless, the potential of these collaborations, in relation to the introduction of emerging digital tools within novel actuation protocols for construction companies, is evident in the significant productivity gains and sustainable results they present (Blanco et al., 2017).

Innochain strives to bridge this gap by merging design, research and production through the consolidation of a training network for Early Stage Researchers (ESRs) developing situated projects through an experimental methodology at the intersection of academia and the construction industry. More specifically, the focus lies within the challenges and opportunities that occur as the new digital chain is established, allowing enhanced tools and concepts to be developed thanks to an interdisciplinary approach, which integrates knowledge and practice from neighbouring fields. This is elaborated through the identification of the three major challenges identified – communicating, simulating and materialising design – and has thrived due to the integration of experimental and interdisciplinary collaborative approaches.

On this basis, relationships between academic and industry partners within the Innochain network are consolidated, and possess transversality in relation to the construction industry. From material development and manufacturing enterprises to leading design and engineering firms, the large number of industry partners as design-active agents in building practice allows the network to reflect the multidisciplinary and multi-scalar fundamentals of research through the digital and physical realms of practice.

Through the development of situated and experimental research and training activities and demonstrators, the network questions the linear process with which the construction industry – like many productive industries – is associated, and creates an opportunity for the application of circular principles to this field.

This allows the projects to demonstrate the importance of a systemic, holistic and integrated approach based on working with design through research and research by design. In addition, experimentation and testing in context operates as a pretext for innovation within the digital chain.

The work offers further resonance for education, reviewing and renewing models in academia in line with principles emerging from the research. This can be appreciated through actions such as the *Computational Bamboo* installation developed and built in July 2018 at the IAAC Global Summer School in Quito, Ecuador, with Innochain researcher Evy L. M. Slabbinck based at the Institute of Building Structures and Structural Design (ITKE), and projects at the City Intelligence Lab of the Austrian Institute of Technology, opened in October 2019, led by Innochain researcher Angelos Chronis.

Through Probes, Pavilions and Exhibitions, the network has taken the scope of the project beyond academic and industrial realms. As demonstrated by the Elytra Filament Pavilion by ITKE and ICCD Stuttgart, commissioned by the V&A museum in 2016, which engaged Innochain researcher James Solly whose work on Coreless Filament Winding (CFW) and their integrated simulation and fabrication strategies is discussed later in this book. Likewise The Bridge Project by Innochain researcher Tom Svilans of CITA with industry partners White and Blumer-Lehmann, which developed an experimental design protocol, informed by the simulation of material performance and integrated feedback loops.

Beyond providing a unique opportunity to merge innovative research practice with industry impact, the Innochain network demonstrates the importance of situated, shared and experimental research protocols within the construction sector. Innochain has defined a circular system combining digital tools, material resources, design protocols, advanced manufacturing and onsite operations.

2. Material experimentation at the Innochain workshop-seminar, 'Materialising Design', developed by IAAC. The seminar introduced novel materials for robotically-steered fabrication, exploring different materials, their formal and structural performance, and how they interact with fabrication requirements.

3. Terraperforma, a large-scale 3D printing project focusing on additive manufacturing of unfired clay and climatic performative design, here experimenting the possibilities of onsite fabrication with the CoGiro robot, a Cable-Driven Parallel Robot (CDPR), at Tecnalia. Developed in IAAC's Open Thesis Fabrication Programme 2016-17.

Displacement of Effort

Ulrika Karlsson
KTH Royal Institute of Technology, Stockholm

The architect and historian Robin Evans described the position and space in which the architect operates on a daily basis as 'displacement of effort' (Evans, 1986). Unlike a painter or sculptor, the architect is always working on some intervening medium, often a drawing, seldom in direct contact with the object of their thought or the material of the outcome. At first, Evans found this displaced position to be to the architect's disadvantage. But he soon observes the enormously generative part played by the intervening medium itself, in this case the architectural drawing. He concludes that the 'displaced' effort of an architect might not always be a disadvantageous position, and that the two different approaches to 'work' might not be incompatible at all. Yet not all things architectural can be derived from drawing. Several of the projects within the Innochain research programme have methods that engage both these positions. This text takes a closer look at one of them (also described on p.122–127 and p.134–135 of this volume), where ice takes the role of formwork.

A refrigerated container is attached to a full-scale material lab at the KTH Royal Institute of Technology Stockholm campus, providing the infrastructure for an

4. Ice Formwork project by Vasily Sitnikov. Main Hall with refrigerated container. Photo: Vasily Sitnikov.

5. Drone Spraying by Stephanie Chaltiel. Photo captured by drone camera at *Practice Futures – Building Design for a new Material Age* exhibition, KADK, 2018.

6. Concrete Deposition by Helena Westerlind displayed at *Practice Futures – Building Design for a new Material Age* exhibition, KADK, 2018. Photo: Anders Ingvartsen.

5

6

alternative material system for the fabrication of pre-cast concrete elements using CNC-milled ice as formwork. The formwork consists of a mould and a counter-mould, made entirely out of CNC-manipulated ice. This research project, led by the architect Vasily Sitnikov, challenges conventional modes of fabrication in which material waste and manual labour lack resourceful considerations. The carefully designed and arranged setup simulates or stages a resourceful manufacturing process of concrete elements, where the traditional formwork material of polystyrene foam has been replaced by a phase-changing material: ice.

First, this method of developing an infrastructure for a full-scale fabrication system removes the need for an intervening medium. It requires weighty physical work and management that give the architect an opportunity to have direct contact with the object of thought and the corporeal material of the outcome. In this case, this means direct contact with, or proximity to, the transformation between states of fluidity and solidity, which are germane to casting. A fabrication method for geometrically-articulated concrete elements.

At the same time, there is an intervening medium: a setup and infrastructure that translate a stack of notations into different carving depths in ice, preparing a series of moulds of ice for concrete casting in climatically-controlled and interlinked rooms. A standard 6m refrigerated shipping container contains a custom-made three-axis computer numerical control (CNC) milling machine, a cyclone extractor to remove the ice dust (the by-product of its milling), equipment for production of low-defect ice stocks, storage of concrete raw materials and a concrete pan-mixer. The container is linked to a material lab at KTH that, for this research project, acts as a control room. This setup is designed for non-human technical and material processes and is linked to a staffed operating room. The assembly of this lab has made it possible to work in direct contact with the material of the outcome – the ice formwork and the cast concrete elements – as well as with the intervening medium and the spatial fabrication system.

It could be argued that the fabrication method is not full-scale and is merely prototypical; however, it uses an industrial system for fabrication. The architectural researcher is still working from a position that is slightly withdrawn from the anticipated industrial object, and, as a result, there is a displacement of effort. This provides a generative space from which iteratively test and modulate the setup of the lab. The carefully crafted and constructed infrastructure or model acts as a basis for running physical simulations. Thus there is potential for the two observational approaches to 'work', a) the researcher working in direct contact with the object of thought and the material of the outcome and b) through an intervening medium.

The displaced effort of the architect when working on an intervening medium, in comparison to working in direct contact with the object of thought, constitute different positions for practice-based research or research in the making. In the ice formwork research project, the toolpaths that the CNC follows are projected through space so that the tip of a cutting tool produces an anticipated form out of the ice. This process produces a mould and a counter mould, in which negative form is translated into concrete. What this suggests, is that instead of a conventional linear process of refinement, we can develop multiple levels of feedback from early stages of design and manufacturing.

It is worth reflecting on the particular condition in which architectural knowledge is produced – in this case, through the staging of an infrastructure for the automated process of fabrication of architectural elements. The position and space in which the architect operates are through an intervening medium and through direct contact with the material of the expected outcome. Both this method and the Innochain project as a whole blur the spatial boundaries between the disciplines of architecture, craft, engineering and construction.

Bibliography

Barbosa, F., Woetzel, J., Mischke, J., Ribeirinho, M.J., Sridhar, M., Parsons, M., Bertram, N. and Brown, S., 2017, *Reinventing Construction: A Route to Higher Productivity*, Washington DC, McKinsey Global Institute.

Beim, A. and Ramsgaard Thomsen, M., 2011, *The Role of Material Evidence in Architectural Research: Drawings, Models, Experiments* (eds.), Copenhagen, School of Architecture Publishers.

Blanco, J.L., Mullin, A., Pandya, K. and Sridhar, M., 2017, *The New Age of Engineering and Construction Technology*. www.mckinsey.com/industries/capital-projects-and-infrastructure/our-insights/the-new-age-of-engineering-and-construction-technology (accessed 12 November 2019).

Duits, T., 2003, *The Origin of Things: Sketches, Models and Prototypes*, Rotterdam, NAi Publishers.

Evans, R., 1986, 'Translations from Drawing to Building' in *AA Files*, no. 12 (Summer), London, Architectural Association School of Architecture, p.4–5.

Rittel, H. and Melvin W., 1973, 'Dilemmas in a General Theory of Planning' in *Policy Sciences*, Vol. 4, p.155–169.

Safford, H. and Brown, A., 2019, 'Communicating Science to Policymakers: Six Strategies for Success', in *Nature*, Vol. 572, p.681–682.

Schön, D., 1983, *The Reflective Practitioner: How Professionals Think in Action*, London, Temple Smith.

1.4 INTRODUCTIONS

Perspectives: Transactions and Trajectories

Bob Sheil
The Bartlett School of Architecture, UCL
Mette Ramsgaard Thomsen
Centre for Information Technology and Architecture (CITA), the Royal Danish Academy of Fine Arts, Schools of Architecture, Design and Conservation

A New Material Age

We may tend to think of transactions as a binary exchange, a deal, a transfer of ownership, the fulfilment of an agreement or indeed an action that assures commitment. While such essential transactions occur in all fields of design, the nature of design transaction as channelled through building procurement has operated in the face of increasingly complex and often contradictory challenges. Regardless of any theoretical orthodoxy, built architectures of numerous creeds have emerged through – and often despite – the circumstances of boom-and-bust. Here we reflect on the notion of transaction through design as fundamental, both through the themes rooted in this book and as an outlook vis-à-vis what might lie ahead.

Within the context of design for the built environment, what matters most?

Size: the construction industry is vast.
Profile: the industry spans from the individual operator to the global conglomerate.
Context: it is thoroughly dispersed.
Protocols: it is interconnected with every facet of regulated economies.
Culture: it is entwined in traditions and methods that arc back centuries.
Processes: some are static, others are evolving at unprecedented pace and more are in development in response to demand.
Operational Skills: shortages are deeply challenging.
Materials: there are consequences to every selection, from scarcity to resilience, from performance to meaning.
Information: there are only pockets of common ground.
Politics: therein lies the power to commission and regulate.
Places: each location for every activity involved has unique coordinates, conditions and aspects.
Environment: we know that we are living with finite resources in a changing climate in which the status quo of building culture cannot be sustained.

Definitions of where design and construction practices begin or end are incrementally evolving. The designer is increasingly in command of data, from how components are manufactured to how they are assembled and perform. Likewise, the contractor's expertise is increasingly relied upon at early stages, including the formation of concept and ideas. Notions of innovation, creativity and genesis are therefore illusive in their origins, as are any hard boundaries between the core disciplines of architecture and engineering. For such close siblings, all design actions are *transactions* and, as such, they are open to translation by the recipient, and very often by the author too. Furthermore, design transactions are more than mere exchanges: they signify a direction of travel, a trajectory.

Connecting research in practice and industry to research in academia, this book examines how advances in digital design tools challenge building culture, enabling more sustainable, more informed and more materially-smart design solutions. The work presented here represents a new generation of interdisciplinary research with a strong industry focus that effects real changes in the way we think, design and build our physical environment. Challenging conventional and mainstream approaches toward design as a linear process of incremental refinement, the work identifies design research potential as a distributed and

1. Nine Bridges Golf Club in Yeoju. Architects: Shingeru Ban. Modelling and Fabrication: Design-to-Production and Blumer Lehmann. Photo: Blumer Lehmann.

2. Fab-Union robotic factory © Ningjue Lyu.

3. Coreless Filament Winding. © ICD/ITKE, University of Stuttgart.

4. Production of physical mockup integrating modelling and feedback methods, by Tom Svilans and CITAstudio.

interdisciplinary activity across the entire production chain. From establishing a multi-stakeholder brief to executing geometries on structures that acknowledge and work with their inherent material properties. Situating feedback between design processes as a key concern for developing holistic and integrated design methods, the work presented here represents new interdisciplinary design methods that integrate advanced simulation and interface with material fabrication.

New Forms of Practice

Architecture and engineering have equally distinguished legacies that arc back thousands of years. Both took a historic step when defining their fields as distinct subjects taught and researched in parallel to professional disciplines, around 175–200 years ago.[1] Ever since, the relationship between academia and the professions has remained intrinsically linked with emergent poles unique to each field. While engineering in academia has remained deeply relevant to professions, it has also developed as a distinct and diverse research industry in which it is common for aspiring general practitioners to be taught by full-time researchers, many of whom are highly specialised. Meanwhile, practitioners tend to be involved as guest speakers with limited student contact, and typically engineering student projects are more likely to be theoretical than 'hands-on'. Engineering departments around the world are thus tasked with balancing the need for core education for an uncertain future with the need to advance high-quality pioneering research that inevitably progresses into increasingly specialised areas, many with the potential to open up new professions and progress others.

With complementary aims, architecture in academia has evolved through a different route whereby many schools are heavily populated with part-time staff who are active practitioners. Aspiring architects are taught by an array of specialised researchers and tutors who draw from their experience in practice. Projects are studio-based, where the fledgling practitioner learns through synthesising simultaneous interests in design, technology, history and theory, practice management, project procurement and so on. Their understanding of the department's research activity is therefore set within the context of its proximity to their exposure to practice, albeit a rehearsal for practice at that. On this basis, it can be common in some universities to find research groups in both engineering and architecture departments with the same agenda (for instance, environmental design

and structural design) yet operating entirely separately, as they are based on, and designed for, different traditions. While this may make sense in some cases locally, for those who have found ways to dissolve such silos the opportunities are extensive, and have never been more urgently required.

All contributions to this book come from, and are representative of, such collaborative trajectories. Few are troubled by labels or being constrained to a box, and perhaps the most common generation they relate to are those who, 200 or so years ago, speculated on where the future of such fundamental disciplines might go.[2] In recent years, and within the context of the disciplines of architecture and engineering, in both academic and professional senses we have witnessed innovative and productive convergence. Design is increasingly recognised as an expertise and a consideration that occurs within all aspects of architectural and engineering practice and is critical to both. Technical understanding and expertise, fuelled and aided by advances in computation, are equally fundamental to both domains. Programmes taught collaboratively between architecture and engineering departments are proliferating, and young university applicants are less likely to define a professional status as their core motivation. Rather, they are more commonly inspired by what they will do as students, what they will be exposed to as learners and researchers, and what it all adds up to as a direction of travel. In short, what is at stake is the challenge to improve both the future of life on the planet and the experience of living here in ways that are sustainable for future generations, while harnessing the talent of complimentary disciplines toward that goal is surely our utmost priority.

The Digital Chain as Common Ground

Contemporary building culture stands before radical changes to its practices and technologies as it struggles to respond to new requirements for energy efficiency, sustainability, and economic and societal change. As our societies are challenged by escalating urbanisation coupled with the energy crisis, we need to create clever solutions that enable smarter material use, higher energy conservation and better social and urban programmes while maintaining high architectural quality and cultural importance. The role of design is to develop solutions that engage the specific challenges of a given site, programme and environment. Until now, such creative inventiveness has been restricted by the mainstream

5

building practices of our modern industrialised building culture. However, with the increasing use of computational design strategies, contemporary building practice is endeavouring to develop new information-based design models that fundamentally challenge the way we think, design and build architecture (Beesley et al., 2004). By establishing a digital chain, digital design tools interface a host of programmes from parallel design fields, enabling new interdisciplinary knowledge transfer. The ability to merge architectural design environments with complex analytical tools for the simulation of force and flow has influenced the thinking of structural design, facilitating the realisation of buildings with a higher degree of formal freedom and structural complexity. Simultaneously, at the other end of design practice, the interfacing of design tools with digital fabrication has led to a profound rethinking of material practice in architecture.

In professional practice, there is an acute awareness of these opportunities.[3] While the field remains novel and methods and tools require maturing, the nascent understanding of the real design-based, technological, economic and environmental possibilities has led to the emergence of a new professional research practice. Design and engineering practices are establishing in-house research environments to develop an understanding of the new tools and investigate how they can benefit from the interdisciplinary collaborations these enable. At the same time, a new cluster of research centres with a strong interdisciplinary focus has been instituted in leading academic environments. These are now examining how computational logics can lead to a rethinking of the basic concepts that define architectural design practice, reconfiguring our representations and challenging fabrication.

Yet, where research cultures of architecture and engineering are aware of each other, communication and knowledge-sharing between the sectors is fragmented and lacks prolific exchange. Scientific progress is urgently required to rethink current building design practice and bring together architects, engineers, design software developers and fabricators to identify novel digital–material relations to reshape how we design and build. Conventional thinking that positions design as a linear process of incremental refinement in which the project is passed between the different building partners is fundamentally challenged in this book. This volume shows how digital tools are being deployed to enable iterative thinking across processes of communication, simulation and materialisation, and asks how these three fundamental axes of design activity can challenge and change building practice.

5. Multi-scalar model for 'Grove', design proposal (2nd place) for the Tallinn Architecture Biennale Installation Competition, 2019, by Paul Poinet and Tom Svilans.

Research Methodology and Approach

The work is interdisciplinary in two ways: first, as a hybrid of architectural and engineering practice; and second as a three-way partnership between academia, practice and industry that also includes the fields of software development and innovative fabrication processes. Involving a relatively large and diverse number of academic and industry partners, it engages with multiple disciplines as well as multiple scales of enterprise. All the projects presented here share an experimental research-by-design methodology, focusing on design-led physical experimentation and full-scale prototyping. Such emphasis offers direct engagement with techniques and technologies all along the digital chain, from design speculation and model analysis to specification and fabrication. This integrated approach positions research inquiries within a web of interconnected and living expertise and practice. Here, material experiments share the empirical data that has been tested, analysed and evaluated by research teams across disciplines, ensuring results are appropriated and implemented in context.

Physical experiments in design act as material research inquiries (Duits, 2003; Beim and Ramsgaard Thomsen 2011) by means of which the concepts and technologies of the design intentions are evaluated. Design as a method of research inquiry is also a reflective practice in which the researcher engages in a dual mode of reflecting *on and through* action (Schön, 1983). Moving between scales and strategies of making, design creates a conversation between the fragmented actions of detailed analysis and critical assessment, with the creative motives of proposition and result. The method is relevant for design-led research in architecture and engineering as it links design creativity and speculation to investigation. Building practice is often classified as a wicked problem in which the 'information needed to understand the problem depends on one's idea for solving it' (Rittel and Melvin, 1973). Design is therefore an active process by which the designer develops the dimensionality of a solution in the context of a given problem. Solutions are assessed not absolutely as correct or incorrect, but rather qualitatively as superior or inferior. Employing a research-by-design methodology therefore allows the individual research project to engage with the solution-led processes of creative troubleshooting that characterise the design process.

Here the work identifies three kinds of material evidence: speculative design probes generating ideation; material prototyping enabling direct full-scale testing of defined design criteria against real-world methods of realisation; and demonstrators acting as proof-of-concept testing design criteria in direct spatial contexts. All three kinds of evidence are seen as sequential, and iterative design phases build on the complexity of the project while addressing different contexts of research thinking. The research method places the exhibitions as central research instruments: beyond acting as a means of public dissemination, they constitute milestones by which research results can be produced, tested and evaluated. The research method is known to the applicant and has been tested and evaluated in prior projects (Ramsgaard Thomsen and Tamke, 2009).

Originality and Innovation

The digitisation of architectural design tools has made a radical impact on building practice. The arrival of computer-aided design (CAD) tools during the 1970s and 1980s and their maturing in the 1990s have resulted in a complete reconfiguration of architectural design practice (Kolarevic, 2003). Computer modelling in architectural design enables the description of variable geometries that calculate the values they embed (Szalapaj, 2005), instigating new practices of algorithmic modelling that actively engage with information, directly calibrating and calculating the impact of a given design decision (Schwitter, 2005). Likewise, in the field of structural engineering, computation has led to new, more efficient and more integrated means of calculating building performance. The digitisation of analysis tools and methods such as Finite Element (FE) analysis, which discretise complex problems into finite numbers of interrelated nodes to compute their force-relations, has revolutionised structural design and the buildings that result from it (Clough and Wilson, 1999).

At the same time, the interfacing of digital design tools with computer numerical control (CNC) fabrication has led to a profound rethinking of material practice in the building realm. Challenging the industrialist paradigm of mass production, practices such as file-to-factory, in which designers directly produce data that drive the CNC machines, and mass-customisation, in which repeatable elements with the same base morphology are differentiated (Scheurer, 2008), enable designers to realise complex structural solutions that optimise material use and therefore address issues of sustainability. Beyond this fundamental reshaping of the tools of our practices, digitisation has also impacted on the boundaries of our professions. By establishing a digital chain that brings together design, analysis, simulation, communication, specification and fabrication in a new integrated sequence (Kolarevic, 2005), building practice is promised the potential of stronger feedback between design phases, better interdisciplinary collaboration, smarter material usage and therefore better, more innovative and more creative design solutions (Mitchell, 2001). At present, the development of digital design tools in architecture is structured around large-scale industry-led efforts that have sought to standardise information and develop shared protocols between interdisciplinary partners (Ramsgaard Thomsen, 2016). However, core industry efforts in the form of building information modelling (BIM) with its overarching aims of unifying design information into a single shared model, remain incapable of tackling the inherent complexity and dynamic nature of building practice (Ramsgaard Thomsen, 2016). The key constraints that limit the fulfilment of integrated digital capability and planning can be summarised as:

A disciplinary separation, whereby building practice has conventionally been conceived as discrete design phases in which the distinct partners (architects, engineers, contractors and fabricators) hold separate design control and responsibility associated with the respective phases. Where current practice retains this siloed understanding of the professions for both legal and practical reasons, the digital design chain as presented here promises a fundamental rethinking of the culture of collaboration. Instead of understanding design methods and their associated tools as particular to each profession, the sector needs to develop new shared and interdisciplinary methods that cross the knowledge spaces of building practice so as to profit from the real potentials of the digital chain.

The impeding of design feedback. The design process is conventionally understood as a process of refinement in which larger-scale problems are solved before smaller-scale ones. This understanding of design as a progression through the scales limits the potential for design innovation, as it excludes our ability to understand how small-scale behaviours and complexities – be they material or detail – can affect large-scale concerns, such as the environment or structure. To support informed decision-making in the early design phase, *Design Transactions: Rethinking Information Modelling for a New Material Age* asserts that we need to develop mechanisms for multi-phased and multi-scalar feedback in which cyclical interdependencies can be analysed and assessed.

A persistence of standardisation. Contemporary building practice relies on the industrialised manufacturing of standardised building materials that can be specified, that exist under legal codes and that ensure economic viability. However, this standardisation is a core restraint in building innovation as it limits the way in which we envisage the processes and materials of buildings. As new approaches employing advanced digital fabrication techniques such as robotics and 3D printing emerge, it becomes important to find new ways to integrate them with – and expand – current building practice.

What is required is a step change in the way that digital design tools are implemented in building practice. We urgently need to reconsider how these tools can inform a culture of collaboration and knowledge-sharing between disciplines. New understandings around how feedback in the design chain can be implemented in meaningful and situated ways is required, and we need to rethink the foundations of the material cultures within which informed designs can be realised. This urgent shift is required to question the linearity of the conventional design chain and instead propose an iterative understanding of the design process, in which the three central concerns of communication, simulation and materialisation appear as recursively distributed and interdisciplinary activities. By reconceiving the design chain in this way, we must allow for new kinds of intersections that merge concerns across the design chain and create opportunities for feedback between otherwise separate design phases.

Modelling Strategies and New Workflows

In the first of three core chapters, 'Modelling Strategies and New Workflows' includes contributions and references to ongoing research within 3XN Architects, ARUP, The Bartlett School of Architecture, BuroHappold, Blumer-Lehmann, CITA at the Royal Danish Academy of Fine Arts Copenhagen, Design-to-Production, Foster + Partners, GXN Innovation, Institute for Advanced Architecture of Catalonia, Proving Ground, str.ucture, Shigeru Ban Architects, University of Applied Arts Vienna and Zaha Hadid Architects, among others. Across their respective presentations, the common trajectory is

6. Flectofold Demonstrator II by Saman Saffarian, ITKE University of Stuttgart at *Practice Futures – Building Design for a new Material Age* Innochain exhibition, Meldahl Smedie Exhibition Hall, KADK, 2018. Photo: Anders Ingvartsen.

one that anticipates the imminent impact of machine learning on processes capable of managing inputs at far greater scale and speed than human-centric teams or processes to date. As the introduction outlines, the maintenance of dynamic datasets has shifted from preservation of geometric rule sets to the modelling of collaborative workflows, dispersed across multiple and simultaneous sources. The heated context for this field of research is ownership of, and responsibility for, data. As transactions occur, responsibilities transfer, and the built environment sector becomes fraught with debate on risk and liability. Consequently, physical output is less than half the story, as for each manifestation of a built component there are multiple digital records of its design-to-implementation pathway. What is emerging here is a call for open-source solutions, maintained through co-creation partnerships committed to investing the expertise of the user/adapter/designer within computation tooling – what Poinet and Fisher call a computational ecosystem. Such avenues would enable digital tooling to be tailored around projects and their particular objectives, and encourage an acceptance that software development expertise exists in abundance across industries and is not confined to software houses, which seem bent on developing ever more generic software tooling.

Design Integration

Following on from these challenges, Chapter 2, 'Design Integration', includes contributions regarding ongoing research within Aalborg University, The Bartlett School of Architecture, UCL, BIG, BuroHappold, CITA at the Royal Danish Academy of Fine Arts Copenhagen, Foster + Partners, Institute for Advanced Architecture of Catalonia, Institute for Building Structures and Structural Design (ITKE) at the University of Stuttgart, KTH Royal Institute of Technology Stockholm, ROK, S-Form, Tongji University China, and White Arkitekter, among others. Central to the cumulative weight of these works is a vehement conviction that design is an overarching practice and expertise that not only must prevail across all phases of procuring built environment projects, but has also reached an unprecedented position whereby such oversight and engagement are possible.

One example of this shift is the prolific and rapid introduction of robotics into leading schools of architecture worldwide, where automated tooling is, in itself, of no new significance. What *is* significant, however, is how robotics in design research and design practice challenges the designer to be engaged across the full spectrum of operations, from conceptual thinking, to creation of code, to material performance and material science, to tooling (effector) design, to production environment design, to the choreography of assembly and integration of feedback at every stage. In this sense, the contemporary design researcher is offered both the challenge and the means to occupy a position of influence where previously they were excluded – an opportunity to put theoretical skill and expertise into practice. What follows from this is a fundamental rethink regarding the destiny of graduates, one that may occupy a far broader scope than that of previous generations. Design research, whether developed in formal academic settings or industrial contexts, has escaped the narrow grasp of the professions and their silos, and offers new ground for harnessing the deeply underutilised potential of the construction industry.

Novel Strategies for Materialisation

Our third core chapter, 'Novel Strategies for Materialisation', includes contributions referring to ongoing research at AKT II, Arts et Métiers-ParisTech, The Bartlett School of Architecture, UCL, BIG, BuroHappold, CITA at the Royal Danish Academy of Fine Arts Copenhagen, Foster + Partners, Henn, Institute for Advanced Architecture of Catalonia, Institute for Building Structures and Structural Design (ITKE) at the University of Stuttgart, Robots in Architecture, KTH Royal Institute of Technology Stockholm and XtreeE, among others.

Here, design research as a prospective practice is laid bare as the agency for pioneering and speculative creative invention. Vital exposure and access to advanced modelling and fabrication resources trigger an abundance of experimentation and prototyping. Just as any trading enterprise must calculate the return on investment value of capital expenditure, often over a greater period of time than the potential redundancy of the acquired assets, likewise science-based research academies predominantly regard capital investment as serving a predetermined need to support research – that is, only acquiring the 'right' tool for the job. Design research, however, often excels with the unexpected tool, the unlikely process or the surprise result. Pioneering design research thrives when located within the midst and proximity of facilitating assets for which, at the critical early stages of research, there is often no known required application. Just as a modeller needs modelling software rich in capability, so too does a designer–maker need access to a wide variety of manufacturing processes. It is through such potential to speculate that the designer looks upon a robotic arm as a means to weave fibre into complex structural forms, or concrete printing as a means to create an artificial coral reef, or sets autonomous tooling the task of carving oak with the same dexterity and skill as a master maker – and even perhaps one specific maker, too.

Design Transactions: Rethinking Information Modelling for a New Material Age sets forth a challenge to both the construction industry and the academic community to deploy the abundance of capability, talent, and knowledge they share as an agency for collaborative transformation. The new work and, more importantly, the new partnerships that have emerged here not only represent tempting possibility, but also signal the urgency of taking a new direction. Offering sobering context to these arguments is the daunting acceleration of the global ecological crisis – a deterioration of future generations' prospects and rights in which our industry has much to account for and rectify.

Notes

1. For example, The Royal Institute of British Architects (RIBA) was founded in 1836, and four years later the first university-based Professorship in Architecture was established at King's College London, and a year later at UCL.

2. In his inaugural address (1841), Thomas Leverton Donaldson, UCL's first Professor of Architecture, described architecture as 'wandering in a labyrinth of experiments'.

3. See, for example, the series of FABRICATE conferences and their associated publications:

> Sheil, R. and Glynn, R. (eds.), 2011, *Fabricate: Making Digital Architecture*, London, UCL Press.
>
> Gramazio, F., Kohler, M. and Langenberg, S. (eds.), 2014 *Fabricate: Negotiating Design & Making*, London, UCL Press.
>
> Sheil, R., Glynn, R., Menges, A. and Skavara, M. (eds.), 2017, *Fabricate: Rethinking Design and Construction*, London, UCL Press.
>
> Sheil, R., Burry, J. and Sabin, J. (eds.), 2020, *Fabricate: Design Meets Industry*, London, UCL Press.

Bibliography

Beesley, P., Cheng, N. and Williamson, R.S. (eds.), 2004, *Fabrication: Examining the Digital Practice of Architecture, Proceedings of the 23rd Annual Conference of the Association for Computer Aided Design in Architecture and the 2004 Conference of the AIA Technology in Architectural Practice Knowledge Community*, Toronto, Riverside Architectural Press.

Beim, A. and Ramsgaard Thomsen, M. (eds.), 2011, *The Role of Material Evidence in Architectural Research: Drawings, Models, Experiments*, Copenhagen, Royal Danish Academy of Fine Arts.

Clough, R.W. and Wilson, E.L., 1999, 'Early Finite Element Research at Berkeley' in *Proc. 5th US National Conference Computational Mechanics*, Boulder, Colorado.

Duits, T., 2003, *The Origin of Things: Sketches, Models and Prototypes*, Rotterdam, NAi Publishers.

Kolarevic, B., 2003, 'Digital Morphogenesis' in Kolarevic, B. (ed.), *Architecture in the Digital Age: Design and Manufacture*, New York, Spon Press, p.13.

Kolarevic, B., 2005, 'Information Master Builders' in Kolarevic, B. (ed.), *Architecture in the Digital Age: Design and Manufacture*, London, Taylor & Francis, p.58.

Mitchell, W.J., 2001, 'Roll Over Euclid: How Frank Gehry Designs and Builds' in J. Fiona Ragheb (ed.), *Frank Gehry Architect*, New York, Solomon R. Guggenheim Foundation, p.354.

Ramsgaard Thomsen, M., 2016, 'Complex Modelling: Questioning the Infrastructures of Information Modelling', in Herneoja, A., Österlund, T. and Markkanen, P. (eds.), *Proceedings of the 34th International Conference on Education and Research in Computer Aided Architectural Design in Europe: Complexity & Simplicity*, eCAADe (Education and Research in Computer Aided Architectural Design in Europe), p.33–42.

Ramsgaard Thomsen, M. and Tamke, M., 2009, 'Narratives of Making: Thinking Practice-Led Research in Architecture' (conference paper) in *Communicating (by) Design, International Conference on Research and Practice in Architecture and Design*, Brussels, Belgium.

Rittel, H. and Melvin W., 1973, 'Dilemmas in a General Theory of Planning' in *Policy Sciences*, Vol. 4, No. 2, p.155–169.

Scheurer, F., 2008, 'Architectural CAD/CAM: Pushing the Boundaries of CNC-Fabrication in Building' in Kolarevic, B. and Klinger, K. (eds.), *Manufacturing Material Effects: Rethinking Design and Making in Architecture*, New York, Routledge, p.211–222.

Schön, D.A., 1983, *The Reflective Practitioner: How Professionals Think in Action*, New York, Basic Books.

Schwitter, C., 2005, 'Engineering Complexity: Performance-Based Design in Use' in Kolarevic, B. and Malkawi, A. (eds.), *Performative Architecture: Beyond Instrumentality*, New York, Spon Press.

Szalapaj, P., 2005, *Contemporary Architecture and the Digital Design Process*, Burlington, MA, Architectural Press (Elsevier).

Modelling Strategies and New Workflows

2.1 MODELLING STRATEGIES AND NEW WORKFLOWS

New Paradigms for Digital Prefabrication in Architecture

Fabian Scheurer and Hanno Stehling
Design-to-Production

Context

In the early 21st century, the building industry is facing some tough challenges. Ongoing urbanisation demands huge volumes of new housing and infrastructure in inner cities, but ageing societies can hardly provide the workforce to plan and build at the necessary pace (Farmer, 2016). In contrast to other economic sectors, where labour productivity has been growing for years and at astonishing rates (in Germany, for example, it has grown by 90% outside the construction industry since 1991), the architecture, engineering and construction (AEC) sector is dramatically lagging behind and has not yet managed to benefit substantially from the 'digital revolution'.[1]

A number of recent studies are urgently seeking a paradigm shift in the AEC industry worldwide – one that includes a turn toward prefabrication and industrialised processes, the subsequent front-loading of planning efforts and the seamless application of digital tools along the whole process chain, increasing the vertical integration of the supply chain and the implementation of 'lean production principles' (Rodrigues de Almeida et al., 2016; Barbosa et al., 2017). Most of this correlates with concepts such as Integrated Project Delivery (IPD) and Building Information Modelling (BIM) that have been discussed in industry since the 1990s but have only recently gained momentum. The intended benefit of shifting the planning effort forward, in an attempt to increase the impact and reduce the cost of decisions, is shown in fig.1.

While fig.1 explains the chronological effects of front-loaded digital design, the discussion about BIM and prefabrication in architecture has, until now, fallen short of addressing changes regarding the content underneath these two bell-curves. Inevitably, replacing the traditional onsite building process with industrialised prefabrication is leading to different requirements for the planning process as well. Merely shifting the planning efforts forward in time and answering the same questions earlier will not deliver the desired results but just lead to the same problems more quickly. Changing the building process requires the problem to be reframed and reordered in its entirety.

Sustainable Digital Prefabrication

In the wake of IPD and BIM, building with timber is preferred for a number of reasons. First, prefabrication has always been the default mode of operation in carpentry and, due to the weight of wood, is perfectly suited to the prefabrication of relatively large and highly-integrated building elements offsite. Second, digital fabrication was an established technology in working with timber for years before planners finally started to adopt the BIM method: CNC-joinery machines are now ubiquitous, even in small-to-medium-sized carpentry firms. Third, and increasingly important in times of accelerating climate change, extracting carbon dioxide from the atmosphere and embedding it as wood in a building has a positive long-term effect. Recently, legal and economic boundaries have started to change in favour of large-scale timber buildings. Freeform timber projects like the Centre Pompidou Metz, La Seine Musicale or the recently-finished Swatch headquarters have changed public perception and paved the way toward orthogonal, pragmatic timber buildings. In this context, here we try to extract some findings from these significant projects and ask how digital planning and production for prefabricated timber could become 'roadworthy'.

Industrialised Lean Production

Timber columns, beams, slabs and wall elements can be detailed and pre-assembled offsite in the controlled environment of a factory. After a thorough quality check, the different elements are transported to the building site and 'snapped' together to erect a building. Typically, most parts of such complex elements are produced using CNC machinery and are occasionally assembled by robots. The higher the degree of prefabrication, the more complexity is shifted from onsite installation to offsite assembly, which allows for more controlled processes and higher quality, but this improvement, in turn, brings new challenges. To avoid idle times, the whole chain – from ordering raw material to installation onsite – needs to be orchestrated to guarantee delivery of the required components at a specific moment and in the desired place, resulting in significantly shorter building times. Since the time needed for installing prefabricated elements is typically shorter than the time needed for their pre-assembly, continuous workflows need to be organised by 'pulling' from the back-end rather than 'pushing' from the front of the process, following the so-called 'lean principle'.[2] To enable continuous installation onsite, the whole process needs to be synchronised or pre-assembly must build up stocks before installation starts. This complex supply chain management initially appears to add a lot of overhead costs, but we would argue that industrialised and controlled processes outweigh this effort with increased safety and reliability.

Planning Tectonics: Defining Interfaces Instead of Elements

The traditional AEC approach of 'check dimensions onsite, then build' inevitably kills all attempts at lean, just-in-time, prefabrication. In such a reactive workflow, time-consuming production can only start once the preceding trade has left its measurable traces on the site. Parametric digital models allow quick adaptation to changing needs, but they cannot speed up the physical production processes, and, without real parallelisation, the main benefit of prefabrication is lost. In order for parts to fit into their designated locations, dimensions need to be defined and tolerances negotiated during the planning process, and checked throughout fabrication, assembly and installation. This requires a clear definition of responsibilities and interfaces between the different trades, not only on a process level but also within the digital building models that inform those processes. Abstract hull volumes can demarcate working spaces for different planners in a common reference model – in the same way that interface definitions make possible the modular implementation of large-scale software projects. Today, digital building models are, however, mainly focused on building parts and not on the interfaces and connections between them.[3] It could be argued that 'architectural tectonics', as defined by German architect Gottfried Semper (1803–79), have yet to attain the conceptual level of BIM.

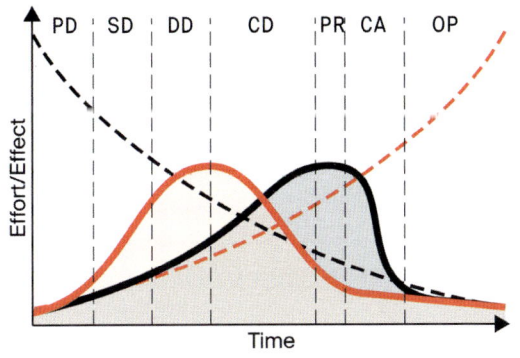 

1. MacLeamy diagram showing the effect of front-loaded planning (Davis, 2011).

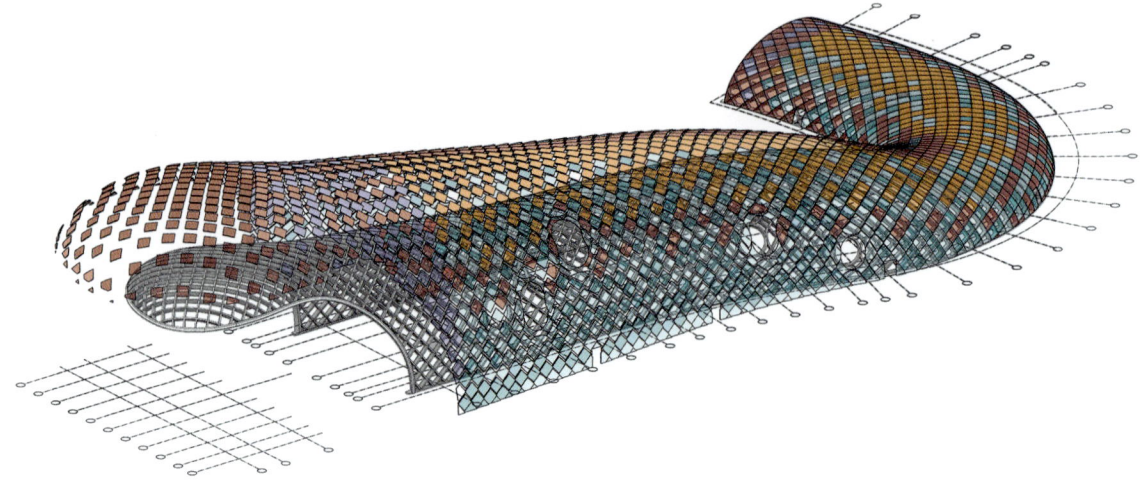

2

Design for Manufacture and Assembly: Prefab Means Product Development

In a prefabrication project, every design decision needs to be checked against manufacture and assembly, ideally in an automated fashion within the digital representation of the building. This requires connections to be modelled not just to simulate their structural performance (as is common in engineering) but also to describe their behaviour during assembly and installation.

From which direction is a connection engaged and how does this influence the assembly sequence? How does the cost of fabricating the connection compare to the cost of assembly? How can that be optimised globally? The message of the MacLeamy diagram becomes clear: design needs to take fabrication and assembly seriously at an early stage of the process, to avoid unexpected delays and costs later on. In product design, this is called 'Design for Manufacture and Assembly' (DfMA), and has been an established field of research since the late 1980s (Andreasen et al., 1988). In AEC today, these questions are implicitly resolved by the fabricator at the engineering stage of a project or after tender, with no chance to optimise the design. In future industrialised building processes, DfMA needs to be applied methodically at early stages, because the development of prefabricated components is, in fact, product design.

BIM-to-Fabrication, In Place of Shotgun Modelling

Even though more and more building projects are digitally planned, the biggest impediment to digital fabrication is still a lack of usable data. The main reason for this is a lack of focus. Building information models

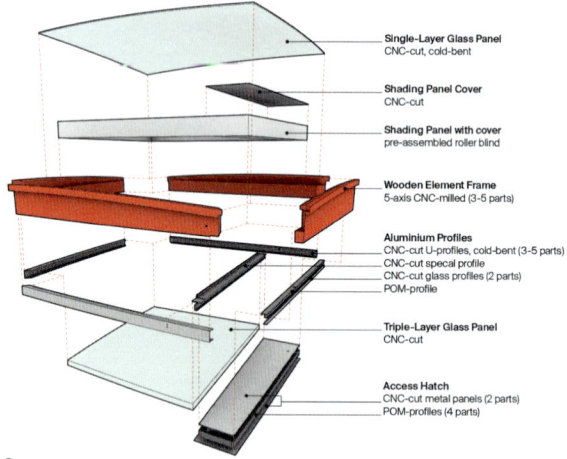

3

2. Swatch building coordination model. The geometric interface between the timber structure and the façade was defined at the tender stage of the project by creating a '3D-hull volume'. In an additional round of coordination, ports for air and electricity inlets and outlets were added to the hull models so that installation cut-outs in the timber structure could be coordinated with mechanical, electrical and plumbing (MEP) features and the respective connection points of the façade elements.

3 & 4. Swatch glass element, exploded and installed. Nine different types of façade elements were developed as parametric 'products' so that 2,800 of them could be preassembled offsite and installed on the timber structure. The most challenging were 470 closed-cavity glass elements with a cold-bent single glass panel on the outside, a geometrically-complex shading mechanism and a triple-glass panel on the inside, connected by a CNC-milled wooden frame.

are typically developed from front to back, driven by project development and design coordination but with limited knowledge about the fabrication environment. Without a clearly-defined objective, almost all planning models miss the target of being usable for production. Instead, fabricators start remodelling their digital model from scratch when they finally become involved in the process. The phenomenon of dumping and remodelling information at every process stage has been described by Borrmann et al. (2015).

Practical experience shows that digital information handed-down from previous planning stages is too detailed and unreliable. Since it is hard to determine which parts of 'shotgun models' are trustworthy, the pragmatic and safe approach is to throw the input away and rebuild altogether. In summary, all discussions about the continuous use of digital information throughout a multi-year planning process need to address the topic of model quality in at least two different dimensions: accuracy and reliability.

Parametric Models: Accuracy and Reliability by Default

A typical timber CNC-machine works with a fabrication tolerance in the range of 0.5mm and this accuracy is necessary to fabricate structurally-sound fitting details, e.g. slotted plates fixed to timber parts by steel dowels. A digital model that is to directly control such a machine must be at least as accurate as this, but expecting this level of precision at an early stage of the design process is unrealistic. Uncertainty and change will always be part of every planning process, resulting in multiple iterations. In this context, models cannot be efficiently created with conventional 'manual' methods, but rather need to be generated based on parametric rules. This allows them to stay flexible and adapt to changing parameter values but, at the same time, prove highly accurate after each update. Creating such models requires a high degree of systematisation to untangle and prioritise dependencies; therefore, decisions need to be made about the underlying rules and structures. On the upside, due to this systematic approach, parametric models are not only accurate but are also reliable; the validity of the results depends more on the rules and inputs than the variable caffeine level of the individual modeller.

Machine-Readable Models: The Industrialisation of Planning

The main benefit of working with digital models is their 'machine-readability'. Instead of needing an experienced human to interpret a plan drawing, digital models can be read, checked and manipulated by algorithms. Models themselves can serve as input for new models, which is the core feature of the productivity leap expected from digitalisation. But when high levels of responsibility and risk are involved – like in the AEC industry – all digital tools we currently use rely on well-structured data. Even though processing of unstructured data by means of

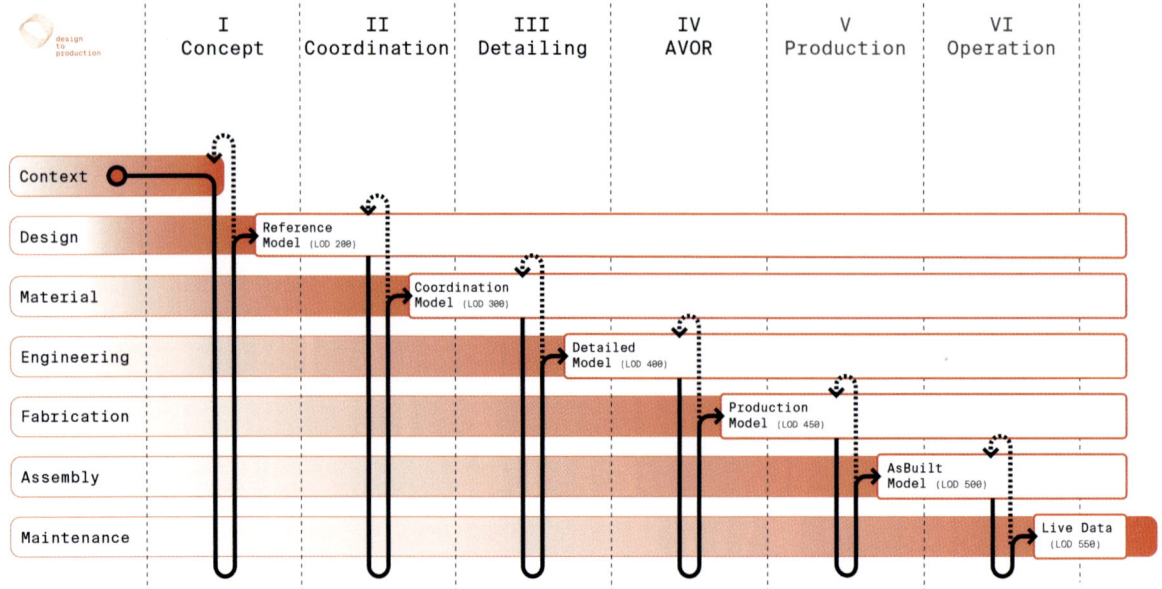

5

artificial intelligence has made some progress in recent years, vague or contradicting building instructions are still dangerous. To unambiguously encode information about a complex building into a set of digital models used by multiple parties for very different purposes, a myriad of very precise agreements are necessary, regarding ontologies of model objects, naming conventions, types and so on. Standardised data formats such as IFC are helping with this, but still leave a lot of work and responsibility for BIM management, a profession still in its formation phase.

```
Small is Beautiful:
Multiple Minimal Models
```

By definition, a model is an abstract description of a part of the real world. A manageable digital model is one that contains as little information as necessary to serve its purpose, without creating redundancies and inconsistencies. The decisive and recurring question during the process of modelling is: What information from the real world should be included in the model? The answer depends on its purpose, which leads to a number of consequences. First, the purpose of a model needs to be clearly defined (see 'shotgun models', as mentioned earlier). Second, for different purposes there will be multiple models of a building that cannot be integrated into one single model without violating the minimum rule. When multiple models are used to describe the same building from different points of view, they need to reference each other or a common base model to avoid inconsistencies, otherwise it cannot be guaranteed that they do not actually describe different

5. Agile Design-to-Production process model. The diagram shows a planning process through different stages in time (from left to right) and varying abstraction levels (from top to bottom).

6. Reference models for the Swatch building, including grid, surface and beam axis. It includes a naming and numbering concept for all beams and façade elements from the beginning of the project until the end, which has remained unchanged for five years.

buildings. What BIM needs is a modelling environment on an organisational and a technological level that handles multiple connected models in a controlled and safe fashion.

Multi-Scalar Models

On an organisational level, planning processes in the AEC industry often follow the so-called 'waterfall model'. Starting at a conceptual level and progressing to the production stage, increasingly 'concrete' topics are investigated, such as materiality, structure, fabrication, assembly and maintenance, while integrating larger amounts of information into more detailed data models. Neglecting practical questions for the first two or three rounds of planning is obviously not compatible with the requirements of DfMA, but on closer inspection there is also a modelling problem. In the waterfall approach, the model with a higher level of detail (LOD) typically replaces the less-detailed version. The aim of parametric modelling is to automatically generate the next level of detail from the previous model, but this becomes impossible once the most important input – the lower-detail model – has been declared 'outdated'. To automate modelling, we not only need to handle multiple models for different purposes but also for multiple levels of scale or abstraction.

Design to Production and Back

A different process model has been developed after more than a decade of experience in freeform timber projects and continuous discussions on the aforementioned modelling conundrums.

All topics, from the abstract context to concrete fabrication, assembly and maintenance, are addressed from the outset in an 'agile' fashion to provide a viable solution at every stage. This requires enough knowledge about production to be brought upstream to inform the design regarding smart integrated opportunities, either by tapping into the know-how of production specialists at early project stages or by developing and following common DfMA guidelines for timber prefabrication.

To efficiently arrive at a high-quality model, the volume of information needs to be kept to a minimum. Only the decisions made and justified at any given stage need to be reflected in the data, thus the process 're-surfaces' to the appropriate level after each round. In addition, the 'abstract' models are not replaced by the more 'detailed' model at the next stage, but instead are kept alive and extended by the additional information. This requires updates to be made to the abstract model in conjunction with later findings, while therefore the probability of change at later stages should also be addressed before adding to any model.

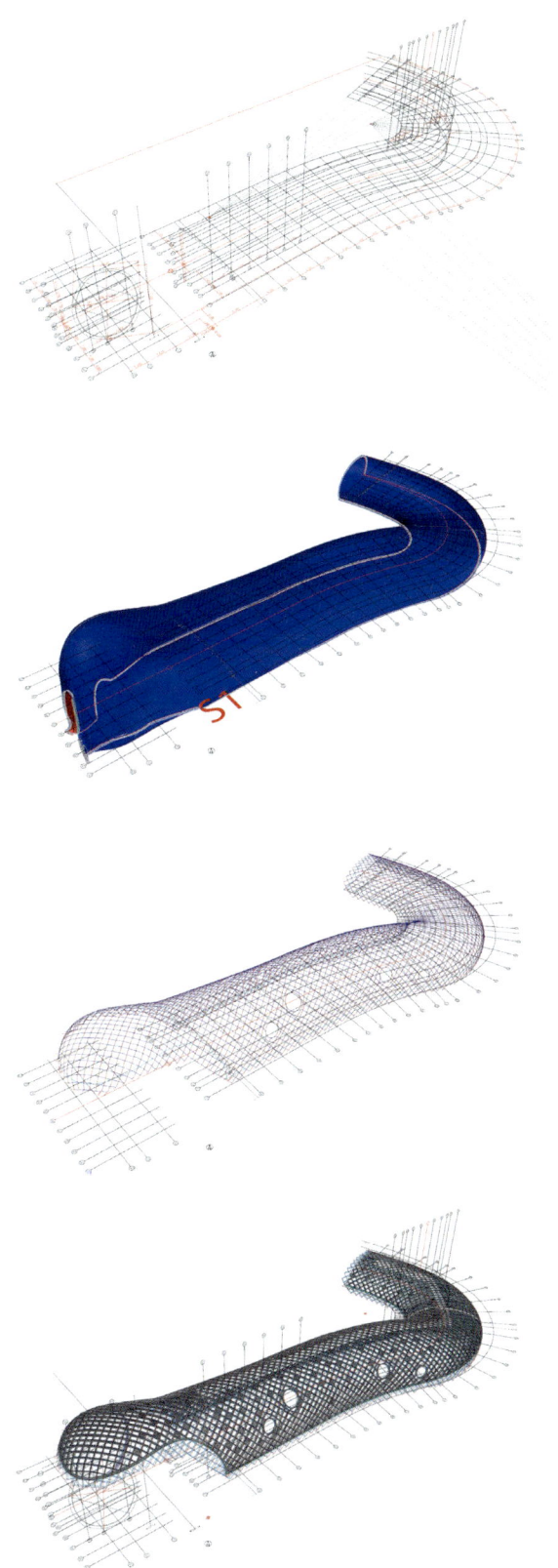

Conclusions

The aforementioned topics are crucial for utilising the potential of digitalisation within the AEC industry. We have been wrestling with, and partly solving, issues in non-standard 'curvy' projects since 2007, in a somewhat experimental fashion. Today, it is exciting to see such discussions happening at a much larger scale, namely around standard 'orthogonal' buildings.

Prefabrication is slowly gaining traction but is still an 'alien' concept in many parts of the AEC industry, particularly as it does not fit many of the traditional approaches for scheduling, the handling of tolerances and the development of details. BIM is becoming more common but the continuous use and coordination of digital data models needs to be extended all the way from design to digital fabrication and assembly processes. The modelling paradigms of BIM are largely concerned with building components but do not define interfaces and connections. Multi-scalar parametric modelling is not yet implemented, either in the workflows, tools or standards.

Outlook

Prefabricated timber provides a chance to finally accomplish the digital turn in AEC with real industrialised processes and a productivity that catches up with that of other fields. But to successfully exploit the already existing digital production facilities at the end of the process, the planning at the start needs to focus on what is needed for an industrialised, lean production of buildings – and to come up with new paradigms to digitally model those processes.

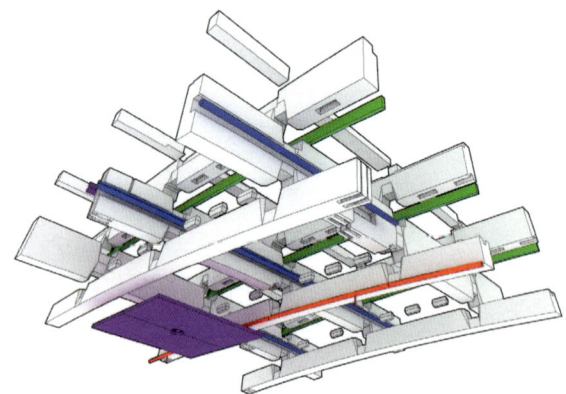

7

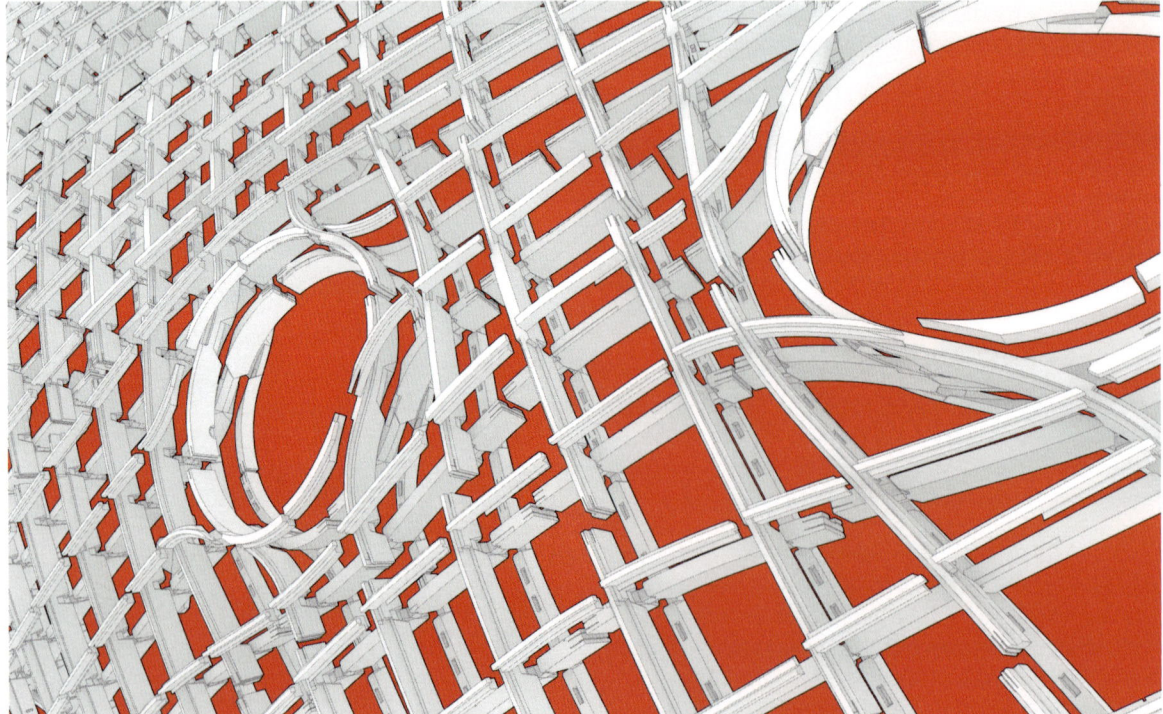

9

7. Detailed model of four fields, showing building parts close to their final physical form. Due to the increased amount of data, detailed models are often subdivided according to assembly sectors, component types or other criteria. Given that all parts respect the boundaries defined by the preceding coordination model, interfaces between different detailed models can be kept to a minimum.

8. Explosion Drawing of detailed timber structure.

9. Swatch headquarters. The timber structure and façade comprise approximately 75,000 bespoke components, prefabricated in more than 20 locations. Most of these components were preassembled offsite into 4,600 beam segments and 2,800 façade elements and were then delivered to site immediately before their installation.

Bibliography

Andreasen, M., Kahler, S., Lund, T. and Swift, K., 1988, *Design for Assembly*, New York, Springer-Verlag.

Barbosa, F., Woetzel, J., Mischke, J., Ribeirinho, M.J., Sridhar, M., Parsons, M., Bertram, N. and Brown, S., 2017, *Reinventing Construction: A Route to Higher Productivity*, Washington DC, McKinsey Global Institute.

Borrmann, A., König, M., Koch, C. and Beetz, J., 2015, *Building Information Modeling*, Wiesbaden, Springer.

buildingSMART International Ltd., 2019, *Industry Foundation Classes Version 4.1.0.0*, https://standards.buildingsmart.org/IFC/RELEASE/IFC4_1/FINAL/HTML (accessed 10 December 2019).

Davis, D., 2011, *The MacLeamy Curve* (blog entry). www.danieldavis.com/macleamy (accessed 10 December 2019).

Farmer, M., 2016, *The Farmer Review of the UK Construction Labour Model*, London, Construction Leadership Council (CLC). www.cast-consultancy.com/news-casts/farmer-review-uk-construction-labour-model-3 (accessed 10 December 2019).

Rodrigues de Almeida, P., Gerbert, P., Castagnino, S. and Rothballer, C., 2016, *Shaping the Future of Construction – A Landscape in Transformation: An Introduction*, Geneva, World Economic Forum. www3.weforum.org/docs/WEF_Shaping_the_Future_of_Construction.pdf (accessed 10 December 2019).

Semper, G., 1860, *Der Stil in den technischen und tektonischen Künsten*, Frankfurt a.M., Verlag für Kunst und Wiss.

Statistisches Bundesamt, 2019, *Fachserie 18, Reihe 1.5, Tabelle 2.14*. https://www.destatis.de/EN/Themes/Society-Environment/Sustainable-Development-Indicators/Publications/Downloads/data-relating-indicator-report-2018.pdf (accessed 10 February 2020).

Notes

1. Statistisches Bundesamt, 2017.

2. www.lean.org/whatslean/principles.cfm

3. The BIM standard IFCx4 (Industry Foundation Classes) contains 137 subclasses of *IfcElement* for defining 'components that make up an AEC product' but only three classes underneath *IfcRelConnectsElements* to define 'connectivity between elements'. Furthermore, IFC-connections cannot be defined by types, nor can they contain parameters (buildingSMART International Ltd, 2019).

2.2 MODELLING STRATEGIES AND NEW WORKFLOWS

Information-Rich Exploration in the Early Design Phase

Zeynep Aksöz
University of Applied Arts, Vienna

Introduction

As computational analysis accelerates in visualising performance objectives, the integration of generative design and metaheuristic search tools, which are designed for systematic problem-solving, is shifting to the early stages of the design process (Harding and Shepherd, 2014). The strength of these tools in generating and evaluating design solutions offers a new perspective on the conceptualisation phase, where it is approached as a problem-solving process.

The first requirement for successful problem-solving is a clear and rational definition of the problem that is to be solved. This calls for clearly-defined variables and goals, addressing all aspects of the problem, hence the problem becomes a multi objective optimisation problem. In conventional problem-solving processes for optimisation, metaheuristic solvers iteratively generate and evaluate different solutions, searching for optimal solutions that address all the selected goals. However, in working with multiple objectives, the selected goals can be in conflict. This means that to improve one of the objectives can result in a reduction of the other objectives. Consequently, the 'optimal solutions' discovered by the solver satisfy all the goals equally, considering all the trade-offs between the objectives.

Design, however, is a process of dealing with situations involving uncertainty, uniqueness and conflict (Fischer et al., 1991). The early design process is evolutionary, by its very nature. Through continuous evaluation and reflection, concepts are revised, reframed or completely discarded (Mothersill and Bove, 2017). Early design is thus an ambiguous phase, where there are no definitive formulations and no rational rules to define and evaluate a design problem.

Here, understanding the design problem is equal to solving it (Rittel, 1972). The role of the designer is, therefore, not only to find the correct solution but to find the right question to ask: finding the correct design variables and design goals to proceed with generative exploration is an exploratory process in itself.

In optimisation, aspects of a problem are incorporated to create one or more measures of effectiveness, which ultimately become the criteria by which design solutions are evaluated. Here, the decision-making process is informed by analysis and simulation, motivating designers to define and evaluate goals early on. With this approach comes a particular obsession with numbers and quantities, where qualitative aspects can easily be mixed with quantitative performance (Harding and Shepherd, 2014). The integration of metaheuristic solvers in earlier phases of design can help the designer to explore multiple solutions. However, this exploration only takes place in the realm of quantifiable goals, where qualitative aspects – which are not easy to measure – may be overlooked.

The objective of this research project is to explore and develop multiple-criteria search strategies that are suited to the early design process. Creative exploration is accepted as an ambiguous and messy process, where the design goals are mutable and fluid. The research, therefore, investigates processes that can accommodate ambiguity and imprecision, while providing the designer with a 'playful' environment through which to develop the conceptual framework of the design problem. Instead of avoiding metaheuristics and the intelligent processes offered by advancing computational power, the research utilises the benefits of these technologies to establish new processes that help designers formulate their concepts.

For successful problem-formulation, a complete understanding of the design, with all aspects involved, needs to be outlined. As design is a linear process, the information gathered in the later stages of design development typically vanishes with each new project. By contrast, the technologies employed in the scope of this research utilise previous experiences, harvesting information gathered in the later stages of design and integrating it into subsequent early phases, to establish information-rich environments using the reoccurring routine processes involved in design.

This research aims to bring a new perspective to the early design process, where creative exploration emerges out of a collaboration between designer and computer. The following sections explain the processes developed within the scope of a project in collaboration with structural design specialists str.ucture. Existing and newly developed methods are evaluated for their accessibility and usability within the design environment, as well as the reliability of these tools in real-life projects.

```
Case Study: Triangulated
Textile Façade for a Car Park
```

Using the industry collaboration with str.ucture as a tangible example, the benefits and limitations of a workflow using generative design are outlined here. The problem was to design a triangulated textile façade that would function as the skin of an existing concrete structure for a car park. The triangulated structure was to be designed in consideration of the geometric limitations of a steel form-fit connection, which was previously developed as a façade detail by str.ucture and Design-to-Production. The joining system consisted of form-fit cog connections on a circular laser-cut steel plate. As the façade design was dependent on the system's geometric limitations, it was essential to develop a design workflow that accommodated the freedom of early exploration, while generating geometries that remained within the fabrication domain.

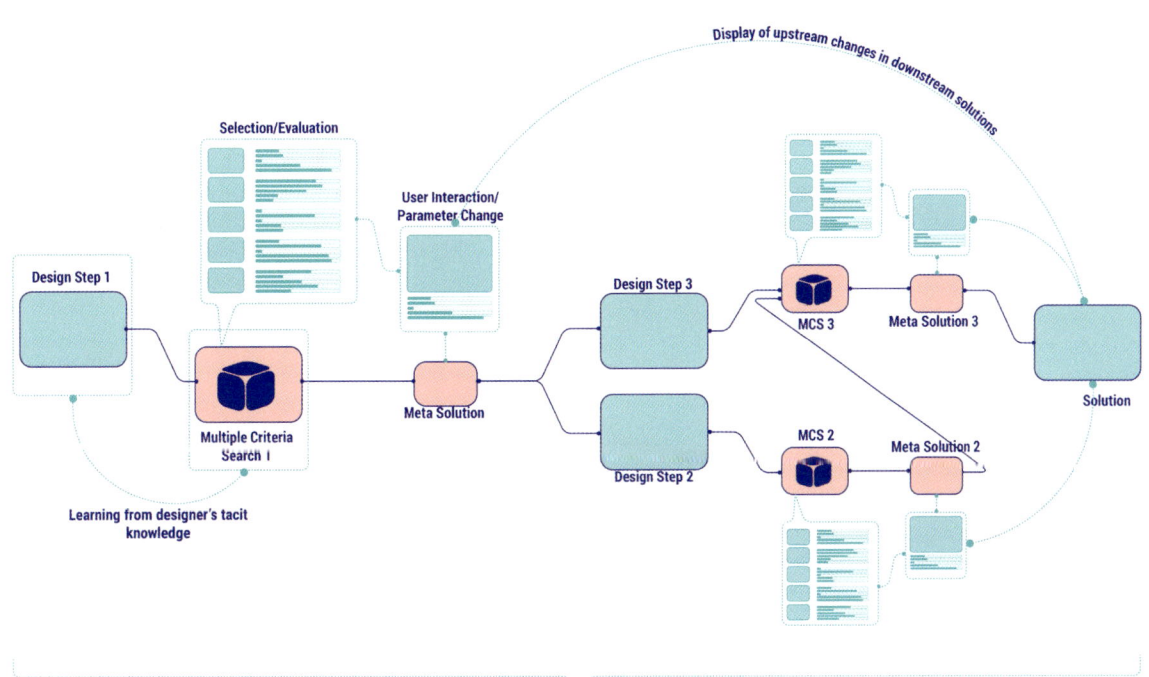

1

1. The pseudo-code of the multiple-criteria solver, Albert, was developed alongside the research. In addition to the conventional features of a Genetic Algorithm, Albert enables the direct interaction of the user with the optimisation process, through selection and user-induced mutation.

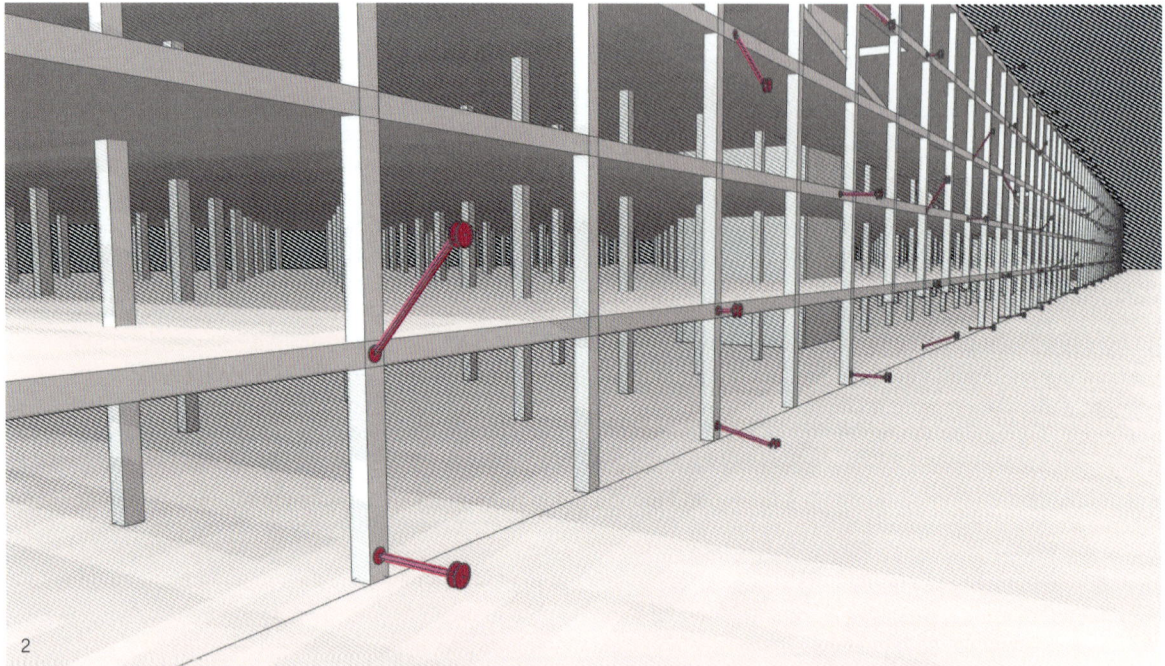

2 & 3. The façade consists of a form-fit cog joining system that connects triangular elements. These figures illustrate different phases of the system, where the joints are installed on the existing construction of the building and the triangle panels are installed around the joints.

4. The pre-defined constraints of the design problem.

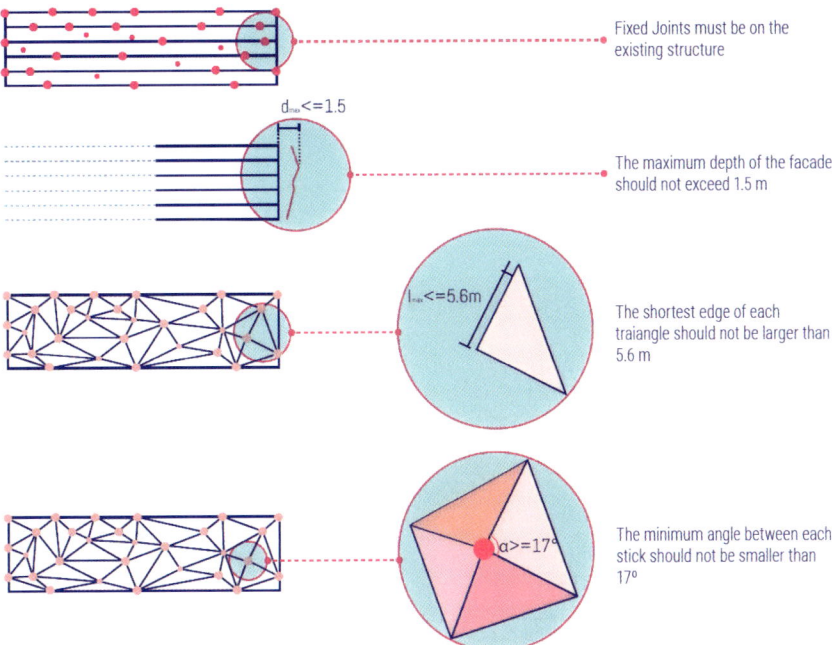

4

The flexibility of the laser-cutting process allowed the façade system to accommodate differentiated triangles, although a minimum angle between the elements had to be considered to avoid collisions. Another limitation was defined by the membrane fabricator, regarding the length of the edges, which could not exceed the maximum cut-edge of the fabric roll. The existing structure of the car park was used as a framework onto which to attach the façade. Some joints, therefore, had to be installed on the existing construction, while the façade depth could not exceed 1.5m (fig.3). The objectives were defined considering the fabrication constraints, structural stiffness and cost-effectiveness of the system.

Although this optimisation problem seems clearly defined through the given fabrication constraints, the parametrisation process, to select appropriate design variables and objectives, also involved lengthy exploration and evaluation of the different methods of problem formulation. It was essential to find a set of parameters that would successfully control the top-down global geometry and bottom-up sizing of elements and angles between the aspects of the problem, simultaneously. Finally, the optimisation process would require us to optimise the size of the elements and the angles between them, and to generate geometries that met the aesthetic aims of the team, which cannot be measured in the design code itself.

Different methods of parametrisation were tested and evaluated vis-à-vis the aesthetic output, and the optimisation problem was, consequently, divided into two sections. A set of variables controlled the global geometry of the façade by varying the frequency and amplitude of four sine curves along the floorplates of the existing structure, generating a doubly-curved surface. Another set of variables controlled the number of pieces and locations of the joints on the surface, within the limitations of the existing construction. The joints were added as vertices that defined the triangulated geometry using the Delaunay triangulation method (Gärtner and Hoffmann, 2013) (fig.4). Using a particle springs system, a method for structural form finding, where a collection of points are connected by linear elastic springs, in Kangaroo (Piker, 2013), the ideal location for each joint was defined using the given fabrication constraints. Due to conflicting criteria, however, Kangaroo could not instantly output an optimal geometry, since this was dependent on the amplitudes of the variables. A heuristic method was integrated to explore different states of the variables in relation to objectives. Genetic Algorithm (GA)-based multiple criteria search-solver Octopus (Vierlinger, 2013) was implemented into the workflow to navigate possible solutions. By merging heuristics with a constraint-based solver, different global geometries could be iteratively generated by GA. While Kangaroo was controlling the constraints, the generated solutions were evaluated by GA, measuring the failures occurring in the system regarding fabrication constraints.

One of the major components in the evaluation of the selected problem-formulation is visual access to the generated solutions. Long optimisation runs could result

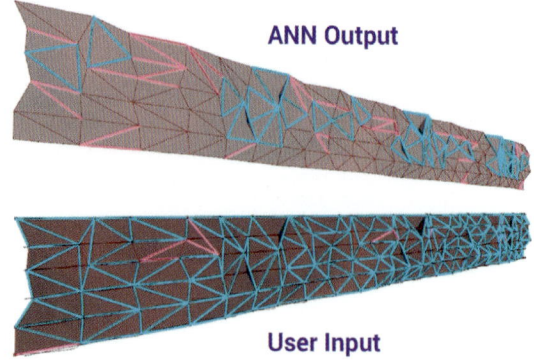

5

in a convergence toward mathematically 'good' solutions that are physically impossible to fabricate. The reason for this lies in the multiple-criteria nature of the problem, where each objective is equally unsatisfied. The Pareto front displays a set of 'optimum solutions' for selected objectives that discard geometric constraints to satisfy other criteria. A lack of visual representation and user interaction with the search process results in the establishment of solutions that appear to meet the quantitative goals, yet these solutions are completely irrational. For example, in one case the solver succeeded in avoiding any large structural members (in this case, rods) and any acute angles between them, while it minimised the cost by not generating any façade components. This indicates two problems: first, the parameters and objectives are ill-defined and, second, the designer has access to the solutions too late to be able to change the selected problem formulation. Ultimately, this process is overly time-consuming and is therefore usually avoided in the early design phase.

In this context, the performance of the platform is not the only issue; the manner in which a playful and intuitive design approach vanishes with the integration of generative tools is also of concern. Do we have to hand over our decisions to the computer to discover novel solutions? Achieving novelty through generative search seems persuasive, but these processes can only find solutions within the limitations of design variables and quantitative goals, which are usually related to performance. Evaluating design solutions solely by considering quantifiable goals disregards the vital qualitative aspects of the design process, since these cannot be measured by any metric. Yet the conceptual idea of design is more than its quantitative performance; the aesthetic judgement of each designer must also be considered. Conversely, sometimes the aesthetic quality becomes so important that the quantitative goals can be completely overlooked. Hence, the early creative process is a negotiation between qualitative and quantitative goals, and the qualitative decision still lies in the hands of the designer. Instead of completely replacing creative exploration with generative design, these tools should become an *amplification* of the creative process, giving the designer the scope to intervene and change the selected parametric setup along the way. Thus, we should use generative design as an extension of creative exploration, and approach these methods as tools of communication rather than decision-making tools. Accordingly, they should help us to formulate questions rather than find answers.

Albert – a multiple-criteria search tool developed during the scope of the research project – reflects on these meditations. Albert prioritises direct interaction between the designer and an evolutionary algorithm to train the system to execute solutions that are customised to designers' preferences (Aksöz, 2019). It provides a graphical user interface (GUI) with which the designer can easily compare different design variations by reviewing visual representations and their relative performance. Through direct interaction, the designer can compose sets of preferred solutions and manipulate computer-generated solutions. By merging interactive evolution with the manual intervention of the designer, an environment of exploration and negotiation is established that smoothly integrates with the early design phase. This avoids long calculation periods and the potential isolation of the designer from the exploration process. Thanks to rapid evaluation, designers can make decisions regarding which parameters and objectives to select for the preferred design goals, and subsequently update or restructure the parametric model.

Although this method can be readily integrated into creative exploration, there are limitations to a parametric approach to design. To successfully implement an exploratory method, one still has to define the design parametrically. Establishing a model from very early on can be challenging and also restricting, since only the domain of exploration remains within the boundaries of selected variables. Therefore, in the very early explorations, designers still prefer to work with 3D modelling as a method of sketching, since it provides more flexibility and supports ambiguity. How can we integrate information technologies into such an intuitive process that keeps the designers aware of the performance without demanding a parametrisation of the design problem? Here, another type of interaction can be discussed, whereby both designer and computer can influence design outcome on different layers of complexity, emphasising their individual qualities. The designer has the ability to control the creative process from a holistic point of view. The computer, on the other hand, can process complex calculations in a very short period of time. With the integration of machine learning, especially Artificial Neural Networks (ANNs), these calculations can be learnt, based on experience, without being explicitly programmed. ANNs are able to quickly execute results in parallel, while the computer can conduct adjustments, changes or improvements, in detail, informed by previous experiences.

The different levels of design can be distinguished as 'global' and 'local'. While the designer is intuitively exploring the global design outcome, the computer can focus on the local details and execute solutions regarding performative goals. To summarise this process, we can go back to the parametrisation of the project. In this context, the designer can control the overall curvature, the overall geometry and the triangulation strategy of the façade, while the computer can operate in detail, fixing the element sizes and improving structural performance. Instead of using a constraint-based solver that can only adjust the geometry in line with given constraints, the ANNs can be trained to execute solutions regarding multiple criteria, not only based on geometry. The problem description becomes so generic that the same ANN can be used on different projects, executing completely different solutions. Consequently, instead of a problem-specific approach, a domain-specific approach can be developed that can prove more sustainable for the overall design workflow.

Conclusions

The integration of machine learning and artificial intelligence-based processes encourages a shift in computational design. Designers are confronted with a new approach that challenges traditional methods of thinking by motivating them to focus on design performance early on. This approach can be beneficial, integrating harvested data with creative exploration. Awareness of design performance can thus be raised, which helps reduce long optimisation cycles in later stages. These systems should be approached critically, however, and used as tools to *negotiate between* the quantitative and qualitative goals. They should remain an extension and an amplification of creative exploration that supports the designers in their creative nature. The underlying question, then, becomes: 'How can we establish a fusion between the ambiguous nature of early design exploration and the computer-aided processes that smoothly migrate into this phase?'

Thesis

Aksöz, Z., 2019, *Reflections on Multiple Criteria Optimization in Early Design Phase Through Applications of AI and Machine Learning for Human Machine Collaboration*, University of Applied Arts Vienna. Supervisor: Prof Klaus Bollinger. Industrial partner: Dr Julian Lienhard, str.ucture, Lightweight Design made in Stuttgart.

Bibliography

Fischer, G., McCall, R. and Mørch, A., 1991, 'Making Argumentation Serve Design', in *Human–Computer Interaction*, Vol. 6, No. 3–4, p.393–419. doi: 10.1080/07370024.1991.9667173

Gärtner, B. and Hoffmann, M., 2013, 'Computational Geometry Lecture Notes HS 2012: Voronoi Diagrams'. www.ti.inf.ethz.ch/ew/Lehre/CG13/lecture/cg-2012.pdf (accessed 7 February 2020).

Harding, J., and Shepherd, P., 2014, 'Meta-Parametric Design' in *Design Studies*, Volume 52, September 2017, p.73–95. https://doi.org/10.1016/j.destud.2016.09.005 (accessed 7 February 2020).

Mothersill, P. and Bove, V.M., 2017, 'Humans, Machines and the Design Process: Exploring the Role of Computation in the Early Phases of Creation', in *The Design Journal*, Vol. 20, Sup.1, p.S3899–S3913. doi: 10.1080/14606925.2017.1352892

Piker, D., 2013, 'Kangaroo: Form Finding with Computational Physics', in *Architectural Design*, Vol. 83, p.136–137. doi:10.1002/ad.1569

Rittel, H., 1972, 'On the Planning Crisis: Systems Analysis of the "First and Second Generations"', in *Bedriftsokonomen*, Vol. 8, p.390–396.

Vierlinger, R., 2013, 'Multi Objective Design Interface', Technical University of Vienna. doi: 10.13140/RG.2.1.3401.0324

5. Diagram showing the overlaying of user input and the output of the ANN. The input represents the structural information; this is extrapolated to show ideal local geometries.

2.3 MODELLING STRATEGIES AND NEW WORKFLOWS

Computational Extensibility and Mass Participation in Design

Paul Poinet
The Bartlett School of Architecture, UCL
Al Fisher
BuroHappold Engineering

Introduction

In order to manage the design-to-fabrication process of large-scale and complex architectural projects, Architecture, Engineering and Construction (AEC) companies have been independently optimising custom in-house processes, as well as the delivery of data to external partners (Deutsch, 2017). These self-organised ways of improving workflows can take different shapes, depending on the company's specific activities. For example, companies that conduct construction-related tasks and deal with large and complex datasets at late stages can be seen to primarily focus on developing tailored scripts based on existing software platforms (e.g. Design-to-Production, Front Inc., Woods Bagot) that curate the generated data from early to late stages until the completion of the building. Meanwhile, many consultants and AEC software developers have built custom interoperability tools to bridge the communication gap between different software platforms and, further, aim to genericise these tools by developing larger frameworks that could be useful for the broader community (e.g. Proving Ground's plug-ins). Even though all these custom processes, tools and software are valuable in solving immediate and critical issues related to the conception and construction of a particular building project, working in isolation they are naturally not focused on – and therefore cannot address the wider challenges of – data interchange, collaboration and inefficiency across the complete supply chain.

The objective of the work described in this chapter is use design and code experimentation to solve local problems related to development, deployment and reuse within the practices mentioned above; and, importantly, with increased transparency and participation at every

1. The SchemaBuilder user interface enables the end user to create hierarchical relationships between Rhino3D objects on-the-fly. This results in a specific user-defined schema containing different objects and sub-objects, which can be sent to a Speckle server.

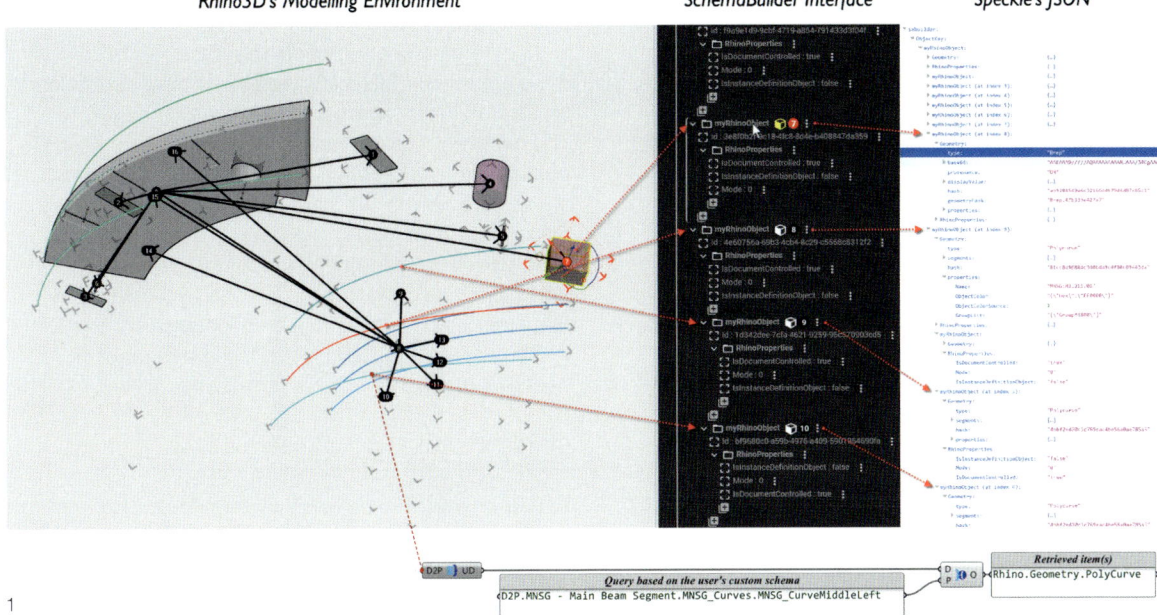

1

stage. For the AEC industry this means open-source platforms for combining the efforts of the programmer, computational designer, engineer and architect in an accessible computational design and coding ecosystem.

Open-Source Frameworks: Enablers of Mass Participation and Computational Extensibility in Design Practices

The challenges for achieving the widespread adoption of computational methodologies are threefold:

1. Construction of design project and system architecture to sustainably facilitate use;
2. Skilling of core competencies in leadership and team behaviours;
3. A technology platform that facilitates and reinforces distributed development, co-creation, system redundancy and flexibility, while nurturing innovation through prototyping.

These challenges necessitate the development of new coding and novel collaboration paradigms, the details of which are compatible with mass-distributed co-creative processes. These are demonstrated in the three case studies here, which range from modelling experiments to more robust prototypical applications.

Two innovative open-source code frameworks have been used – separately or orchestrated together – in order to demonstrate the potential of computational extensibility (enabling better transparency and interaction between the different design actors at every stage) and mass participation in design practice: Buildings and Habitats object Model (BHoM) and Speckle:

- BHoM has been designed as a hybrid model for code architecture, integrating a number of concepts across existing languages and platforms. The BHoM has a data structure and manipulation strategy that is directly compatible with both visual flow-based programming (such as in Grasshopper3D and/or Dynamo) and text-based imperative code. Practically, the BHoM offers a neutral schema to define design objects that can be converted to and from various software platforms. In this neutral environment proprietary software functionality can be extended by adding and calling generic methods through system reflection.
- Speckle is an extensible and scalable design and AEC data communication protocol and platform. It offers a neutral schema for the specification and creation of basic geometry types, as well as a federated server architecture to send and receive streams that collect various geometrical datasets defined by the user within different software platforms.[3]

Prototypical Applications

The three case studies described here gradually tackle different scales, from local object level to macro project level. As the scale increases, more design participants become involved in the process, resulting in complex design workflows and behaviours. These prototypical experiments respectively highlight three main points:

1. Extensibility and flexibility of the object's schema;
2. Cross-practice collaboration and interoperability;
3. Project and process mapping at scale.

Flexible and Extensible Object Schemas

Design object flexibility and extensibility are crucial aspects to be enabled during the conception of large-scale digital workflows. This means that any data schema needs to be flexible enough to adapt its representation to any unknown future change or requirement throughout the design process, without losing its core abstract definition necessary for robust interoperability and sharing across all required software platforms. In order to explore designer control of such object customisation, a prototypical application entitled SchemaBuilder has been developed. SchemaBuilder's main goal is to allow the user to build custom-nested hierarchies of geometrical objects. The user is able to select geometries directly from the viewport in Rhino3D and aggregate them within a directory tree structure[4] from which custom properties and 'parent-child' relationships can be defined. As the hierarchy is being built, a corresponding graph highlighting the current dependencies can be previewed within the viewport. Once the user is satisfied with the object's schema, the latter can be shared on an online server using the Speckle plug-in for Rhino3D.

SchemaBuilder focuses exclusively on the object's properties and metadata. Other strategies have looked at similar extensibility of an object's methods and behaviours. The BHoM framework enables the injection and exposition of an object's methods, as well as its properties. Exposed in a visual programming User Interface (UI), the user is similarly able to navigate a tree of objects and call a specific object's methods. Methods that can be injected into the object from multiple authors, across separate modular code projects, open the door to mass customisation for disparate purposes.

In both the SchemaBuilder interface and the BHoM code framework, flexibility and extensibility have been tackled on the local, small-scale level of the object. The next step is to demonstrate the benefits of adaptive object schemas[5] through a cross-collaboration case study that involves two different collaborators working on a common object. This context is illustrated by the next modelling experiment, which is a speculative cross-practice collaboration between BuroHappold Engineering (an engineering practice based in London) and Design-to-Production (a consultancy practice based in Zurich).

Cross-Practice Collaboration

To demonstrate the potential of the previous experiment within a collaborative scenario, the following speculative experiment attempts to integrate the communication and collaboration processes between Design-to-Production and BuroHappold Engineering through schema-based workflows, using a specific example of a timber assembly modelled by the former. In this experiment, a common schema has been shared between the two practices, which are working toward a common project goal but with different design objectives: while Design-to-Production is generating full geometrical descriptions of each architectural component, BuroHappold Engineering is mainly focusing on obtaining precise structural analysis results. To perform the latter, BuroHappold Engineering uses the BHoM platform, allowing seamless data transfer from the Grasshopper canvas – considered here as a main UI interface of the BHoM – to Autodesk's Robot Structural Analysis[6] software package. The retained common schema was discussed by both partners, who agreed on the minimum information necessary to generate their respective data: a series of different planes informing on the directionality of the beam assembly, allowing further geometrical generation and structural analysis. Such agreement on a common-object model enables a bi-directional

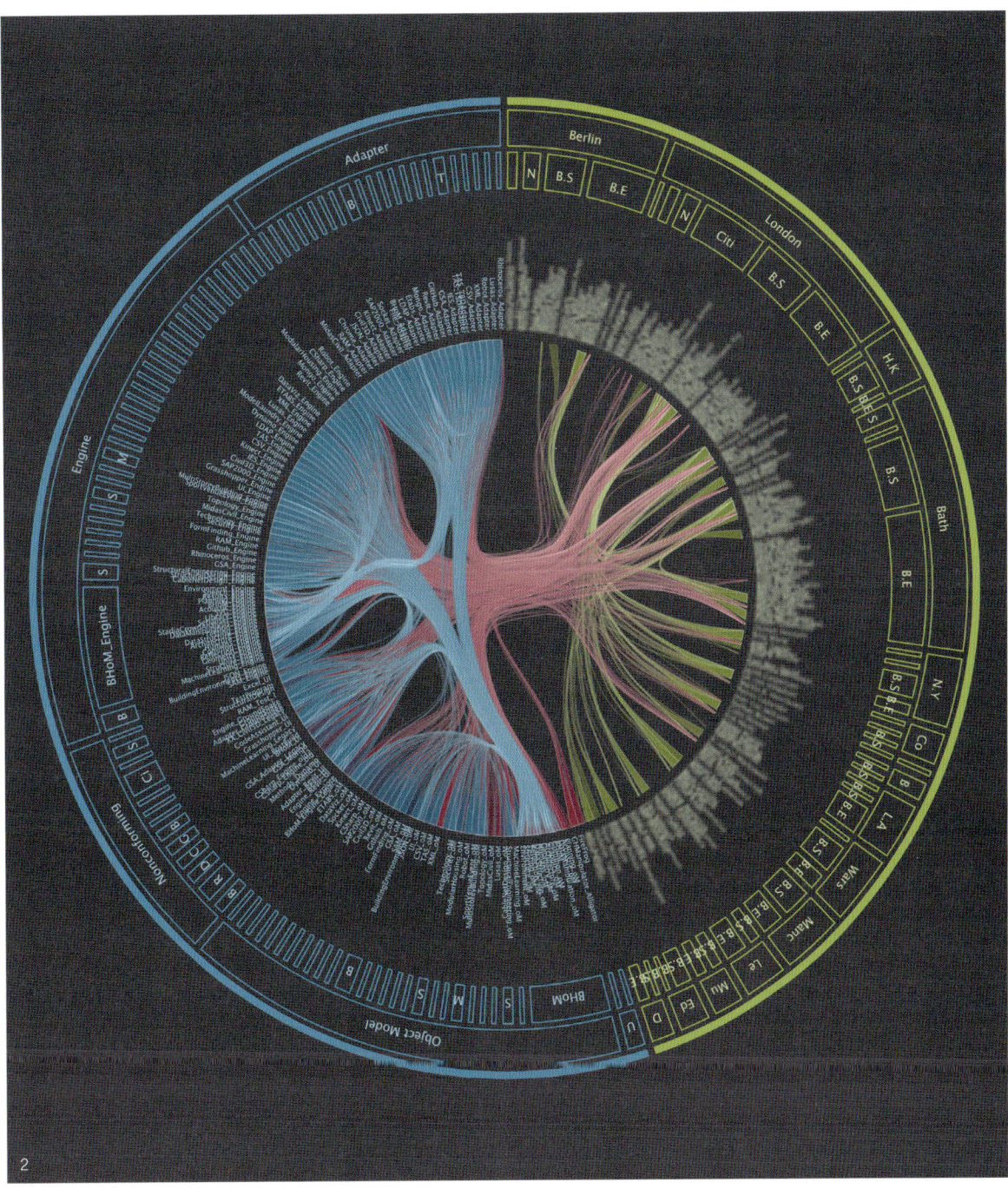

2. Mapping of the BHoM code base and the contributors. Left, in blue, are the modules of code on GitHub with the connections showing the code dependencies; right, in green, are the people who have contributed and their location in the world; in red are the human contributions to each piece of code. Image: BuroHappold.

workflow from which data can be transferred seamlessly between the respective working environments of the two companies.

This scenario shows how a single data-rich object is able to adapt to two different paradigms, from engineering to fabrication concerns. The third experiment of this series aims to scale this speculative design workflow further by shifting the focus from the object to the project scale.

From the Object Level to the Project and Process Scales

Visualising and mapping a large number of object instances from an entire project can be quite challenging, especially for complex modelling consultancies like Design-to-Production with requirements to describe at full fabrication resolution all necessary parts of a building. In order to ease the design process, therefore, an interface entitled LayerStalker has been prototyped, presenting an alternative means of rendering object dependencies and exploring complex datasets and geometrical information of large-scale projects. A sunburst diagram is used to visualise the hierarchical structure of the layer table from Rhino3D. 'Child' layers are represented as offsets of their respective 'parent' layer, situated more toward the centre of the diagram. Each level is subdivided by 'sibling' layers.

Through the LayerStalker interface, the user is able to perform unstructured queries using specific tags ('detailed volume', 'dowel', 'drill', 'axis', 'connector', etc.) to search the local database, to display all objects with layer names that contain the exact same tag within the application's viewport. Although acting here on a local database only, the LayerStalker interface could be implemented within either the BHoM or Speckle frameworks to operate web-based queries, enabling clear design communication and mass participation in design practice at a larger scale.

Conclusion: Toward Mass Participation

The three examples outlined in this chapter focused on the local adaptive object schema, its transfer between different modelling environments and its instantiation at the project scale. Merging these three concepts enables cross-practice collaboration at scale, whereby multiple parties can seek to exchange complex data schemas and (sub-)models in a project.

This principle was explored during the 2018 Innochain Simulation for Architecture + Urban Design (SimAUD) workshop taught by Dimitrie Stefanescu and Paul Poinet. The workshop aimed to introduce the Speckle open-source framework and focused on open, collaborative design and modelling workflows. As part of the exercise, a predefined modelling workflow consisting of generating a complex network of freeform timber beam elements was segregated into six distinct modelling pipelines that was shared amongst the six workshop participants through Grasshopper files. Those files were linked through Speckle senders and receivers. The geometrical data was incrementally streamed to a Speckle viewer at each data transaction. The streams could also be aggregated and displayed within a common viewer accessible to all participants. Each time that pipelines were connected through the object streams, the overall workflow's map could be visualised in real-time through a global, higher-level graph displaying the input–output connections between the different pipelines. It is this 'metagraph' that is the key concept here, keeping track of both the object and the process and, crucially, human dependencies that exist, adapt and change throughout the evolution of a project.

As previously mentioned and observed in all the above modelling experiments, the human factor cannot be neglected in favour of a purely automated technological paradigm, and must be considered throughout all aspects of the design process. In order to enable mass participation in design at scale, co-creation and co-authorship behaviours need to be engendered, both in terms of project architecture and team competencies.

Competencies and Behaviours

To enable this continuum of participation from entry-level computational skills to advanced development, BuroHappold Engineering has developed a series of Computational Competencies, ranging from Level 1:

'Appreciation of Visual Programming' to Level 4: 'Expert Knowledge of Text-based Programming'. The former focuses on Grasshopper and Dynamo and the abstract concept of flow-based programming, while the latter, relates to advanced, well-structured modular C# code, co-created through collaborative behaviours facilitated through platforms like GitHub. The important intermediate levels 2 and 3 ensure the co-creation, sharing and reuse of VP scripts, and a smooth transition to basic coding.

A continuous range of computational skillsets enables mass participation in computational design, both in terms of usage and authorship. The distributed co-creation of the BHoM code base brings the benefits of the creators' diversity, resilience in development and greater relevance for adoption.

Project Architecture

With both an increased talent pool and a technology platform crafted for deployment at scale, the key to enabling effective utilisation is to ensure development is in context – that it is distributed on projects and, in the case of large multidisciplinary firms, across both project teams and disciplines. This requires the formulation of a project architecture and a project team and leadership that are equipped to facilitate development and ensure effective and appropriate use.

Instilling cultural change across all three of the above pillars enables a foundational change in an organisation's computational capabilities. In a similar way that DevOps (Development and Operations) has been seen as unifying software development and operations, the authors see computational engineering as a conscious unifying of continuous computational development and utilisation of code on projects, driven by project needs and performance outcomes.

The natural implication of a distributed development approach, such as that proposed by this essay, is the exploitation of network effects, increasing collective intelligence and – through improved communication – participation, access and the means to utilise this as collective know-how. The series of modelling experiments and prototypical applications described here present the progress made toward establishing such an approach.

Bibliography

Deutsch, R., 2017, *Convergence: The Redesign of Design (AD Smart)*. Hoboken, NJ, John Wiley & Sons Ltd.

Scheurer, F., 2012, 'From Thinking to Modeling to Building' in Marble, S. (ed.), *Digital Workflows in Architecture: Design-Assembly-Industry*, p.110–131, Basel, Birkhäuser.

Speckle: Open Digital Infrastructure for Designing, Making and Operating the Built Environment, 2018. https://speckle.works (accessed 7 February 2020).

The Buildings and Habitats Object Model: Sustainable Code at Scale, 2018. https://bhom.xyz (accessed 7 February 2020).

van der Heijden, R., Levelle E. and Riese, M., 2015, 'Parametric Building Information Generation for Design and Construction' in *Computational Ecologies: Design in the Anthropocene: Proceedings of the 35th Annual Conference of the Association for Computer Aided Design in Architecture (ACADIA), Cincinnati, Ohio*. http://papers.cumincad.org/data/works/att/acadia15_417.pdf (accessed 7 February 2020).

Notes

1. In computer science, a visual programming (VP) environment enables the user to create programmes by manipulating elements graphically rather than by specifying them textually.

2. Imperative programming is a programming paradigm that uses textual statements to modify a programme's state.

3. See p.62–67 and p.80–81 of this volume.

4. In computer science, a directory structure is the way an operating system's file system and its files are displayed to the end user.

5. While object schemas are usually static and specified by an object-oriented programming language and/or a software vendor, the authors argue here for dynamic object schemas that can be changed and specified on-the-fly by end-users.

6. www.autodesk.co.uk/products/robot-structural-analysis/overview

2.4 MODELLING STRATEGIES AND NEW WORKFLOWS

Alternative Means of Digital Design Communication

Dimitrie Stefanescu
The Bartlett School of Architecture, UCL

Introduction

Design, in general, is charged with solving ill-defined, or 'wicked', problems, the understanding of which is concomitant with the act of their resolution. In the words of Rittel and Webber, 'the information needed to understand the problem depends on one's idea of solving it' (Rittel and Webber, 1973; Crowley and Head, 2017; Rith and Dubberly, 2007). As such, the act of design has no definitive stopping rule, and nor can its output be judged by a binary evaluation of good vs. bad. Most importantly, the stakeholders involved in the design process do not necessarily have a shared set of values. Essentially, design can be seen as an iterative act that aims to reduce uncertainty at an ontological level (Hanna, 2014) by simultaneously searching for the appropriate problem-representation and resolution.

The main goal of this research project, as set out in the original Innochain call, is to analyse how complex, digital-based design can be communicated and collated internally, within a design team, and externally, with the various stakeholders involved in the design process. The literature establishes that communication and dialogue constitute the foundation for solving wicked problems, as, through these means, shared understanding can be constructed among the actors involved in the (design) process (Dawes et al., 2009; Lawson, 2005; Roberts, 2000; Conklin, 2005; Walz et al., 1993; Bechky, 2003). In other words, shared understanding can be construed as a set of matching ontological representations of meaning that gradually emerge through a process of conceptual displacement (Koestler, 2014; Schön, 2011, 1991). Communication and dialogue are increasingly reliant on digital means, yet they cannot be fully analysed through the lens of a purely technical model. On this premise, communication is understood as a transactional phenomenon that has both a technical or mechanistic manifestation (digital) and also an intrinsic psycho-social component. The former approach corresponds to the Shannon-Weaver model of communication (Shannon and Weaver, 1963, 1948), while the latter draws from inferential models developed under the philosophy of the natural language communication field (Grice, 1991; Sperber and Wilson, 1995; Wilson and Sperber, 2008).

Consequently, this project aims to investigate critical aspects of design communication, whereby communication is understood as having both technical and social dimensions that reinforce each other (Garfinkel and Rawls, 2006). Following that, at the beginning of the design process, one is bounded by an incomplete definition of the given problem and by the fact that the relationships between actors need to first emerge before subsequent shared ontologies can be defined. With this in mind, three main research directions were selected: (1) data representation and (2) data classification juxtapose different approaches to ontological models of design objects; and, finally, (3) data transaction looks into the mechanisms of interactional exchange and how they change the nature of design communication.

Methodology

The comparative investigation in the three research directions outlined above lacked a feasible alternative to existing digital design communication software. Consequently, this project required a separate software platform to be developed that would offer a valid comparison base. These efforts resulted in the connected design platform named Speckle, which served as base research instrument throughout this project.

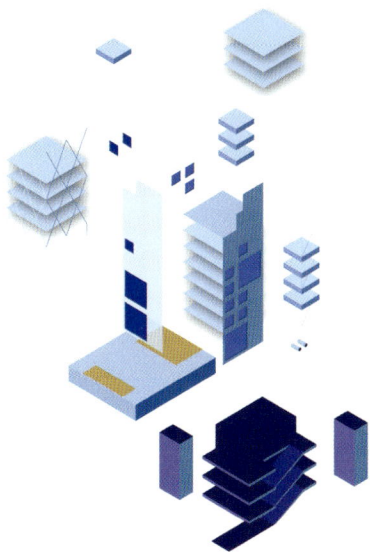 

1

First, the Speckle platform can be described as being schema-agnostic: it does not have a standardised ontology *per se*, but rather a small set of user-defined, composable object models that can be swapped in and out, or used in tandem. Second, Speckle is object-centric, as opposed to file-centric: instead of saving data in monolithic blocks, it stores each object individually (and immutably) and allows for overlapping groupings thereof. Third, Speckle is embodying data: as opposed to existing approaches, where files are just 'shared' and there is no overview of who is consuming the information, nor to what effect, Speckle traces the communicative network and informs end-users of their transactions and the implications of these. Thanks to these characteristics, Speckle enabled theoretical, technical and applied analysis of the aforementioned research questions.

The collaborative network within which this research project was undertaken, Innochain, consisted of both academic and industrial partners. It served as the seed for a living laboratory that grew throughout the project to include many other industry participants. As such, this setting served both as the basis for the technical development and testing of Speckle, as well as the pool from which the quantitative and qualitative data required to investigate the research directions outlined above were gathered.

Research Findings

Regarding the first research direction, (1) *data representation*, it was found that a low-level composable schema provides opportunities for dialogue between stakeholders on the topic of how design objects are defined – essentially, enabling ontological revision at a representational level. Furthermore, existing higher-level object models can be natively supported, including the industry-standard Industry Foundation Classes (IFC), without loss of fidelity and without enforcing an overly strict high-level standard. Nevertheless, one important limitation was the asymmetrical codification and de-codification of objects, which can lead to information loss. Specifically:

- A lower-level, composable object model allows end-users to undergo a productive process of ontological (representational) revision.
- Existing higher-level object models from the industry, such as the BuroHappold Object Model (BHoM) or IFC, can be natively supported, thus allowing for 'backwards-compatibility'.
- Multiple, self-contained object-models can be programmatically supported in a simultaneous and consistent manner in a digitally-enabled design communication process, thus invalidating the industry's assumed need for a singular, unique object model.

1. From a digitally fragmented design process, toward an integrated data platform for the built environment.

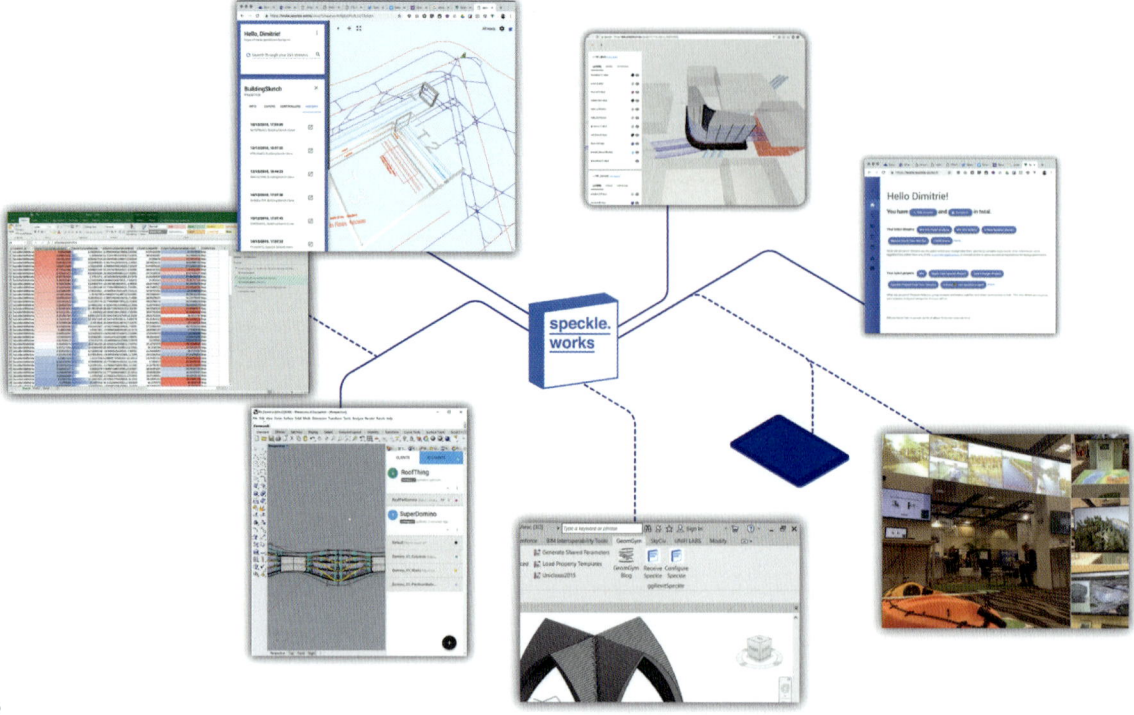

2

In (2) *data classification*, we put forward a curatorial object-centric approach to data storage and classification that mitigates information loss. This was achieved through an approach to object identity that was directly linked with the object's properties, as opposed to a randomly-generated one of the type currently employed in most persistence layers. Furthermore, we showed that, unlike file-centric collaboration methodologies, an object-centric approach imposes ontological revision at the content level by requiring actors to negotiate what information they share and why. In turn, this leads to increased relevance of data and a reduction in overall communication noise: instead of sharing information 'in bulk', any design data that is communicated must have a recipient and a direct use. The findings of this second research strand can be summarised as follows:

- The communicative productivity of an object-based curatorial approach to design data classification has been validated both through qualitative means, by assessing several case studies observed 'in the wild', and through empirical observations based on the monitored usage of Speckle: on average, design models were broken down into 2.47 separate sub-classifications. Furthermore, when taking into account the sources coming into a given model, the average count of both sources and receivers per model was 2.78, highlighting a dynamic process of fragmentation and re-assembly.
- An object-based approach to data persistence is potentially twice as efficient as a file-based one in enabling multiple overlapping classifications of design information. Furthermore, the actual cost of creating new classifications from existing ones is virtually negligible (< 0.1% of the original model size), which facilitates the emergence and evolution of efficient 'informal' communication exchanges.

Finally, in strand (3) *data transaction*, by evaluating key characteristics of the informational flows (their frequency, the potential for meta-information transmission, their relevance outside specialised contexts), we showed that smaller (and thus faster) data transactions increase the velocity of the overall communication process. This determines the rate at which the representational and content-level revisions proceed, and thus represents a critical aspect of digital design communication in terms of enabling the emergence of shared understanding. Among other major findings were:

- The transaction size can be decoupled from the size of the model, thus enabling much smaller, and speedier, change-dependent digital design data exchanges. From a theoretical point of view,

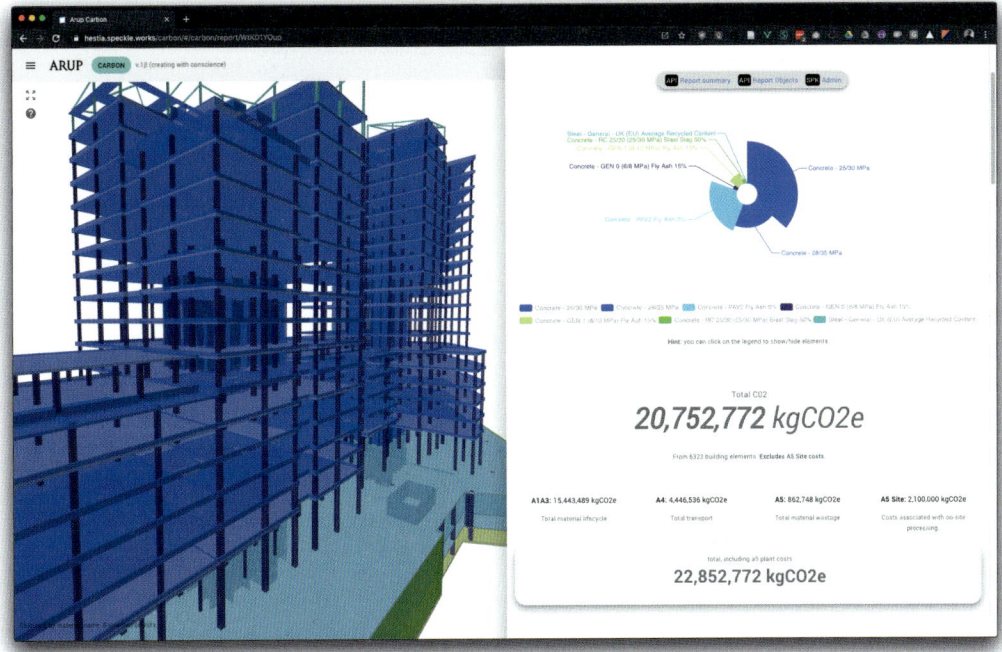

3

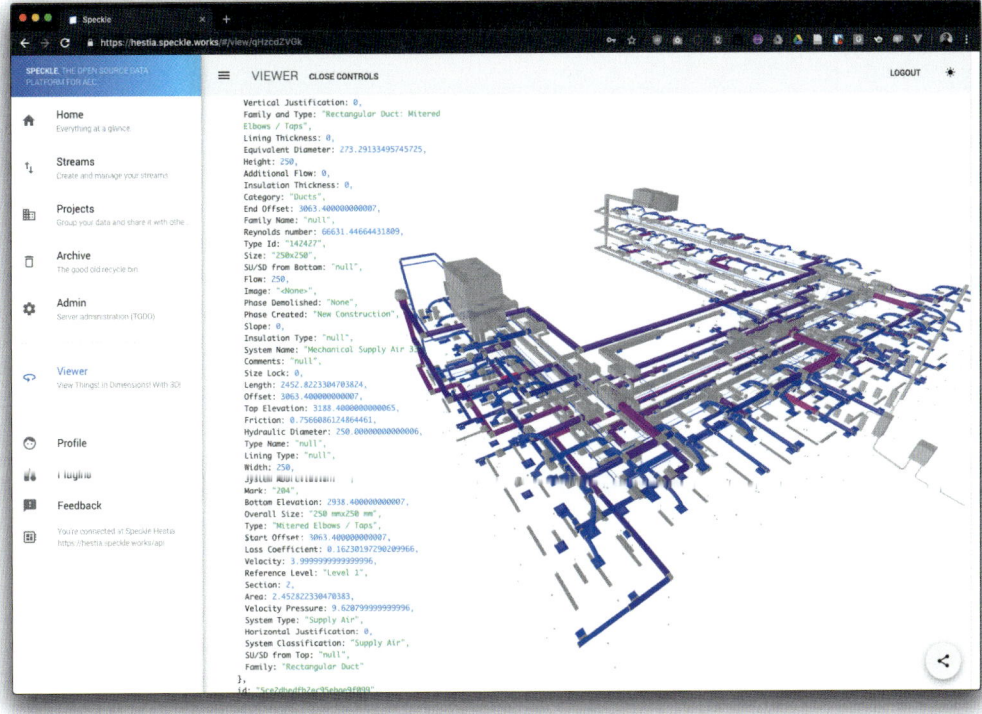

4

2. The Speckle ecosystem connects several software applications and enables customised digital workflows to be assembled.

3. Arup Carbon, a proprietary embedded carbon estimation web application, developed on top of Speckle to provide real-time sustainability insights on designs, © Arup, 2019.

4. Mechanical engineering model and its associated data displayed in the online Speckle viewer.

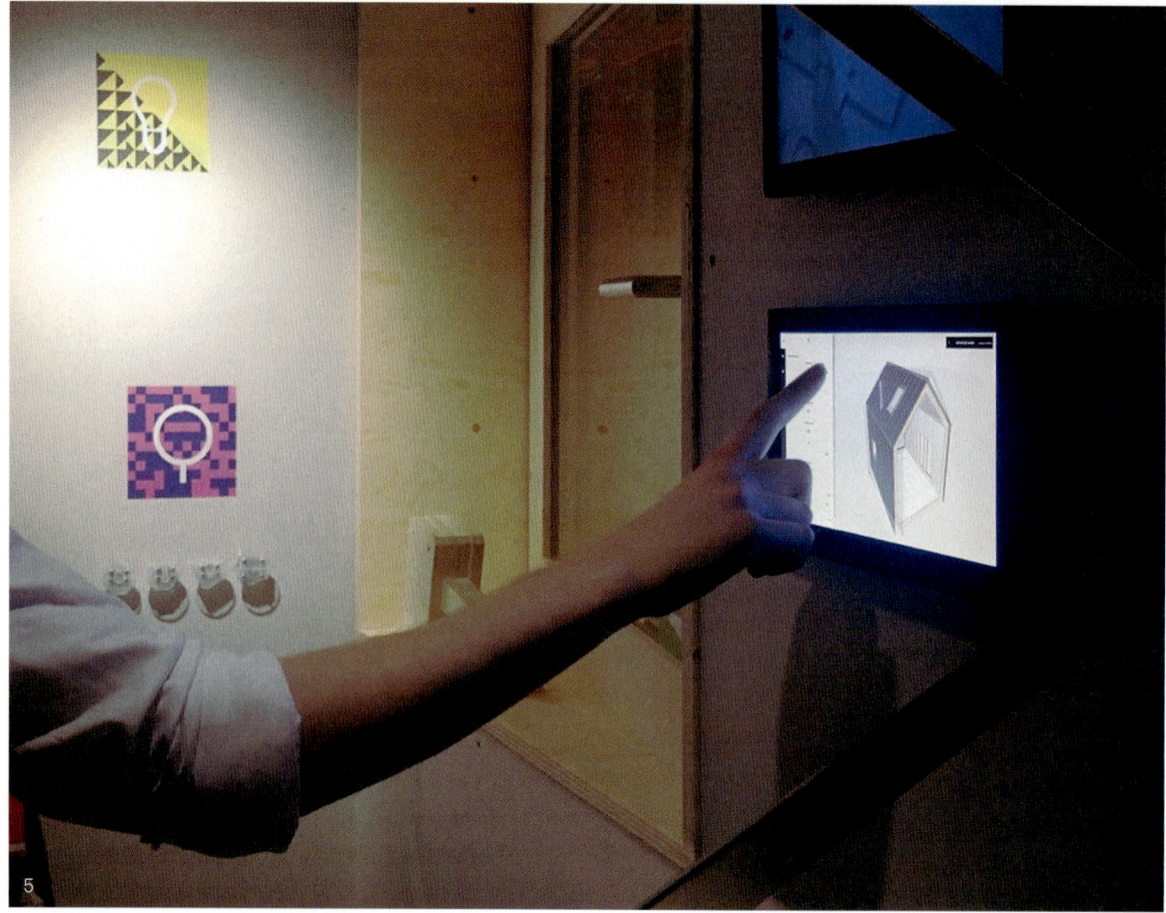

this allows for the reassertion of nextness (adjacency) in a digital design workflow. Empirical observations showed that transactions can be as much as five times faster (by virtue of being five times leaner in size).
- Informing users of who is dependent on their data (as well as when data on which they are depending, coming from a different person, has become stale) establishes a measure of productive sequentiality, which is sufficient for individual tasks. Nevertheless, we identified a need for stakeholders in coordination roles to provide a project-wide overview of the activity network.

Impact and Perspectives

In terms of ongoing academic research, the most recent development is the 'AEC Delta Mobility' grant, funded by Innovate UK in late 2018. Within a consortium consisting of BuroHappold (former Innochain industrial partner), 3D Repo, Rhomberg Sersa Rail UK, Speckle, and The Bartlett School of Construction and Project Management at UCL, the scope of this project is to normalise and specify, using Speckle, an industry standard for design change specification that allows faster and more agile 'delta' updates to replace the file-based exchange mechanisms that are currently prevalent in the AEC industry.

Furthermore, Speckle has been used as a technological base for research in participatory urbanism at the Future Cities Laboratory at the Singapore ETH Centre. The role played by Speckle was twofold. First, it enabled an expert user to define a subset of a design space from a parametric model. Second, it allowed any number of users, without any special technical background, to explore said design space and express their subjective opinion in direct relation with the well-defined (mathematical) parameter values of the model itself. In a paper currently under peer review, Katja Knecht, the lead scientist on the project, concludes that 'it has been shown that the approach of sharing parametric design spaces can facilitate public engagement and support the exchange between expert and laymen in urban design'.

With regard to adoption within industry, a number of international AEC companies have incorporated Speckle at the core of their digital transformation efforts. Among many others, the most prominent firms are HOK, SOM, Arup, RHDV, BVN, Aurecon, Dialog Design and Grimshaw.

Conclusion

Digital communication constitutes a key infrastructural base on which the design process now operates. Within this research project, communication was contextualised as a transactional phenomenon, with both technical and social manifestations that reinforce each other. Accordingly, the contribution made by the project can be summarised as an integrated technical and sociological rethink of communication in the digital design process that challenges the existing status quo of the AEC industry.

By marrying contemporary technical affordances with a user- and industry-centred analysis, this project demonstrates that existing assumptions around the need for centralised high-level standards and workflows discourage meaningful dialogue from happening and exclude vital stakeholders from the design process.

By contrast, a flexible digital communication framework that provides an inferential context for dialogue to take place among design stakeholders, allows for emergence and evolution in the way information is defined and structured, enabling the creation of shared values and meaning. Broadly speaking, the low impact of emerging technologies on the overall productivity and efficiency of the AEC industries (Barbosa et al., 2017; Charef et al., 2019; Dainty et al., 2017; Hong et al., 2019) can be attributed to widespread confusion regarding its communicative processes, and their subsequent distortion through inadequate technological implementations. Nevertheless, this research project concludes that digital technologies can embrace the diversity and richness of the design process, enhance the collaborative aspects of the industry, and, moreover, open an accessible and ethical pathway toward a digitally-integrated built environment.

Bibliography

Barbosa, F., Woetzel, J., Mischke, J., Ribeirinho, M.J., Sridhar, M., Parsons, M., Bertram, N. and Brown, S., 2017, *Reinventing Construction: A Route to Higher Productivity*, Washington DC, McKinsey Global Institute.

Bechky, B.A., 2003. 'Sharing Meaning across Occupational Communities: The Transformation of Understanding on a Production Floor' in *Organization Science*, Vol. 14, p.312–330.

Charef, R., Emmitt, S., Alaka, H. and Fouchal, F., 2019, 'Building Information Modelling Adoption in the European Union: An Overview' in *Journal of Building Engineering*, Vol. 25, 100777.

Conklin, J., 2005. *Dialogue Mapping: Building Shared Understanding of Wicked Problems*. Chichester: Wiley.

Crowley, K. and Head, B.W., 2017. 'The Enduring Challenge of "Wicked Problems": Revisiting Rittel and Webber' in *Policy Sciences*, Vol. 50, p.539–547.

Dawes, S.S., Cresswell, A.M. and Pardo, T.A., 2009, 'From "Need to Know" to "Need to Share": Tangled Problems, Information Boundaries, and the Building of Public Sector Knowledge Networks' in *Public Administration Review*, Vol. 69, No. 2, 392–402.

Dainty, A., Leiringer, R., Fernie, S. and Harty, C., 2017, 'BIM and the Small Construction Firm: A Critical Perspective' in *Building Research & Information*, Vol. 45, No. 6, p.696–709.

Dainty, A., Moore, D. and Murray, M., 2006, *Communication in Construction*. London, Routledge.

Garfinkel, H. and Rawls, A., 2006, *Toward a Sociological Theory of Information*, Boulder, CO, Routledge.

Grice, H.P., 1991, *Studies in the Way of Words*, Cambridge, MA, Harvard University Press.

Hanna, S., 2014. 'Ontological Uncertainty and Design: Requirements for Creative Machines'. Conference paper, Design Creativity Workshop 2014, London.

Hong, Y., Hammad, A.W.A., Sepasgozar, S. and Akbarnezhad, A., 2018, 'BIM Adoption Model for Small and Medium Construction Organisations in Australia' in *Engineering, Construction and Architectural Management*, Vol. 26 No. 2, p.154–183. https://doi.org/10.1108/ECAM-04-2017-0064 (accessed 10 February 2020).

Lawson, B., 2005, *How Designers Think: The Design Process Demystified*, 4th edition, Amsterdam, Routledge.

Koestler, A., 2014, *The Act of Creation*, New York, Last Century Media.

Rith, C. and Dubberly, H., 2007, 'Why Horst W.J. Rittel Matters', in *Design Issues* Vol. 23, No. 1, p.72–91.

Rittel, H.W.J., Webber, M.M., 1973, 'Dilemmas in a General Theory of Planning' in *Policy Sciences*, Vol. 4, p.155–169.

Roberts, N., 2000, 'Wicked Problems and Network Approaches to Resolution', in *International Public Management Review*, Vol. 1, p.1–19.

Schön, D.A., 1991, *The Reflective Practitioner: How Professionals Think in Action*, Farnham, Routledge.

Schön, D.A., 2011, *Displacement of Concepts*, Farnham, Routledge.

Shannon, C.E. and Weaver, W., 1963, *The Mathematical Theory of Communication*, University of Illinois Press.

Sperber, D., and Wilson, D., 1995, *Relevance: Communication and Cognition*, 2 odition, Cambridge, MA, Wiley-Blackwell.

Walz, D.B., Elam, J.J. and Curtis, B., 1993, 'Inside a Software Design Team: Knowledge Acquisition, Sharing, and Integration' in *Communications of the ACM*, Vol. 36, No. 10, p.63–77.

Wilson, D. and Sperber, D., 2008. 'Relevance Theory', in Horn, L.R. and Ward, G. (eds.), *The Handbook of Pragmatics*, Cambridge, MA, Wiley-Blackwell, p.606–632.

5. Speckle in use at the V&A's Arup/WikiHouse exhibition from 2016.

2.5 MODELLING STRATEGIES AND NEW WORKFLOWS

Negotiating Structured Building Information Data

Nathan Miller and David Stasiuk
Proving Ground

The Emergence of Machine Learning

In recent years, applied machine learning techniques and advanced algorithms for data analysis have become increasingly ubiquitous across a wide array of professional and academic practices, ranging from the natural sciences to business and finance. The successful application of these algorithms hinges on their access to large volumes of data describing respective targets of inquiry. In machine learning, input data is organised into features, which may be produced using a variety of independent mechanisms.

The heterogeneity of input data carries both positive potential and risk: while diverse input data may yield better results, it is generally a non-trivial effort to effectively capture, reconcile and integrate multiple discrete data sources. For example, decision support resulting from a sales analysis that relies on the observation of business transactional data may be significantly enhanced or further informed by customer attitudinal profile data; or scientific data describing natural phenomena collected through sensors or other observational techniques may be used in conjunction with data generated through the application of computational simulations. Yet, the synthesis of such distinct datasets into meaningful-feature collections may require manual processing that relies not only on the ability and intuition of the user implementing the algorithm but also the quality and 'cleanliness' of the data itself. The value of these analytical techniques and decision support tools is thus tied to the underlying data, which they rely on being correct, suitably voluminous and well structured.

Challenges for the Application of Machine Learning in Architectural Design

Architects and engineers have an established history of using machine learning algorithms to enhance manufacturing processes (Nicholas, 2017; Brugnaro, 2017; De Leon, 2012), search intractably large design spaces (Stasiuk, 2014; Derix and Thum, 2005), label spatial typologies (Peng, 2017) or even generate building and floor plans (Chaillou, 2019). These techniques have, however, more rarely been applied as decision support tools for associating early-phase design and discovery processes with specified outcome quality, especially related to more subjective performance measures. The relative absence of the use of predictive modelling for evaluating the impact of design decisions on architectural performances stems from multiple challenges.

The first of these relates to problem definition: difficulty in effectively articulating subjective design problems has been considered extensively because the introduction of a design solution may, in fact, introduce new, unforeseen problems (Rittel, 1973). This, in turn, leads to challenges in quantifying performance outcomes relative to these stated problems, especially for those that appear outwardly subjective, such as a user's experience of the space. Furthermore, in practice it is rare for practitioners to maintain or have access to the types of well-structured data needed for training machine learning algorithms to become effective mechanisms for outcomes prediction. As a result, the most abundant examples of applied machine learning in the building sciences tend to focus on the physical characteristics of an assembly, such as its structural or thermal performance, or descriptions of its morphology.

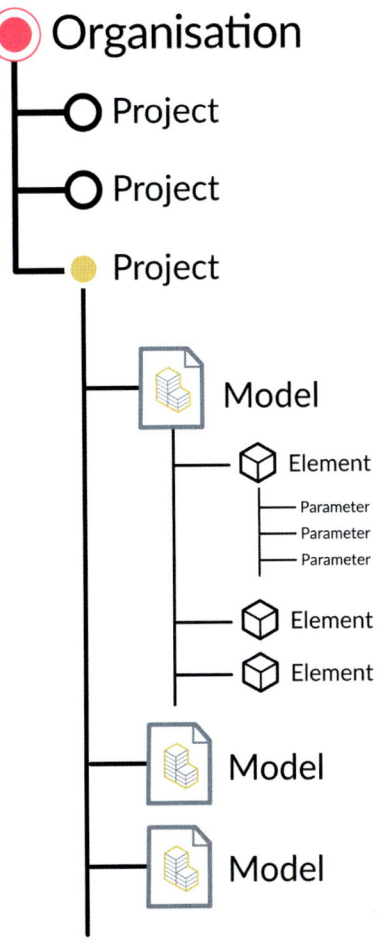

The rare examples that engage in predictive modelling for architectural usage help illuminate reasons why. One such approach has been described by Daniel Davis, where his company WeWork leveraged historical data to optimise its conference-room design methodologies for end-user satisfaction (Davis, 2016). Here, the vertical structure of WeWork – a company that designs, owns and operates its own buildings – facilitates the acquisition and curation of datasets created at different stages along the supply chain. Their relative success relies on the extensive data access afforded by the multi-faceted roles their company plays in the building lifecycle; this underscores the challenges in realising closed-loop predictive analyses faced by more traditional design practices that generally only have access to design-level model data.

Methods for Exploiting Model Resources

Contemporary architectural projects of even the most modest complexity are ubiquitously realised using digital modelling techniques for design authoring and for the production of pertinent representations. While many different approaches may be employed throughout the design cycle, Building Information Modelling (BIM) is a methodology widely used to employ 'a digital representation of physical and functional characteristics of a facility' for design development, documentation and archiving (US national BIM Standard Project Committee). Depending on the size and complexity of a project, a single building may be represented by a series

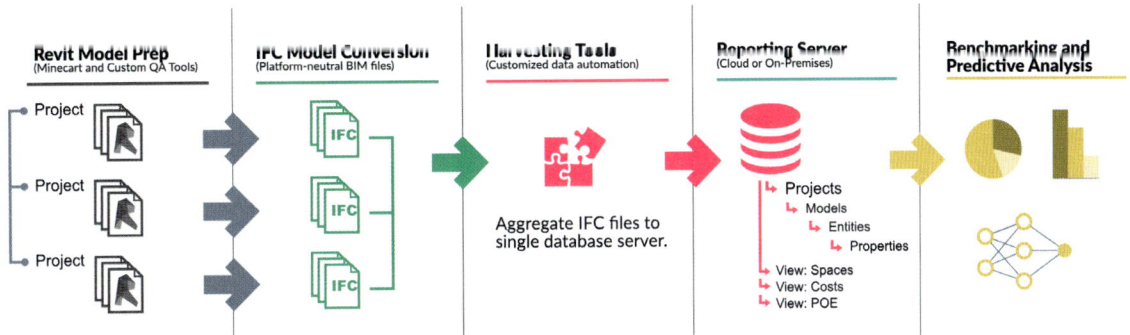

1. Database structure that scales from practice to project, to model, to element.

2. Pipeline for data aggregation and application to machine learning.

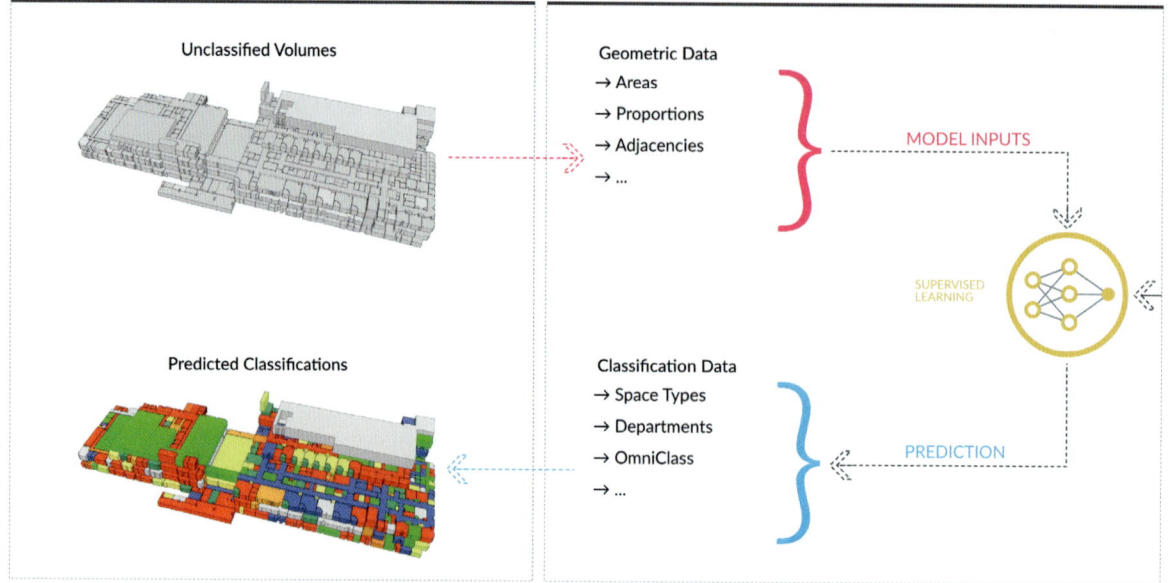

3

(sometimes dozens) of disaggregated model files, based on scope or discipline. Once their role is complete for building production, however, most of these models cease to be used in any way – with some notable exceptions for more sophisticated owners and operators, who may employ them for improved building operations. In the context of leveraging BIM for enhanced design intelligence through machine learning, these historical models constitute an invaluable and largely untapped information resource.

Design of a Relational Database for BIM Aggregation

We present a storage and access strategy that allows for data-mining models across individual and multiple projects (fig.1). Here, we have created and implemented a relational database schema and system for automating its population with model data. The database is designed around the basic entity-relationship hierarchy exhibited within BIM formats such as Revit and IFC, which has been extended to accommodate the information traversal that scales from individual model element all the way up to project levels.

The basic table structure hierarchy reflects this existing information infrastructure and intent for extendibility, encompassing Projects-Documents-Elements-Parameters (PDEP):

- **Projects:** Project information such as client, project name and market classification.
- **Documents:** Document-level data such as file name, location and file size.
- **Elements:** Individual object data, such as names, and categorical classifications, including walls, rooms and equipment.
- **Parameters:** Object properties with storage types for text and numeric properties, including for classifications, areas and quantities.

With a database schema established, tools have been developed to collect and prepare Revit and IFC file data, respectively, and which follow the processing pattern shown in figure 3:

- **File Harvesting:** An automated routine processes a BIM file and establishes a dataset containing tables for document, element and parameter information. Harvester applications have been built both as an add-in for Revit and as a standalone application for IFC.
- **SQL Formatting:** The processed dataset is then automatically formatted as a series of text-file uploads to the database server.
- **Database Upload:** The data files are bulk-uploaded into the relational database tables.

Data Harvesting for Applied Machine Learning

This harvester technology has been used in several professional architecture and engineering practices. This section focuses on its use at HDR Architecture, where it is deployed to support benchmarking analyses across several business sectors, comparing the spatial metrics of real-world projects relative to industry best practices and standards.

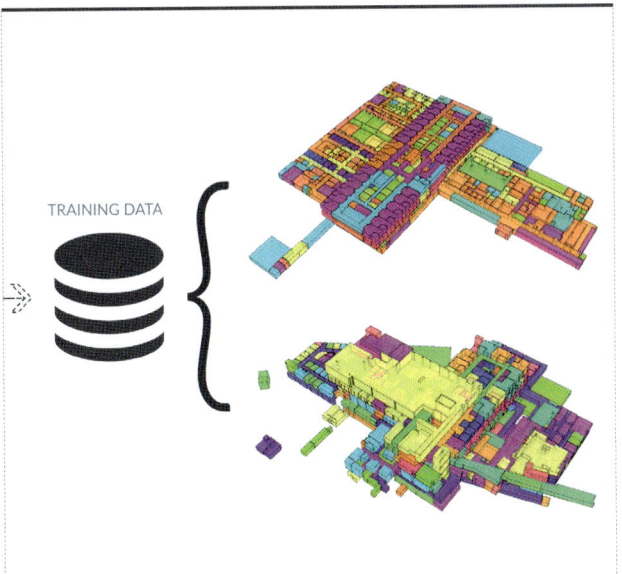

BIM Database

TRAINING DATA

3. Machine learning workflow.

Here, we have created a proof-of-concept prototype that leverages data from three large-scale healthcare projects to train and test a machine learning algorithm (fig.2). (The limited number of models available for this prototype is a result of those made available for our collaboration; the setup is capable of handling thousands of models.) Planning for healthcare projects is accompanied by strict requirements, with individual spaces following specifications that include not only size and shape, but also adjacency to rooms that house related functions, the inclusion of specific medical equipment, and other considerations for patient and provider experience.

Historically, the design processes that aim to reconcile these demands rely heavily on a planner's experience and any heuristics they may employ, and such approaches may be time-consuming in broader application. This prototype positions machine learning as a support tool to facilitate more rapid search efforts and to support designer intuition.

Predictive Modelling Prototype

The learning model uses room-bounding geometry and building-level data to suggest viable OmniClass specifications within the healthcare business sector.[1] We hypothesise that, by training a model based on known prior room-programme assignment with a series of descriptive features discernible from the harvested data, a supervised learning algorithm may provide architects with real-time critical decision support for programming and planning during the design of a new building (fig.3).

Firstly, models in the database are evaluated for their consistency in employing OmniClass labels for room-level programme specification. This type of data-normalisation strategy is essential when project requirements and naming conventions for spaces vary between project teams and according to client requirements.

A first-order feature set is extracted from the database, including room area, level, and department. Grasshopper is then used to extract geometry from the IFC database to derive second-order descriptive features related to room shape and adjacency to other rooms, using spatial analyses based on 3D representations of each room. The OmniClass specification is then used as the labelled or predicted data feature. With these first- and second-order descriptive features, two of the available IFC models are used to train a Naive Bayes Classifier (NBC) learning algorithm, and the third model is reserved to test the viability of the algorithm. NBCs evaluate a series of categorical input features to assign probabilities that a given data point may be of a specific classification. A result of this is that test data points will frequently have several possible outcomes, each attended by a probability as determined by the algorithm. Because NBC relies on categorical inputs for learning, continuous numerical feature data – such as area or aspect ratio of bounding box space – is prepared as a collection of categories (such as variants on 'small', 'medium' or 'large' for room size). Based on this setup, our model demonstrates positive results as a decision support tool, with over 80% of spaces containing in their probable outcomes set their actual OmniClass value (fig.4).

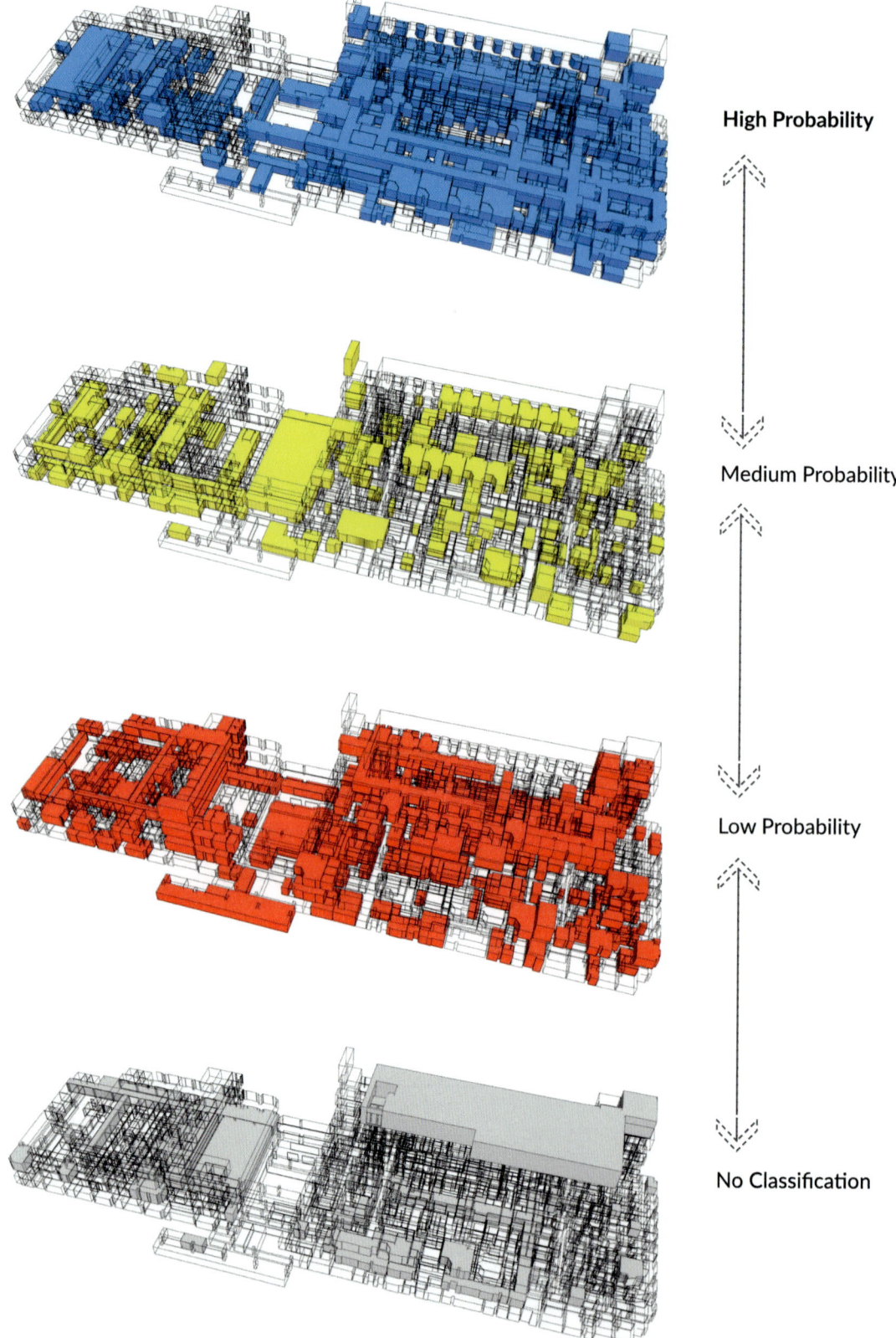

Conclusions and Future Work

Building information models provide a consistent data structure that has been broadly adopted for production but is ultimately under-utilised for data analysis. Our data harvesting techniques allow us to efficiently migrate BIM data into a scalable, centralised database that can be mined to train machine learning algorithms. As these methods of data collection are adopted by building practices, we foresee both the need for greater accountability on the subject of data standards in order to successfully utilise the data for supervised learning, and also for the development and deployment of data remediation techniques for cleaning or repairing older data that may be of poor quality but still contain potentially useful insights for future design efforts.

While this research presents methods and technologies for leveraging building data, it also reveals challenges pertaining to data quality in the construction industry, which remains subject to inconsistent production practices, lack of standardisation, and error-prone data entry methods. Nonetheless, current trends indicate that the continued adoption of BIM-related data standards and the growing market demand for data-rich digital assets should ultimately improve data availability for the enhanced training of machine learning algorithms for early-stage architectural design.

Note

1. OmniClass is a North American construction classification system used for standardising building information that, when deployed, provides a baseline definition that is consistent and project-independent.

Bibliography

Brugnaro, G. and Hanna., S., 2017, 'Adaptive Robotic Training Methods for Subtractive Manufacturing' in *Proceedings of the 37th Annual Conference of the Association for Computer Aided Design in Architecture (ACADIA)*, Acadia Publishing Company, p.164–116.

Chaillou, S., 2019, 'Architecture & Style: A New Frontier for AI in Architecture' in *Towards Data Science*, 2 June 2019. towardsdatascience.com/architecture-style-ded3a2c3998f (accessed 8 February 2020).

Davis, D., 2016, 'Evaluating Buildings with Computation and Machine Learning'. ACADIA/2016: POSTHUMAN FRONTIERS: Data, Designers, and Cognitive Machines. Proceedings of the 36th Annual Conference of the Association for Computer Aided Design in Architecture (ACADIA), Acadia Publishing Company, p.116–123.

Derix, C. and Thum, R., 2000, 'Self-Organising Space (SOS): Artificial Neural Network Spaces', 3rd Generative Art Conference GA2000.

Langley, P., Derix, C. and Coates, P., 2007, 'Meta-Cognitive Mappings: Growing Neural Networks for Generative Urbanism', 10th Generative Art Conference GA2007.

McGraw-Hill Construction, 2012, 'The Business Value of BIM in North America: Multi-Year Trend Analysis and User Ratings (2007–2012)' in *Smart Market Report*, Bedford, MA, McGraw-Hill Construction Research & Analytics.

Nicholas, P., Zwierzycki, M., Clausen Nørgaard, E., Leinweber, S., Stasiuk, S., Thomsen, M.R. and Hutchinson, C., 2017, 'Adaptive Robotic Fabrication for Conditions of Material Inconsistency: Increasing the Geometric Accuracy of Incrementally Formed Metal Panels' in *Fabricate 2017*, London, UCL Press, p.114–121.

Pena, A., 2012, 'Two Case-Studies of Freeform-Facade Rationalization' in Achten, H., Pavlicek, J. Hulin, J. and Matějovska, D. (eds.), *Digital Physicality: Proceedings of the 30th eCAADe Conference, volume*, Vol. 2, p.118.

Peng, W., Zhang, F. and Nagakura, T., 2017. 'Machines' Perception of Space: Employing 3D Isovist Methods and a Convolutional Neural Network in Architectural Space Classification' in *Proceedings of the 37th Annual Conference of the Association for Computer Aided Design in Architecture (ACADIA)*, Acadia Publishing Company, p.104–10.

Rittel, H.W. and Webber, M.M., 1973, '2.3 Planning Problems Are Wicked' in *Polity* 4, p.155–169.

Stasiuk, D., Thomsen, M.R. and Thompson, E.M., 2014, 'Learning to Be a Vault: Implementing Learning Strategies for Design Exploration in Inter-Scalar Systems' in *eCAADe*, Vol. 32, Newcastle upon Tyne, England, CAAD Education, p.381–390.

4. Dataset used for proof-of-concept prototype.

Research Summary
Multiple Criteria Design Exploration in the Early Design Phase

Zeynep Aksöz
Industrial Partners: Foster + Partners, str.ucture GmbH
Academic Institution: Institute of Architecture, University of Applied Arts Vienna

Conventional design practice is often constrained to follow a linear path, starting with an early design sketch, leading to late-stage engineering resolution, design optimisation and execution that may run counter to aspirations defined in earlier stages. Indeed, some early decisions may in fact complicate 'more informed' optimisation procedures in later stages. Such flawed design-to-realisation pathways can be wasteful with an uneven distribution of time for the investigation of novel approaches and solutions.

As computational power increases and data-processing accelerates, the simulation of design performance also becomes faster. Accordingly, the integration of applications for optimisation is moving to earlier stages of design. While opening new horizons for exploration and optimisation, these processes encourage an obsession with numbers and performance, where design is often mistaken for conventional problem-solving. However, early design exploration is actually a stage in which the variables and goals that influence the optimisation and search process are not clearly defined. This stage is, characteristically, a cycle of iterative exploration, evaluation and reflection, where the role of the designer becomes more about framing the questions than finding solutions.

This research project explores design methods and workflows that break the linearity of the traditional design process, while still accommodating the flexible and ambiguous nature of creative exploration. Acknowledging the potentials of technological developments in the field, through the integration of heuristics and machine learning, the research investigates methodologies of collaboration between designer and computer to amplify the creative exploration. It asks how architects and designers can use information-based processes in the early design phase to negotiate between performative design objectives and aesthetic aims, and how this awareness can positively influence optimisation procedures in later stages.

Here, technology is approached as a communication medium rather than a decision-making tool. A new way of thinking is established, integrating generative processes early on. Design outcomes are approached as emergent products of a collaborative system between designer and computer. Design methods are developed that integrate machine learning technologies with heuristics. With this fusion, design-to-realisation processes are transformed into sustainable workflows, with information harvested across design processes and utilised to establish a computational tacit knowledge across projects. Through a feedback loop that integrates this knowledge in the early design exploration, designers are informed of future optimisation goals. The creative exploration is, consequently, expanded into an information-rich process, where the performative goals are considered alongside aesthetic aims. Digital tools developed within the project framework enable design goals to be defined and evaluated at the outset. As a result, a cross-disciplinary dialogue emerges between professionals and stakeholders to understand the nature of the design problem early on.

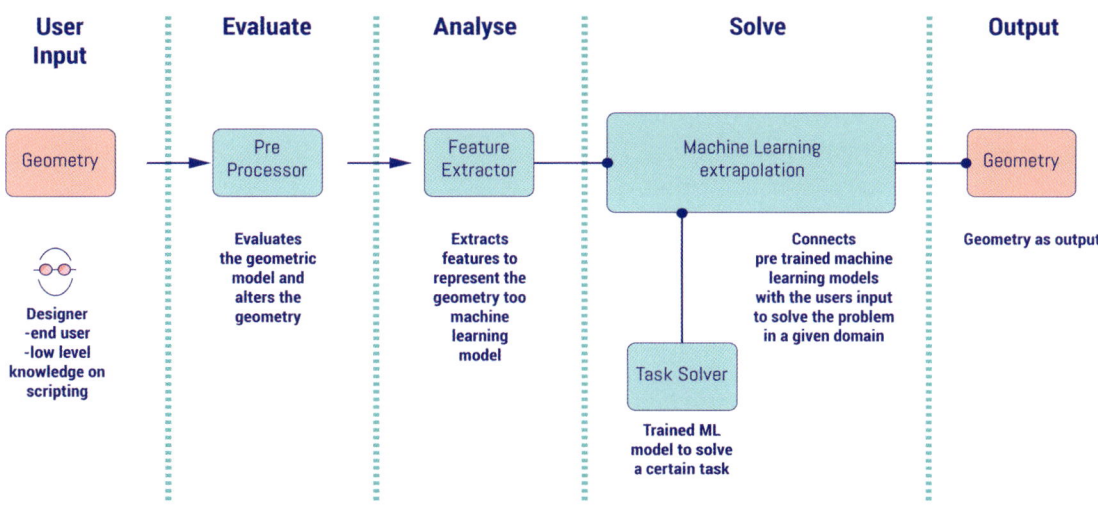

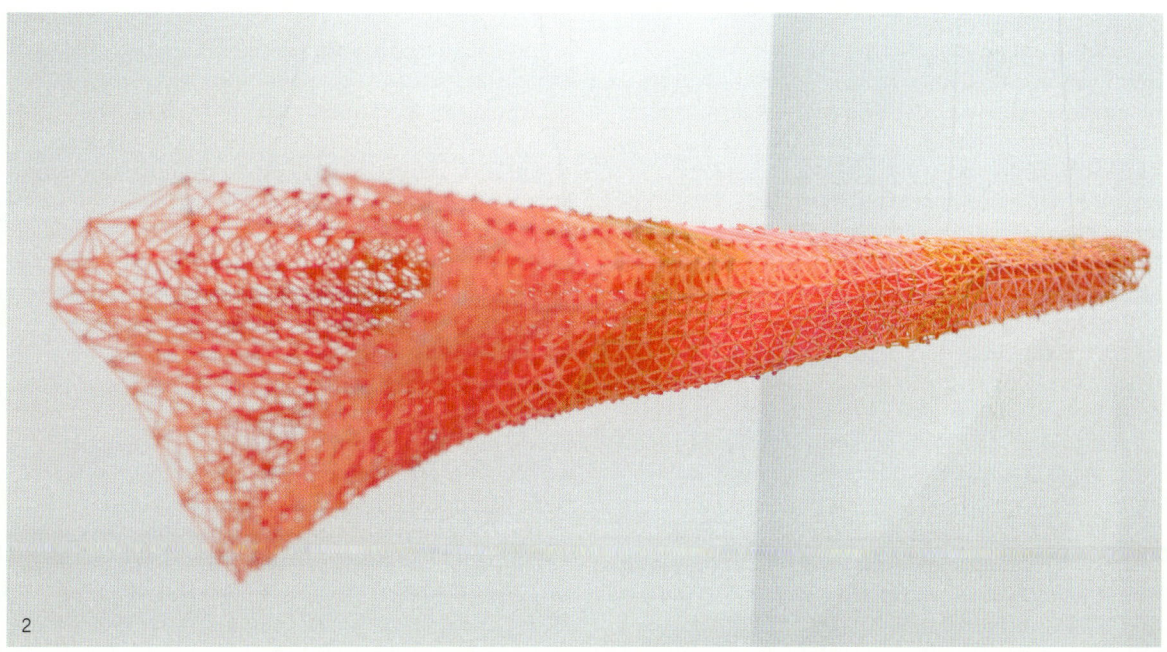

1. An optimisation workflow that utilises a learning strategy instead of an iterative optimisation solver. Instead of a global optimisation strategy that emulates from the global parameter, this method solves the optimisation problem by subsampling the global geometry into independent modules that share the same topology. This way, an Artificial Neural Network that is specially trained for a certain local problem can predict approximations of locally optimal solutions for each singular module.

2. A locally optimised lattice using a local learning strategy. This prototype was the result of the industry collaboration with Foster + Partners and was robotically printed in their office.

MODELLING STRATEGIES AND NEW WORKFLOWS

Research Summary
Morphogenetic Fluid Dynamics

Angelos Chronis
Industrial Partners: Foster + Partners, McNeel
Academic Institution: Institute for Advanced Architecture of Catalonia (IAAC),
Universitat Politècnica de Catalunya

Today, performative morphogenesis provides common ground in avant-garde architectural research and practice. The form-finding design systems that, two decades ago, were envisioned to transform architectural design are now at the forefront of our built environment. Architects can now integrate most environmental forces that define a building's performance into their design systems, enabling them to determine their form. One of the fundamental environmental forces that affects how a building performs – as well as most form-finding methods in other fields – is, however, still largely unaccounted-for.

The flow of air in and around buildings is, undoubtedly, one of the most important aspects of architectural design. As buildings continue to be one of the primary contributors of carbon dioxide emissions that lead to climate change (UNEP, 2016), demand for cooling energy is expected to overtake that for heating energy in the coming decades. This project investigated the potential of wind-driven form-finding in architecture, aimed at optimising the natural ventilation potential of buildings. By integrating Computational Fluid Dynamic (CFD) simulations and shape-optimisation methods, it explored how aerodynamic forces can drive the shape of buildings and augment their ability to cool naturally.

Over the course of the project, a number of integration methods for CFD in computational design were developed and evaluated. Through industrial and academic collaborations, as well as workshops and other dissemination efforts, the project exposed architects and researchers to CFD simulations and wind-driven form-finding. Using design experiments and case studies across scales, ranging from the cooling of the inner chambers of a 3D-printed clay wall (fig.1) to optimising the ventilation of the abandoned inner courtyards of a city, the project explored the potential of wind-driven shape-optimisation in the design workflows of architects today.

Input from the project's research partners – McNeel Europe and Foster + Partners – was instrumental in developing the tools and knowledge to direct the research efforts toward meaningful design problems. The project also established wider collaborations with international industrial and academic partners through the Innochain network, such as RhinoCFD, TU Graz and the host institute, IAAC, all of whom played a crucial role in developing and disseminating the research. Over the course of the project, 15 workshops, full-time seminars and courses were run, engaging more than 300 students, researchers and professionals with wind-driven shape-optimisation techniques. Feedback from these courses, as well as interviews with prominent CFD experts in architectural practices and academics in the field, helped to shape the outcome. In parallel, longer-term research partnerships from projects at other institutions – such as the University of Patras, Greece, the Technical University of Košice, Slovakia, and Innochain partner CITA, Denmark – served as case studies for testing the tools and methods developed.

The collective outcome of this project has demonstrated that architects can apply wind-driven shape-optimisation techniques to augment the natural ventilation performance of our buildings and building components. The complexity of our design problems at the various scales of engagement with airflows revealed that much work remains to be done to fully harness the potential of aerodynamic forces in architecture; nevertheless, we have the instruments to engage and will continue to drive our architectural forms with these forces.

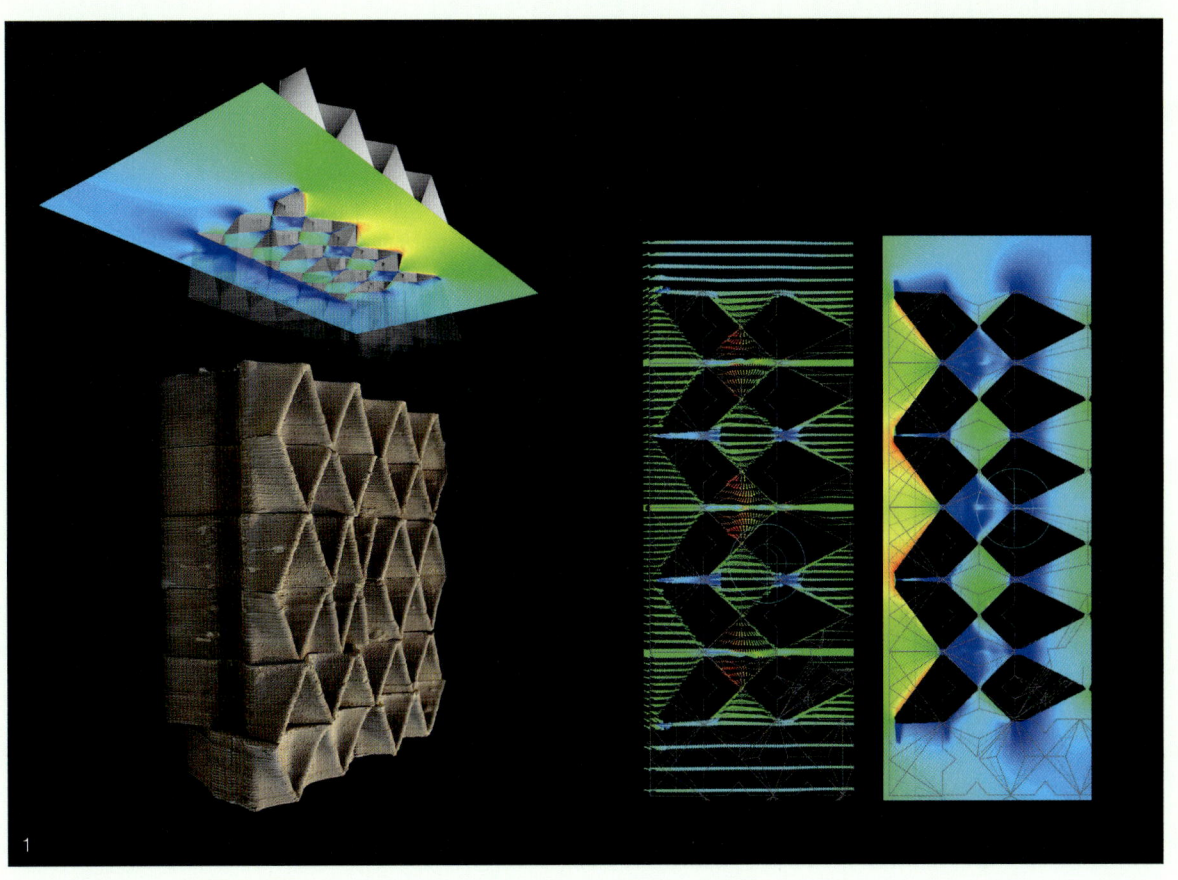

1. Cooling optimisation of the inner chambers of a 3D-printed clay wall.

Bibliography

United Nations Environment Programme (UNEP), 2016, *The Emissions Gap Report 2016*, Nairobi, United Nations Environment Program.

MODELLING STRATEGIES AND NEW WORKFLOWS

Research Summary
Multiple States of Equilibrium for Bending-Active Tensile Structures

Evy L. M. Slabbinck
Industrial Partners: Foster + Partners, McNeel
Academic Institution: Institute of Building Structures and Structural Design (ITKE)
at The University Of Stuttgart

A combination of bending-active elements and a structural membrane introduces new integrative solutions into the design space of adaptive structures by using their potential for multiple states of equilibrium. The particularly complex nature of Bending-Active Tensile Hybrid (BATH) structures affects most aspects of their creation, from modelling and analysis to fabrication, construction and detailing, restricting their adaptivity and the possibility of building them at larger scales. Changing the shape of BATH structures challenges the reciprocal structural equilibrium, namely the membrane and the bending-active elements. There is a need for a new and comprehensive approach to design and fabrication, to enable these hybrid modules to move.

The research was conducted on different levels. First, a literature review was conducted to give context; second, several concepts, strategies and ideas were generated and pooled to answer the following research questions: 'How are BATH systems designed with multiple states of equilibrium to utilise their potential in adaptive architecture?' and 'How can the multiple states of equilibrium be integrated in these BATH structures in such a way that the membrane does not wrinkle or break?' Third, digital simulations and analyses were conducted to compare and examine the different strategies. The results from these analyses were then embedded in three built research projects: BAT_02; the ITECH Research Demonstrator 2017–18; and the computational bamboo installation. Finally, these experiments were analysed, re-simulated and discussed.

The research was performed at the Institute of Building Structures and Structural Design at the University of Stuttgart, under the supervision of Professor Jan Knippers. The Institute has a long history of combining engineering and lightweight architecture, and is a leader in the research of innovative structural systems, high-performance materials and integrated fabrication processes. One of the built research projects, BAT_02, was developed in collaboration with the linked Innochain industry partner, Foster + Partners, which supported and helped frame the architectural context of the research.

The research opens new doors for adaptive architecture and BATH approaches in general, and is a stepping-stone for further investigation and future potential applications. First, the structural systems show that it is possible to create large movements using small and simple actuation forces (ITECH Research Demonstrator 2017–18). Second, the results indicate that structural membranes allowing movement are not a limitation of the system, but rather can act as a structural part that endorses this movement (BAT_02). Third, the structures go beyond merely tubes and membranes, also integrating plates, material gradient, combination of materials and so on, making the design space larger and improving its structural properties (ITECH Research Demonstrator 2017–18, BAT_02, Computational Bamboo).

The BAT_02 project begins to address the need for adaptable architectures in contemporary spaces. With further development, it holds the potential to be applied in real-world contexts today. Further investigation is planned, in particular, regarding the link between construction, system typology and scale. In addition, steps have been taken to integrate the design-to-manufacture process of these structures so that all steps are thought-through in the initial design and form-finding stage: material, actuation, construction, details, stability and fabrication.

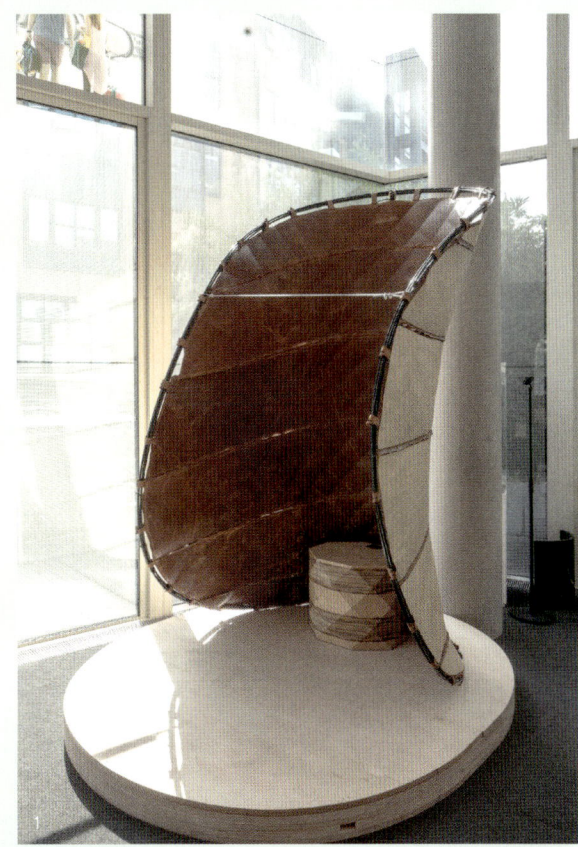

1. BAT_02 at Foster + Partners' office, London.

2. Computational bamboo installation at the Museum of Interactive Science in Quito.

MODELLING STRATEGIES AND NEW WORKFLOWS

Research Summary
Alternative Methods for Data Transaction

Dimitrie Stefanescu
Industrial Partners: Henn Gmbh
Academic Institution: The Bartlett School of Architecture, UCL

This research introduces an integrated socio-technical analysis of communication as applied within the digital design process, which challenges the existing status quo of the building industry. Three critical aspects of a communicative act were explored: data representation, data classification and data transaction. Throughout the project, software instruments, 'Speckle', were developed to enable the research to be validated. By leveraging and expanding the industrial and academic network provided by the project's context, these instruments were continuously tested and iterated-upon during a three-year living laboratory composed of industry specialists.

In 'data representation', the communicative performance of a low-level composable schema is compared to the existing industry standard. It is shown that the ontological revision process at a representational level is better served by the former approach, while the latter impedes meaningful dialogue and excludes stakeholders. 'Data classification', meanwhile, suggests an object-centric approach to data persistence. By comparing existing file-based exchanges to the proposed alternative, it is found that an object-based exchange methodology leads to increased data relevance and a reduction in 'noise'. Instead of sharing information in bulk, any design data that is communicated has an intention attached to it. 'Data transaction' investigates the affordances of the digital medium in supporting communicative contracts between actors that are relevant to the organisational nature of the architecture, engineering and construction industries.

Some of the friction in the contemporary design process can be attributed to the nature of its communicative processes and their subsequent distortion due to inadequate technological implementations. Nevertheless, this research demonstrates that digital technologies can embrace the diversity and richness of the design process, enhance the collaborative aspect of the industry and open an accessible pathway toward a digitally-integrated built environment.

The project was awarded a £1 million follow-up grant, 'AEC Delta Mobility', by Innovate UK. Based on prior work on Speckle, the consortium – comprising The Bartlett School of Construction and Project Management, UCL; BuroHappold; 3D Repo; and Rhomberg Sersa Rail Group – aims to define an industry standard for design change specification that allows faster and more agile 'delta' updates (in which only code is updated) to replace the file-based exchange mechanisms that are currently prevalent in the AEC industry.

Furthermore, Speckle was used as a technological base for research in participatory urbanism at the Future Cities Laboratory at the Singapore ETH Centre. From an academic perspective, the findings of this project can be used to inform further research in digital design collaboration, construction and project management, as well as to revitalise scholarship in the realm of data interoperability in AEC.

At the time of writing, Speckle continues to exert a growing influence beyond academia, on the professional practice of architects, engineers and other stakeholders involved in the design and construction process. It is incorporated into the digital transformation efforts of a number of international AEC companies, among the most prominent of which are HOK, SOM, Arup, Woods Bagot, BVN, Aurecon, DIALOG and Grimshaw Architects.

1. Speckle: digitally connecting the design process.

MODELLING STRATEGIES AND NEW WORKFLOWS

Research Summary
Integrated Material Practice in Freeform Timber Structures

Tom Svilans
Industrial Partners: Blumer Lehmann, Dsearch at White Arkitekter AB
Academic Institution: Centre for Information Technology and Architecture (CITA),
The Royal Danish Academy of Fine Arts, Schools of Architecture, Design and Conservation

Timber as a building material has acquired new relevance, not least in view of the climate crisis and concerns regarding overpopulation. Following new developments in adhesives and process technology, this sustainable, renewable and carbon-storing material has made a return to the forefront of construction. This project examines the design and fabrication of large-scale freeform timber structures by proposing an integrated material practice in which design intent is informed by material and fabrication constraints, and new potential for architectural design is explored.

The significant shift toward automation and prefabrication by the timber industry. opens up a new ability to fabricate components with increased precision and complexity at larger scales, and with greater production volumes. Concurrent developments in engineering and material sciences have enabled the performative capacity of timber to be pushed further and exploited more thoroughly. While these developments have resulted in new and innovative products and structures, engaging with timber properties and fabrication affordances in early design stages remains a challenge. Similarly, the design and engineering of freeform timber components challenge current methods of fabrication that are largely tailored to standardised inputs.

This project was developed in collaboration with Dsearch – the in-house research lab at Sweden's White Arkitekter AB, focusing on integrating computational design strategies within multidisciplinary architectural practice – and with Blumer Lehmann AG – a leading Swiss timber contractor specialising in the planning, development and delivery of complex timber structures. This threeway collaboration positioned the project critically between architectural practice and industrial production. The methodology drew on embedded secondments with industrial partners, material prototyping and the interplay between design-modelling and fabrication. The research was tested and implemented through architectural competition proposals and ongoing design projects in practice.

The focal point and subject of inquiry was the glulam blank: glue-laminated, near-net-shape large-scale timber components. A shift from a subtractive approach in timber processing to one of aggregation, through the development of structural adhesives, has opened up a large field of possibilities for composing precisely-tailored blanks, in response to design or performance criteria. From an architectural and design perspective, the space that the blank occupies – between sawn and graded lumber, and the finished architectural component – holds much potential in yielding new types of timber components and new structural morphologies. Engaging with this space, therefore, required new interfaces for design modelling and new approaches in production.

The project created new ways of augmenting existing design-modelling tools with lightweight material and fabrication-specific information. Deployed in early design stages, these revealed the production implications of design decisions, and allowed an interplay between early development and material performance. By integrating 3D scanning as a key component in the design-to-manufacture process, sensing was used as an integrated tool for material calibration in fabrication. This created a digital link between fabrication data and material reality, towards an encoded awareness of material behaviour during production. The project has the potential to

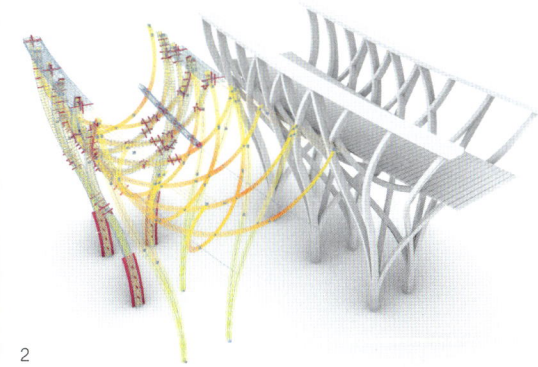

influence how architects and designers may interface with the material and fabrication constraints of engineered timber, and challenges existing industrial workflows by proposing a re-sequencing of the fabrication process and the integration of digital feedback systems. By suggesting new means by which timber architecture can be built, it also presents fresh perspectives on what timber architecture can be, how it can be shaped and what spaces it can engender.

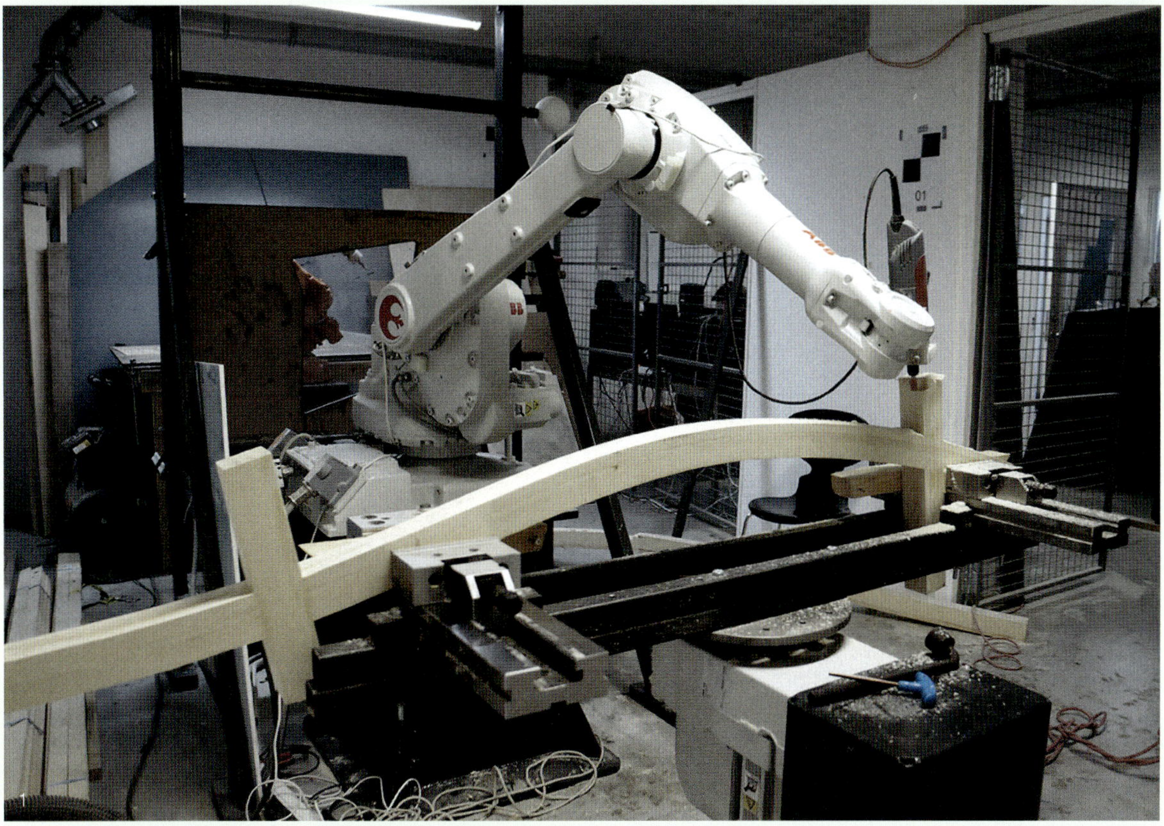

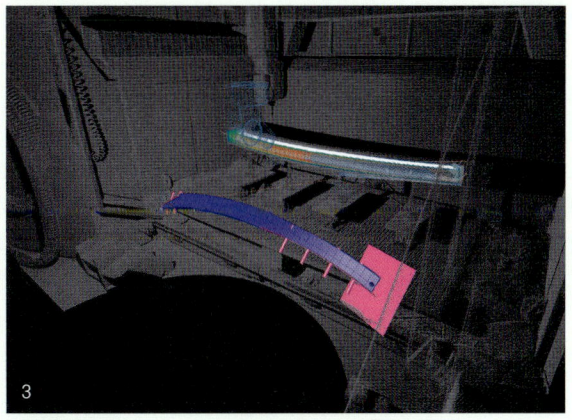

1. Robotic fabrication of glulam prototypes.

2. Augmented modelling tools integrate material properties and fabrication specification.

3. Integrated 3D scanning in multi-axis glulam machining.

MODELLING STRATEGIES AND NEW WORKFLOWS

Further Perspectives
New Workflows and Collaborations

Kenn Clausen
3XN Architects GXN Innovation
Sean Lineham
ARUP
Morten Norman Lund
3XN Architects GXN Innovation
Line Rahbek
Dorte Mandrup
Kåre Stokholm Poulsgaard
3XN Architects GXN Innovation

Introduction

As design modelling evolves, new tools and approaches emerge and, with this, data-driven modelling can integrate the work of interdisciplinary teams. As platforms and approaches proliferate, they pose new challenges to architecture studios. Studios have to integrate tools within workflows that are flexible enough to balance the emerging requirements of the different digital specialisations and the need for interdisciplinary collaboration. As the projects described here show, current practice puts significant demands on the establishment and maintenance of dynamic data models, as modelling practice expands from being centred around geometry to include the modelling of collaborative workflows (Garber, 2017).

Dorte Mandrup

In 2008, while working for Zaha Hadid Architects, Line Rahbek found that Building Information Modelling (BIM) software was being challenged by the geometry of building designs and it had become necessary to move between different software environments to achieve the best results. While these workflows seemed pioneering at the time, a few years later, similar workflows were being built into the leading software platforms. The effort invested was rewarded, but often the path was not directly from A to B. Thinking outside the box, therefore, became a necessary tool for success.

The Opal IDA project – designed by Dorte Mandrup for the Danish Society of Engineers – is a suspended structure on the Copenhagen harbour front. A freeform landmark, it has an almost weightless quality to its structure. At an early stage in the project, ideas were generated on how the different contractors could take the advanced model, or parts of it, to develop shop drawings. To control the freeform geometry and also to share information with Søren Jensen Engineering Consultants, the building model was based on a 3D-point set via high-speed data-transfer (Flux). The point set was the basis for both the architectural design of the façade panels and the engineering design of the structural elements, with both sharing a common naming convention (fig.2).

The Icefjord Centre is a visitor and research centre on a UNESCO-protected site in Ilulissat in Greenland. Its structure uses gently-tilted frames that blend into the landscape as a path. The complex twisting shape meant that sharing a dataset with Søren Jensen Engineering Consultants was an advantage as it helped maximise precision and efficiency. The dataset – consisting of freeform curves – defined the geometry of the building and the movement of its edges, and was as important as the traditional building grid (fig.3).

Some of the new workflows, such as cloud sharing of live datasets between professions and systemising through cloud-based parametric-driven collaboration, were first implemented on The Opal and the Icefjord projects.

3XN Architects and GXN Innovation

The new International Olympic Committee (IOC) headquarters opened in summer 2019, designed by 3XN Architects. With its design for a dynamic façade, the building will look different from all angles, conveying the energy of an athlete in motion. Each element of the façade needed to be unique in its shape and its relationship to neighbouring elements, and this posed

1. EFFEKT – Camp Adventure Tower.
Image courtesy of Rasmus Hjortshøj – COAST.

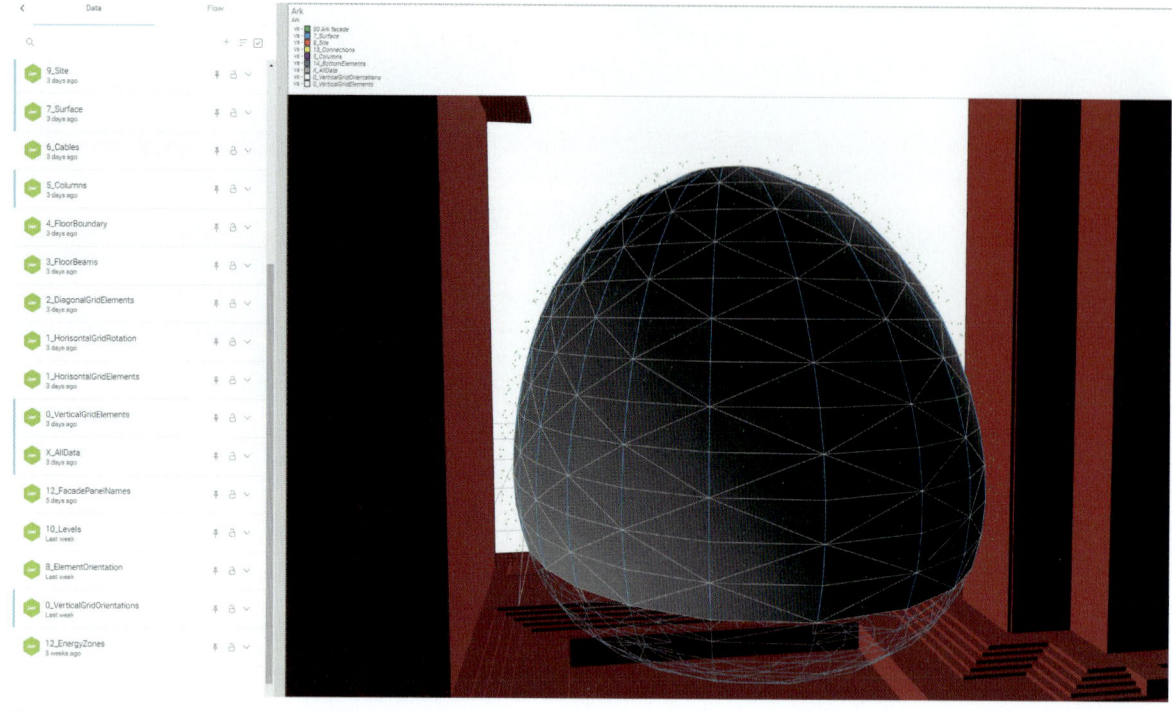

2

significant challenges for the 3XN team and their collaborators during design development. Iterations could have unpredictable consequences and affect geometric integration of elements, structural integrity of the full façade, aesthetics and building performance.

To understand and manage relationships under strict deadlines, the 3XN team needed a robust digital workflow that could tie the expertise of design and building information modelling into an efficiently-working whole. GXN's Digital Design team established a data structure linking the façade model across Rhino and Revit, using Grasshopper, Dynamo and scripting to create a two-way data link. Updates in one modelling environment could continuously feed into the other, enabling the different members of the project team to work simultaneously and efficiently across software.

The efficiency of the data structure relied on a grid that allowed the 3XN and GXN teams to identify and link each individual element across modelling environments. This shift toward control of workflows via an explicit data structure enabled rapid analysis and exchange of building information during design development. It also enabled collaborators to work on problems at different resolutions and scales simultaneously. Structural and façade engineers could solve localised structural issues by inputting data on boundary conditions and constraints, while 3XN managed the integration of these, in keeping with the overall form and design intent of the project.

4. Dorte Mandrup – IDA – The Opal. Screenshot from Flux, a cloud-based platform. The image shows the grid controlling the freeform on which both architect and engineer based their geometry.

5. Dorte Mandrup – Icefjord Ilulissat. Icefjord Centre in Ilulissat, Greenland. BIM model illustrating some of the information you would extract from one of the façade panels.

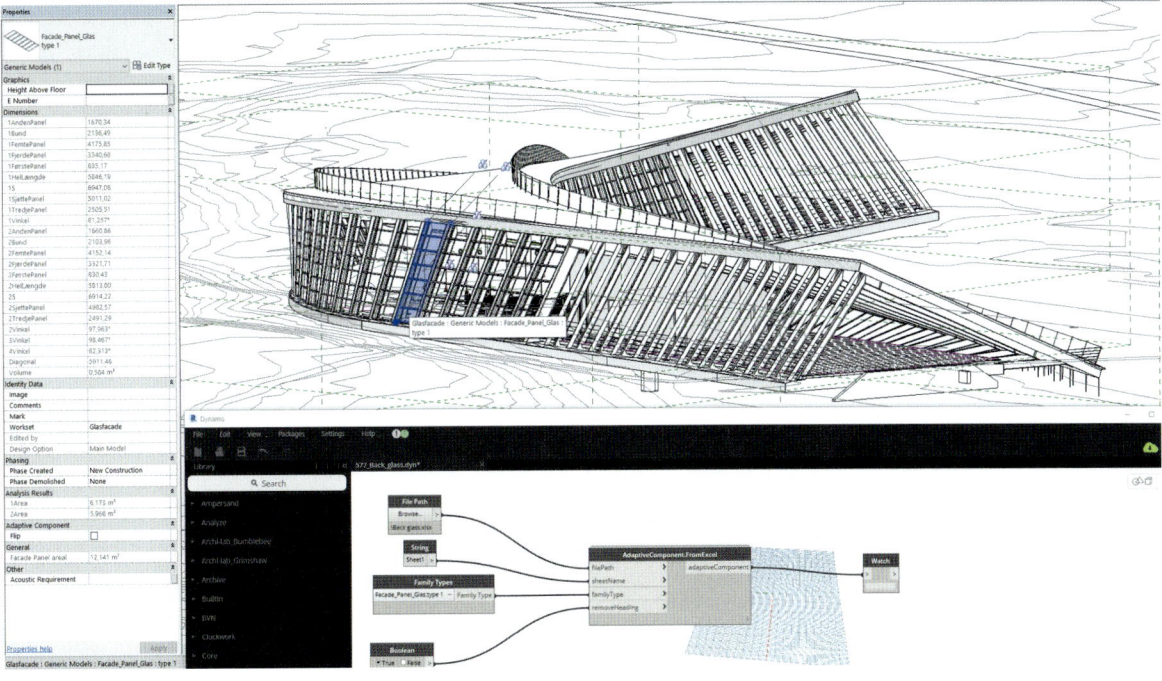

3

Data-driven collaboration proved to be dynamic and relatively platform-agnostic, as the methodology was applicable to different project and software environments in the studio. The model expanded from an environment for iterative-design exploration, to a data-driven setup that serviced project partners with divergent requirements. The 3XN team retained control of design and geometry by using data to structure collaboration with partners through all phases of design development and construction.

Arup

Digital tools and new approaches to workflows open fantastic opportunities in the building-design process. They allow us to create and explore design in new ways and can aid the collaborative effort between engineer, architect and contractor. Using parametric design in engineering helps us to engage more closely and actively with the architecture and the overarching concept of the design.

A strong case study on workflows and collaborations is the Camp Adventure Tower, a unique installation designed to enable visitors to experience the protected forest at Gisselfeld Kloster, one hour south of Copenhagen. The development comprises a walkway that gives visitors access to the preserved forest, before ascending above the trees, up a spiralling 45m-tall hyperboloid diagrid tower designed by Arup and EFFEKT architects (fig.1).

To deliver the novel structure, the project required closely integrated architect–engineer collaboration and design workflow thinking. The design was conducted using a fully parametric workflow in Grasshopper with an array of interoperable plug-ins. The degree of integration between structural analysis, design and delivery in the parametric framework was extremely high. The setting-out of the geometry and the architect–engineer coordination was conducted exclusively in code: the architectural, geometric and engineering-design principles were collectively defined in one single Grasshopper environment.

Collaborating in code and developing workflows as a close architect–engineer team ensured that all consequent analysis models, architectural depictions and BIM deliverables were accurate and perfectly coordinated. Additionally, the use of parametric tools promoted ease and speed in testing design alternatives, with a focus on determining an option that met the client's budget requirements. A major advantage of this workflow was that it allowed more time for establishing the details, such as the complex steel connections, and devoted less time to producing information or models.

The success of the project was achieved by establishing a collective digital workflow for the main geometry early on, allowing time to refine and develop the detailing in coordination with the contractor.

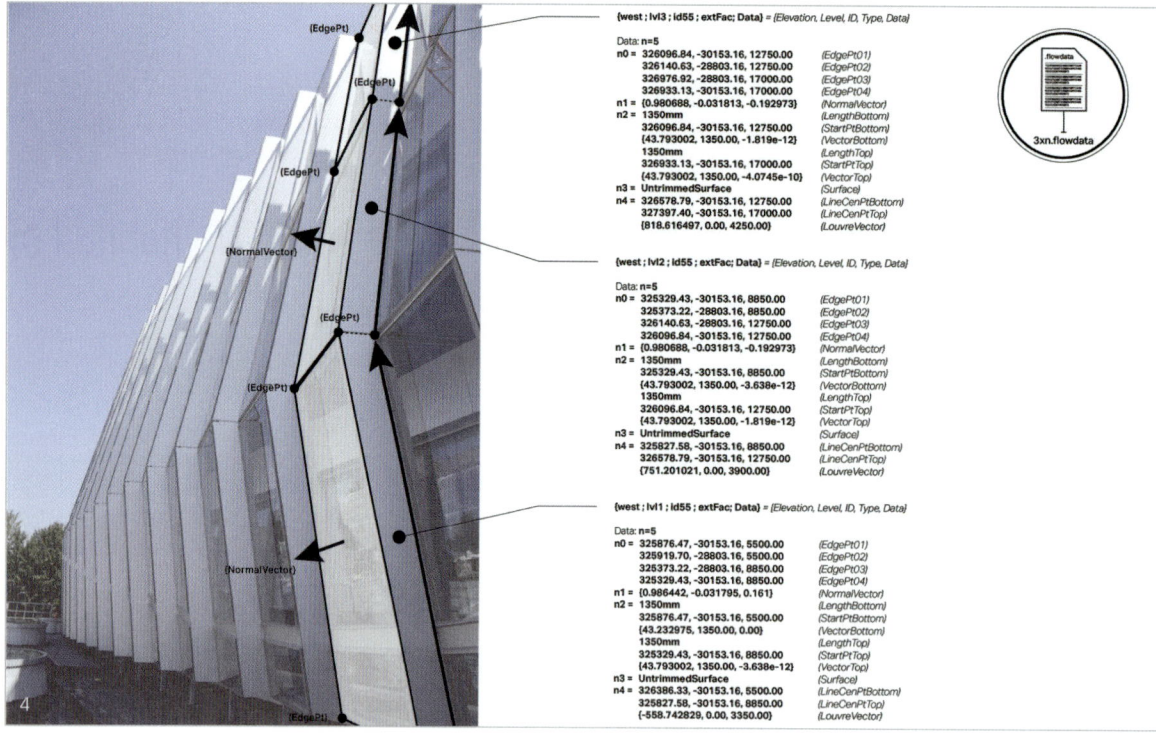

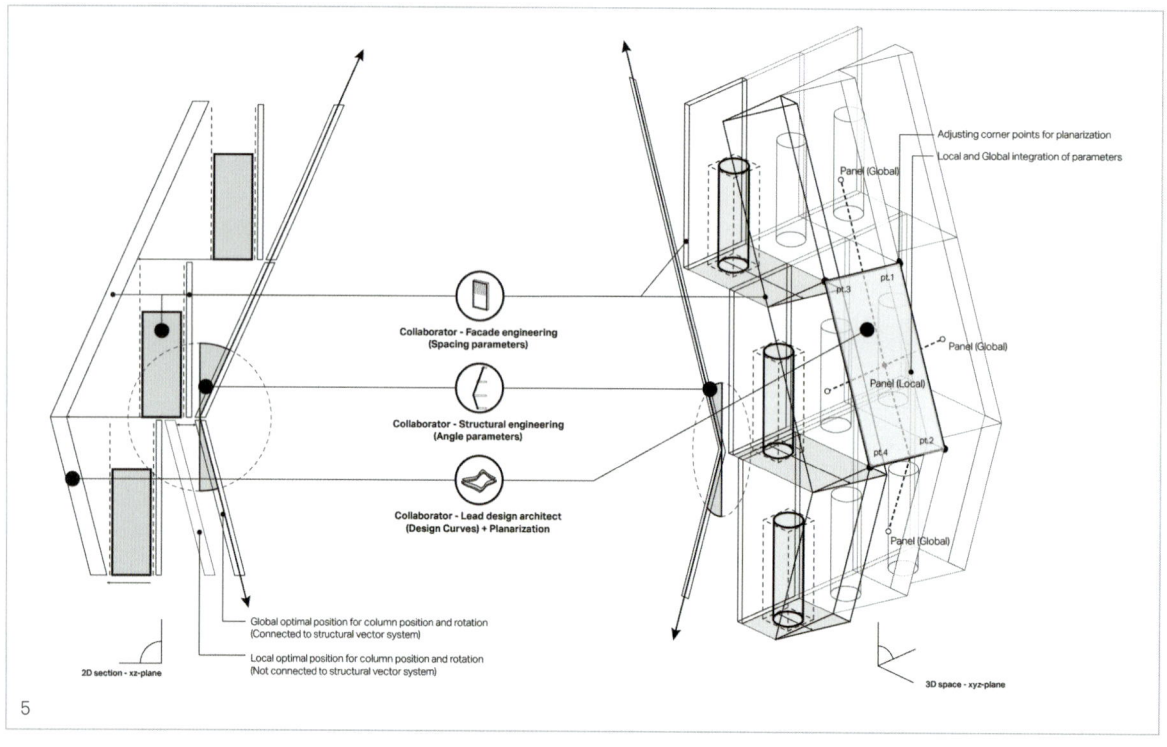

Conclusion: Data-Driven Collaborative Workflows

Promising convergence and greater interconnectivity (Deutsch, 2017), the current complexity of computational modelling means there are now innumerable information, software environments and practices. Scripting has empowered a new generation of architecture and engineering tool-users to become tool-makers (Burry, 2011), but the proliferation of approaches risks undermining the coherence of collaborative workflows as they expand in reach and scope.

Digital workflows and BIM provide teams with the ability to coordinate collaborative-working prior to, and during, construction (Garber, 2014), but integration between software environments remains challenging. The database/BIM standard is not yet structured and differs between offices and countries.

Interoperability and collaboration are core concerns for studios seeking to expand information modelling. As the quantity of information expands, it can be difficult to maintain quality and to filter relevant information within the model. Software has made these information-rich models attainable, but often by emulating older workflows and hiding data under user interfaces. Efficient methods for filtering and sorting data are urgently needed for close collaboration in interdisciplinary project teams.

The concept of BIM showed the way forward, and today the potential of integrating more data-driven approaches into practice is changing the way we think about our designs, communication and professional interaction with collaborators. Expanding information modelling promises a platform-agnostic and dynamic approach to collaboration that no single software environment can offer at present. The strength lies in the data structure and protocols developed for individual projects, which enable dynamic exchanges and allow collaborators to work on global design and construction-detailing simultaneously.

Bibliography

Burry, M., 2011, *Scripting Cultures: Architecture Design and Programming*, Hoboken, NJ, John Wiley & Sons Inc.

Deutsch, R., 2017, *Convergence: The Redesign of Design*, Hoboken, NJ, John Wiley & Sons Inc.

Garber, R., 2014, *BIM Design: Realising the Creative Potential of Building Information Modelling* (second edition), Hoboken, NJ, John Wiley & Sons Inc.

Garber, R., 2017, *Workflows: Expanding Architecture's Territory in the Design and Delivery of Buildings*, Hoboken, NJ, John Wiley & Sons Inc.

2. Local and global integration of structural principles and design parameters across 2D and 3D environments. Image courtesy of 3XN Architects.

3. Predefined data structure, linking elements across modelling environments. Image courtesy of 3XN Architects.

Design Integration

3.1 DESIGN INTEGRATION

Design Integration: Global Technological Advancement and Local Culture

In dialogue:
Areti Markopoulou
Institute for Advanced Architecture of Catalonia (IAAC), Universitat Politècnica de Catalunya
Philip F. Yuan
Tongji University, Shanghai

Areti Markopoulou (AM): In an era of increased urbanisation, digitisation and exponential risk, the practices of digital design and manufacturing are expected to change not only our built environment and the business around it but, more than anything, the way we live and how we participate and interact within it. In this context, we discuss the applications and implications of integrating digital design and manufacturing technologies with strategies of sustainability that involve local resources, culture and craft.

The impact of unsustainable materials and processes on the environment highlights the urgency for optimised design and manufacture. It provokes a rethinking of the form and kinds of materials that should be used in making our environments. Steel, concrete (cement) and plastic are the building materials that dominate the construction industry today, with cement – which relies on coal and petroleum for its manufacture – being the most energy-intensive of all materials. The construction industry is the biggest generator of waste in these materials globally, and sustainable alternative material, design and manufacturing models urgently need to be established in the mainstream.

New construction practices and processes are being researched in which negative impact is reduced, with a focus on natural resources, advancements in synthetically engineered zero-waste materials and an increased awareness of the importance of circular design strategies.[1] Alongside this, advancements in digital design and fabrication offer potential for material, structural and construction optimisation, opening up possibilities for more sustainable, faster-to-produce and, in some cases, cheaper constructs.

Techniques such as additive manufacturing can be simulated in the design process to deposit material only when needed, without the need for a mould or the creation of waste. Material libraries are shifting toward more sustainable, organic and natural consistencies, as well as natural materials found close to the construction site, which boosts new circular design strategies. Automation and the creative use of robots – industrial, mobile and aerial – play a critical role in this change, as do onsite, robotic manufacturing technologies and pop-up factories, as opposed to the expensive and environmentally costly modes of transportation needed for offsite construction methods. In this new material age, the architect-as-protagonist in the creation of urban, built and public spaces can guide us toward more responsible choices, integrating digital design with local material, culture and craft. Can each of these elements merge in emergent projects and research?

Philip F. Yuan (PFY): Key here is how we use traditional craft and local material when adopting new tools of design and fabrication. An example of how this process might be realised can be found in the rural construction project 'In Bamboo', designed by Archi-Union and constructed by Fab-Union in Daoming Town, Sichuan Province, China, in 2017. A multi-functional rural community cultural centre with facilities for exhibitions, conferences, dining and recreation, which integrates new construction technology with locally sourced wood and bamboo, and traditional construction techniques with prefabricated industrialisation.

The architecture, landscaping and interior were completed in 52 days, which was more rushed than initially imagined. By using digitally prefabricated structural wood components that were nested, volume transportation of bulk material was reduced and the

1. 3D-printed settlements made from locally sourced earth materials and customised by local users. Image: IAAC, Open Thesis Fabrication, 2019.

2. Weaving installation integrating digital fabrication technology with local craft.
© Bian Lin.

speed of assembly was increased. In the development of this project, research from many years of experimenting with digital fabrication technology for wood structures was put to use at full scale. The gestural interweaving roof is a construction of prefabricated parts, delivered to the site ready for quick assembly. The Mobius-shaped roof is supported by a light prefabricated steel frame and is finished with local ceramic tiles. The efficiency afforded by pre-fabricating components made the creation of this complex geometry possible in the short construction period.

Such new modes of construction offer the possibility to reinvent traditional building materials and have challenged our understanding of a building as a fixed, solid entity. From your perspective, how do transformable tectonics/materials/assemblages reshape the living environment to confront current global issues, such as the environmental crisis?

AM: In response to possibilities arising from a new digital and material age, part of the research developed at IAAC explores the use of locally sourced, natural and recyclable materials for housing solutions. Earth-based materials are combined with 3D printing to produce complex geometries for climatic and structural performance using algorithmic design, and the potential of robotic technologies is used to improve the construction site using onsite robotics.

In collaboration with UN Habitat, IAAC developed sustainable housing solutions on three sites in Africa that make excellent case studies. The collaboration revealed that onsite robotic manufacturing with earth-based materials could provide solutions for affordable housing (Kakuma Refugee Camp, Kenya), urban flood protection (Suleja River, Nigeria) and sound protection during the construction of highways (Yaounde, Cameroon). Furthermore, the research has developed based on the engagement of residents with the construction process, as well as the possibility of responding to complex humanitarian situations with the new generation of social, economic and environmental capital.

IAAC's 3D printing projects use earth-based materials and provide zero-emission construction solutions while engaging users and local craft in their development. Robots are adapted for onsite construction, creating new possibilities for remote areas where resources are scarce. Natural materials are combined with digital design and robotic manufacturing to produce contemporary structures that combine aesthetic qualities with embedded performance that would have previously been computationally simulated. Furthermore, the results demonstrate the potential of 3D-printed earth architecture to adapt to site-specific resources, climate, community and culture. From your experience, do you think that the use of locally sourced materials can bring people closer to constructions? And how can culture and tradition inform design and manufacturing?

PFY: Robotic fabrication and other new technologies could result in more meaningful and lasting changes for the rural construction industry. New technology shouldn't replace traditional craft construction tied to rural life and industry; instead, we should consider opportunities for innovation and improvement that might integrate existing construction methods with new technology.

China's rural industrialisation process is yet to begin, as urban gentrification and modernisation overwhelms the advancement of production systems in the countryside. It is startling how difficult it is to find a worker in the countryside under the age of 40, as the traditional architecture industry has no means of attracting the younger generation. Right now, prefabrication for use in rural areas could redefine and upgrade traditional construction.

Daoming Town is well known for its enduring tradition of bamboo weaving, which is integral to how families spend time together and neighbours interact. A traditional craft, it is also a living cultural heritage with much to offer contemporary ways of living and making. For *In Bamboo*, we researched local architecture and the limitations of using bamboo as the primary structure system. We learned that bamboo performs very well as a protective sheathing on the exterior façade of a building. Working with a local artisan, we modelled over 20 different variations of weaving patterns with thin strips of bamboo that could be used on the façade. This produces the experience of seeing something familiar but encountering it in a new context.

Industrial robots are the revolutionary construction platform of the digital era; offsite prefabrication technology and in-situ robotic construction not only give traditional craftsmanship a new identity but also

3. Interlocking-curved roof of the In-Bamboo project. © Li Han.

4a & 4b. Fab-Union in-situ construction robot series. © Philip F. Yuan.

5. Urban simulator of networked buildings, processing infrastructural data, user desires and urban-planning scenarios. Image: IAAC, City & Technology, Internet of Buildings, 2019.

6. *Superbarrio* is an open-source virtual-gaming interface for citizens to engage with public-space design. Image: IAAC, City & Technology, 2016.

make open-ended mass production and customisation possible. In your view, how could our living environment be reformed by the responsive construction process, which is highly sensitive to human beings, in both temporary and spatial dimensions? How do you think the public contribution could improve the current relationship between research and practice in our discipline?

AM: History indicates that any profound social change happens in circular feedback with a technological revolution, meaning that one is both fuelling and being fuelled by the other. According to the authors and researchers Erik Brynjolfsson and Andrew McAfee, the advancement of digital technologies is affecting mental power in the same magnitude that the steam engine affected muscle power. All agents involved in contemporary design, including architects, manufacturers and users, are gradually shifting their modes of operation, inhabitation and interaction.

Increasing digital connections and the rise of Web 2.0 have boosted a highly participatory culture. More and more people are becoming familiar with the design and production of their surroundings. Open-source design and customised manufacturing technologies enhance the possibilities for participation. Within this context, the architectural discipline encompasses new design and making processes. For an urban project developed in Barcelona and Mumbai by IAAC, virtual gaming platforms and virtual reality technologies were used to engage citizens with the design of the public space and the new buildings in their neighbourhood. Machine learning and Artificial Intelligence (AI) were used to analyse data to create an urban simulator for more informed decision-making processes in the urban environment. Similarly, in the 3D-printed earth project, users could customise the design of their home based on their personal criteria, as well as on the material properties and environmental performance of the final form defined by digital simulations.

Similar to the effects of the Industrial Revolution, architecture in the current digital age is evolving to become a natural nexus between bits (digital world) and atoms (physical world), while cognitive decisions, cultural aspects and crowd wisdom merge in a unique way with computational simulations, predictions and manufacturing processes. The new design paradigm emerging in architecture promotes novel design processes in which designers, users, environment, materials and digital codes play a fundamental role. It promotes the designer as the creator of an open-ended system able to provide the rules for a variety of evolutionary forms to emerge, where final decisions are made by the resonance and collective intelligence of multiple agents, including codes, humans and machines, rather than a top-down unique design and final form. In your view, what kind of new collaborations could emerge from such a paradigm? How can designers augment their capacities to work with machines?

PFY: According to the philosopher Andy Clark, as human beings we are 'natural-born cyborgs'. The development of increasingly sophisticated digital tools and prostheses – from robotic fabrication to AI – have been making us ever-more cyborg-like. In this post-humanist view, we adapt to new tools so that they become absorbed within our body schemas. There is no longer a one-way relationship between architects and digital tools, as the former adapts to digital technology.

Furthermore, with industrial robots as the revolutionary construction platform in the digital era, the architectural profession is experiencing a paradigm shift from traditional craft and industrial reproduction to cyborg craftsmanship techniques, combining human-to-machine and human-to-human collaborations. New possibilities for collaboration, made possible by this robotic platform, challenge traditional design authorship and question authority within the cycle of architectural design and construction. Both offsite prefabrication technology and onsite robotic construction make 'architecture without architects' a possibility. A tendency toward de-professionalisation within the building industry emerges through the reciprocal feedback loop between cloud computation and production.

Shared knowledge and the fresh creativity liberated by the platform between robots and humans encourage citizens to contribute to the constant building process in the living environment. In this way, construction tools have a kind of reversed adaptivity, too. Processes, interfaces and systems of fabrication can be customised or modified according to the intention of the user. Based on robotic platforms and AI, customised fabrication technology introduces a highly adaptive prefabrication system, which is distinguished from the assembly system based on mechanical reproduction in the post-war period. With this upgrade of the construction system, triggered by customised reproduction, the feedback loop between tool and user will become highly differentiated. These differential feedbacks are inserted into the social production system, and a new relationship between architects, technology and the building industry would be established. How architects participate in digital technology adaptation thus becomes an essential question for the future.

Bibliography

Brynjolfsson E. and McAfee A., 2014, *The Second Machine Age: Work, Progress, and Prosperity in a Time of Brilliant Technologies*, New York, W.W. Norton & Company.

Clark A., 2003, *Natural-Born Cyborgs: Minds, Technologies, and the Future of Human Intelligence*, Oxford, Oxford University Press.

Dubor, A., Izard, J.B., Cabay, E., Sollazzo, A., Markopoulou, A. and Rodriguez, M., 2018, 'On-Site Robotics for Sustainable Construction' in Willmann, J., Block, P., Hutter, M., Byrne, K. and Schork, T. (eds.), *Robotic Fabrication in Architecture, Art and Design 2018*, Cham, Switzerland, Springer International, p.390–404.

Ellen MacArthur Foundation, 2012, *Towards the Circular Economy: An Economic and Business Rationale for an Accelerated Transition*, Isle of Wight, Ellen MacArthur Foundation.

Gausa M., Markopoulou A. and Vivaldi J., 2019, *Black Ecologies*, Barcelona, Actar Publishers.

Surowiecki J., 2005 (second edition), *The Wisdom of Crowds*, New York, Anchor.

Note

1. Circular design systems aim to prevent or limit material and resource loss, and have the potential to minimise waste, using this as a resource in itself.

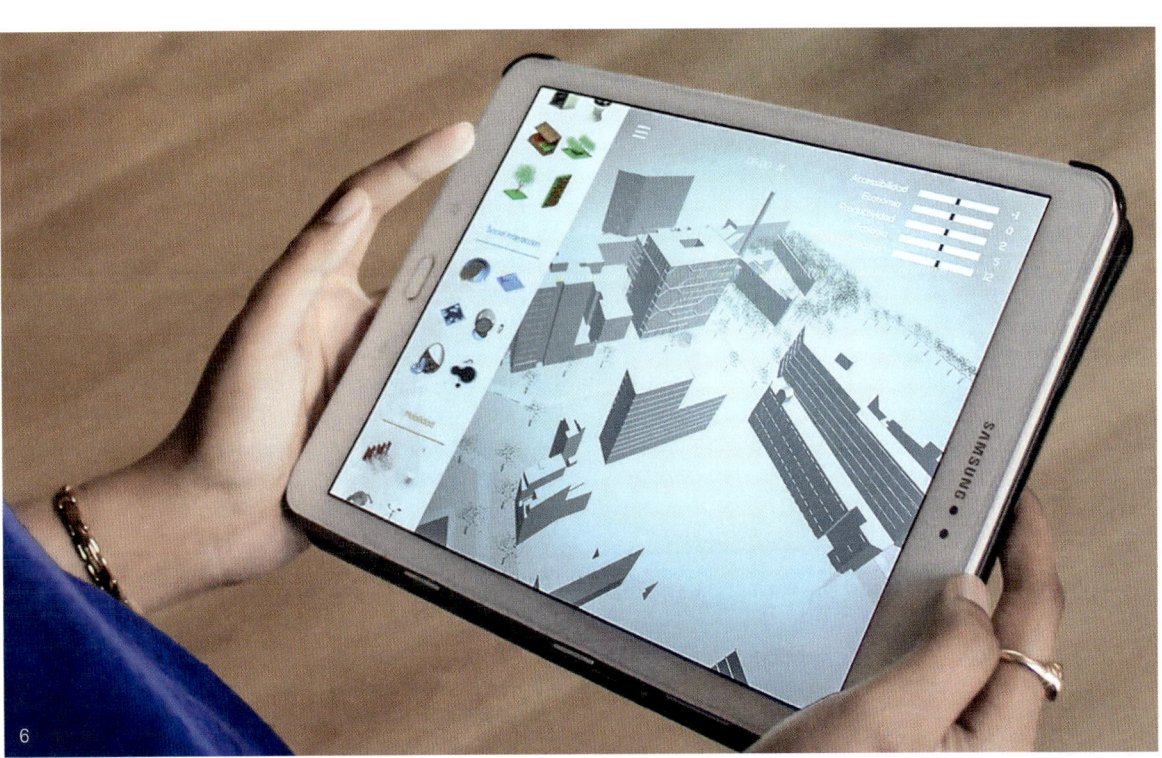

6

3.2 DESIGN INTEGRATION

Agency of Material Production Feedback in Architectural Practice

Tom Svilans
Centre for Information Technology and Architecture (CITA),
The Royal Danish Academy of Fine Arts
Jonas Runberger
White Arkitekter AB, Stockholm, Sweden
Kai Strehlke
Blumer Lehmann AG, Gossau, Switzerland

Introduction

With the introduction of automation, computation and large-scale engineered timber, contemporary timber design and fabrication have evolved from earlier craft-based traditions. Projects have grown in scale and complexity with this evolution, facilitating new forms of building and uses for timber in architecture and construction. The complex nature of wood – a live and organic material – presents challenges for fabricators and designers, however, due to its tendency to change form in response to environmental and inherent factors. This is especially felt in the development and construction of large-scale, freeform timber buildings, where the performative demands of wood are much higher. Advances in computational workflows and machine technology have opened up the possibility of using real material behaviour as an input to both the control systems involved in fabrication, as well as the early design stages and digital models of an architectural project. This presents opportunities for new types of flexible and materially-aware design-to-fabrication paradigms at an industrial scale.

This integration of material behaviour and performance in the design and fabrication of freeform timber structures is the focus of a partnership between an Innochain Early-Stage Researcher (ESR), Dsearch – the computational design team at White Arkitekter AB – and Blumer Lehmann AG – a timber contractor specialising in the development and production of complex timber projects. Here, we present a case study from this collaboration: the design and development of a timber bridge in Stockholm, Sweden, informed by two industry secondments with both industrial partners over several months. The key point of focus is how research can be conducted within the contrasting settings of industrial timber fabrication and multidisciplinary architectural practice during live projects, allowing material performance and feedback to be integrated in both domains. A secondary focus is to show how research conducted in parallel industry environments (architectural practice and production) can broker expertise between these environments, as exemplified in the production feedback in early-stage design in architecture.

Integrating Material Performance

Using a multi-scalar approach, we consider different forms of feedback: feedback in design through computational models and augmented modelling tools; direct feedback in production through the integration of sensors and 3D scanning in the timber production process; and organisational feedback in the timber supply chain through the exploration of iterative, integrated gluing and machining processes (Svilans et al., 2019). Previous work has explored the application of multi-scalar modelling for the design and fabrication of complex timber structures in the context of Innochain and other research collaborations (Svilans, et al., 2018). This case study, however, focuses on the transference of research results to immediate applications within industry. The relevance of this is augmented by the larger shift in architecture toward an integration of design tools and methods of production: the 'digital continuum' between design and construction (Kolarevic, 2003).

This continuum has been extended beyond methods of production to encompass the design of materials and harnessing of their behaviours. Using digital simulation as an integrated component of the design-to-fabrication process has resulted in new material practices that

1. The physical mockup of a portion of Version 3 at the Innochain exhibition 'Practice Futures – Building Design for a New Material Age'.
Photos: Anders Ingvartsen.

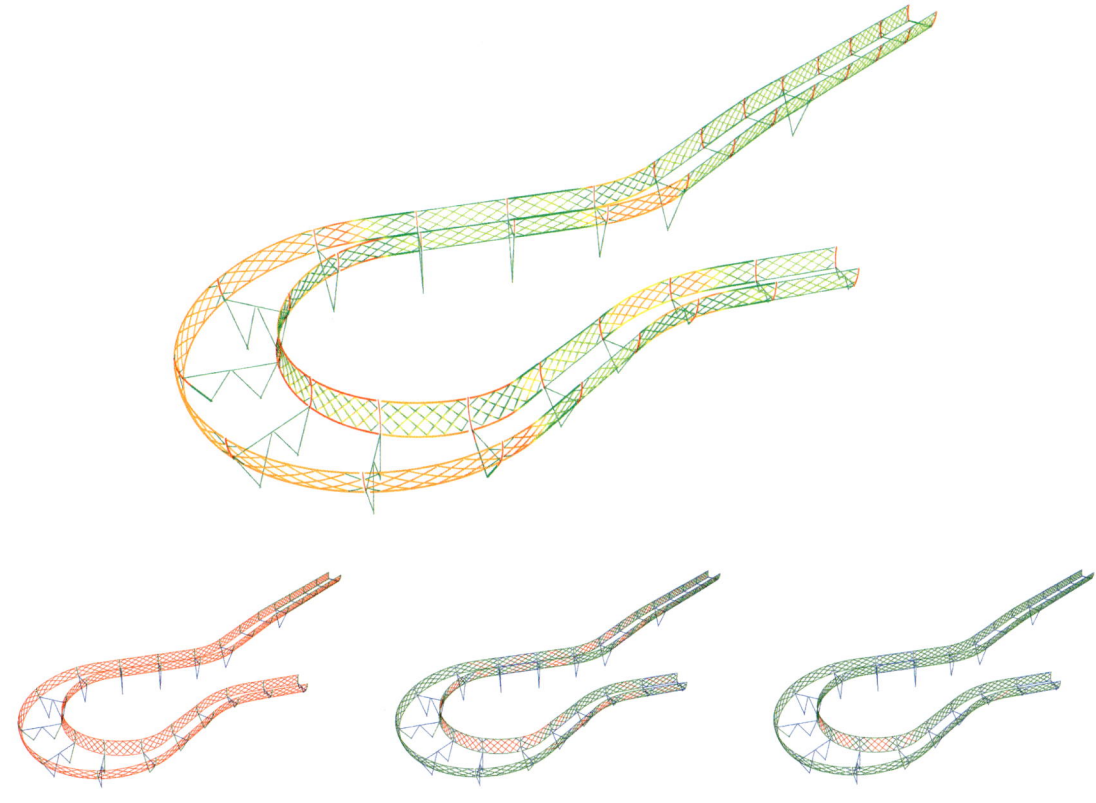

3

2. Rendered visualisations of the Magelungen Park Bridge, Version 0 (starting point), Version 1 (initial concept) and Version 2 (developed version for planning).

3. The curvature analysis of the Version 2 railing trusses provided valuable insight into repeatable elements, as well as the potential to replace curved glulam elements with straight members with a machined outer edge for visual consistency. By allowing a deviation of 5–10mm from the element centrelines (bottom), the need for expensive double-curved elements (red) can be minimised, potentially reducing the glulam lamination cost by ca. 40%.

4. The physical mockup explores the production and assembly of a fragment from Version 3 of the bridge. Exhibited at Practice Futures – Building Design for a new Material Age Innochain exhibition, Meldahl Smedie Exhibition Hall, KADK, 2018. Photo: Bob Sheil.

embrace material feedback, and rich opportunities for new tectonic logics and optimised usage of material resources (Tamke et al., 2012). This is particularly relevant for the design and construction of timber buildings: wood is a complex, live material, an aspect which is often made painfully apparent during its processing and usage. The underlying question is how these modes of thinking can find purchase within established, multi-disciplinary and industrial contexts, and contribute to existing workflows in a productive way.

Feedback in Production

One of the main sources of difficulty during the production of freeform timber elements is their highly irregular and non-orientable geometry. This affects their logistics and handling, quality control and fabricability. Verifying dimensions and comparing the received glulam material to the digital production model become non-trivial tasks, and can require the use of templates, jigs, and slow and delicate contact measurement. The somewhat unpredictable nature of wood machining compounds these difficulties, especially when the high-volume removal of wood releases internal tensions within the glulam, leading to springback and deformation of the component during production.

To address this, a secondment at Blumer Lehmann AG explored the application of different types of 3D data-gathering to the production workflow through a series of experiments. The primary goal was to establish a better routine for registering the freeform elements on the machining bed, creating a link to the digital production model and allowing it to be aligned with the material. The experiments were initially simple, with minimal change to the production workflow, and progressed to more complex integrations of different scanning technologies with a closer relationship to the digital production model (Svilans et al., 2019).

The extreme cost of downtime made choreographing the experiments around active production schedules a challenge. The research strategy, therefore, became one of 'shadowing' the production through parallel development of the scanning experiments, with short and focused testing periods at key points within the production schedule. If providing immediate and positive impact on production, they were implemented, and, if not, they could be easily rolled back. This allowed the continuous parallel experimental research to be tested within the scope of production, allowing flexible development with very clear performance criteria while avoiding the need for a dedicated production setup.

4

These experiments were the first steps toward a tighter integration of material behaviour and the development of a more fluid continuum between model and material in an industrial timber context. This has two main implications, the first being the development of an 'adaptive fabrication model', where dimensional changes in material can be addressed and responded to during linear production. Production often runs in a kind of 'fire and forget' mode: material is ordered, the production data is generated, and then the processing is blindly trusted to the performance of the machine and the accuracy of the material. 'Eyes' that link the ongoing processing with the digital production model in real-time or at discrete intervals minimise the risk and unpredictability involved. Responding to dynamic material behaviours would reduce risk and improve the overall quality of machining, as well as lessen the time spent estimating, checking and cautiously moving forward. The second opportunity is that of an 'encoded experience' through the gathering of sensor data across projects and over longer periods of time. This would allow both the fabricator and designer to extract insights through statistical means about the types of input geometry, material and production strategies, and how they impact on performance. For producers, this would provide a much more accurate assessment of risk and expected quality.

For designers, it would serve as a sounding board for testing design ideas, as well as providing a good base of principles for freeform timber design. The geometry and curvature of freeform glulam elements have a direct impact on their cost, structural performance and visual appearance. The composition of elements and the way in which they are processed affects their form stability and end quality. Extracting these principles and insights at an early design stage, therefore, becomes a priority for the design and construction of smarter and more efficient timber structures.

Material Performance in Early-Stage Design in Architectural Practice

The Dsearch team members at White Arkitekter perform various different roles: from back-end method development to support and design-lead on projects. The ESR secondment with Dsearch coincided with the initiation and development of a pedestrian bridge for the Magelungen Park Project in Stockholm, featuring landscaping and five different residential developments. The bridge will provide pedestrian and bicycle access between two separate forested areas, bridging over a road, a set of commuter-train tracks, and pedestrian/biking paths, with a height difference of approximately 10m from start to end, requiring it to be extended into a nearby wooded grove in order to achieve a maximum slope of 5% and comply with accessibility requirements.

Initially planned as a standard bridge in steel or concrete, eventually timber was selected as the preferred material. The research/practice collaboration enabled an improved design outcome, and gradually introduced client and stakeholders to this more advanced structure of higher architectural merit and better use of resources, while maintaining cost efficiency. The methods developed by the ESR could be directly applied in the well-established computational workflows of Dsearch (Runberger et al., 2015), facilitating the direct transfer of research into practice. The role of the ESR here shifted from a 'shadowing' approach to an active collaborative design role, followed by a divergence into two parallel development trajectories, resulting in Versions 2 and 3. The planning process for the bridge is still ongoing at the time of writing, with forthcoming steps to be based on the research outcome presented below.

Version 0 can be seen as the starting point and a point of reference for the more refined versions. The curving form is dependent on the need to extend the bridge to allow the maximum 5% incline.

In Version 1 the researcher proposed a first conceptual principle using curved glulam beams as well as timber panels. At this stage, the different structural needs – due to differences in spans of approximately 30m across the road and railway, versus 9m over land in the grove – were identified but not resolved. The structure of the bridge was configured as repeated V-formed columns, carrying horizontal glulam elements that formed the edges of the bridge, with timber elements between the edge-beams to create the floor. The longer spans were provided by a shift of structure, from very short spans distributing the load to a truss based on a central beam across the road.

Version 2 was repositioned onsite according to 3D-scanned data, avoiding damage to high-value oak trees. The railing became structural, using trusses that minimised the depth across the highest point over the railway, and allowing the minimum free height to be achieved without further extending the bridge in plan. In the initial iteration, the trusses of the bridge railing were clad with external vertical panels. In the second iteration, the structure was inverted, with an externally-curved truss and internal cladding, allowing end wood elements to be properly covered and a simpler solution for the inside of the railing to discourage climbing. The analysis of all glulam elements provided by the ESR led to a potential solution where beams of lesser curvature could be replaced with straight beams with a machined outer edge. As a result, the initial estimate of 61 straight, 73 single-curved and 654 double-curved elements could be adapted to 268, 500 and 20 respectively, with a potential glulam lamination cost saving of around 40%.

Version 3 put the focus on utilising more of the structural potential of curved glulam elements by aligning the grain closer to the overall form of the

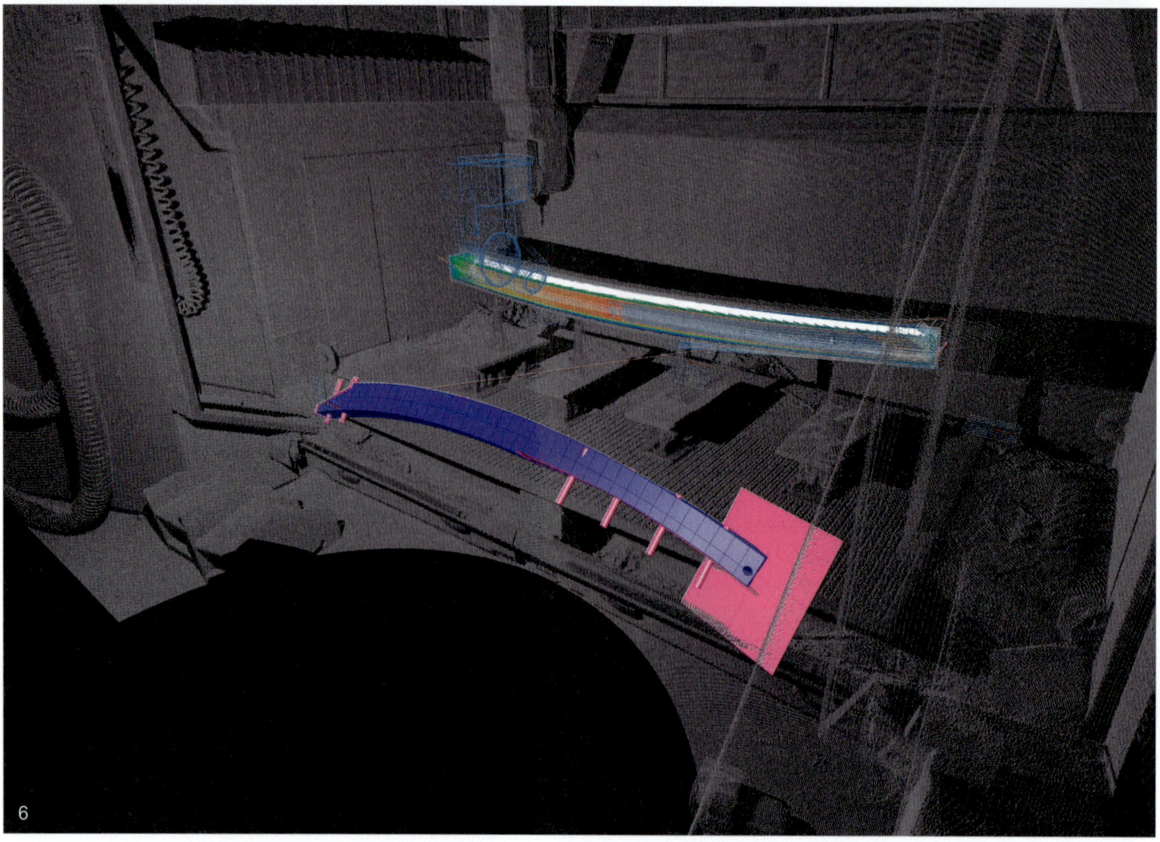

bridge, and testing the design-to-fabrication workflow and toolkit developed in both secondments. The goal here was to arrive at a physical mockup that would demonstrate the feasibility of the integrated approach, linking material feedback and production concerns to the design modelling and overall bridge scheme of the Magelungen Bridge. As such, the design involved more use of single- and double-curved glulam elements that were modelled and rationalised using the design modelling tools. For example, the overall geometry was constrained so that most blanks could be single-curved with minimal cutting of double-curved surfaces, and to maximise the thickness of individual lamellae to make production easier. The direct feedback techniques developed at Blumer Lehmann were applied to locate and verify the material during machining, facilitating the processing of the freeform elements. The final physical prototype was fabricated by the ESR in an environment that mimicked the production context at Blumer Lehmann but on a smaller scale: an industrial five-axis wood processing centre using standard G-code.

Conclusion

The chronology of the secondments progressed, in a way, in reverse: starting with a 'shadowing' role in production and ending with a collaborative-design role in architectural practice. This order was intentional and facilitated a valuable transfer of expertise from production to design, providing the ESR a unique role when entering the practice context. The value of this transfer, as well as computational toolkits relating to material performance – from fabrication and production to early-stage design – could be identified in several ways in the given example. The possibility to develop the design at a conceptual stage while being directly informed by the constraints of production and material performance aspects of bent, laminated wood was crucial to the project. The iterative development allowed the shift of scope in the project, from a standard bridge to an advanced glulam timber bridge, in a way that allowed stakeholders and decision-makers to initially accept and, later, promote the proposal. The potential 40% cost reduction for glulam production further supports this decision. These aspects can be seen as ways to control risk while facilitating imaginative innovation in practice (Marble, 2010). The use of mockups remains particularly important in freeform timber structures and, although much can be simulated and predicted, the final performance depends on many factors that simply have to be explored through making. Verification through physical prototyping is, therefore, necessary at key points within this iterative design process. The preliminary outcome of the conceptual design and analysis stages will depend on the further use of prototypes and mockups.

Acknowledgements

This project was undertaken at CITA, KADK, as part of the Innochain Early Training Network. The Doctoral Thesis of the ESR was supervised by Mette Ramsgaard Thomsen and Martin Tamke (CITA) with additional industry supervision by Kai Strehlke (Blumer Lehmann), Jonas Runberger (White Arkitekter), and Martin Antemann (Design-to-Production). Thanks to the staff and faculty at Aarhus Architecture School for their contribution toward the fabrication of the physical mockup.

All images copyright Tom Svilans, Blumer Lehmann AG or White Arkitekter AB, unless otherwise stated.

Bibliography

Kolarevic, B., 2003, 'Introduction' in Kolarevic, B. (ed.), *Architecture in the Digital Age: Design and Manufacturing*, Didcot, Taylor & Francis, p.3–10.

Marble, S., 2010, 'Imagining Risk' in Deamer, P. and Bernstein, P.G. (eds.), *Building (In) the Future: Recasting Labor in Architecture*, Princeton, NJ, Princeton Architectural Press, p.39–43.

Runberger, J. and Magnusson, F., 2015, 'Harnessing the Informal Processes around the Computational Design Model' in Thomsen, M., Tamke, M., Gengnagel, C., Faircloth, B. and Scheurer, F. (eds.), *Modelling Behaviour*, New York, Springer, p.329–339.

Tamke, M., Hernández, E.L., Deleuran, A.H., Gengnagel, C., Burry, M. and Thomsen, M.R., 2012, 'A New Material Practice: Integrating Design and Material Behavior', in *Symposium on Simulation for Architecture and Urban Design '12*, p.1–9. http://dl.acm.org/citation.cfm?id=2339456 (accessed 8 February 2020).

Svilans, T., Poinet, P., Tamke, M. and Thomsen, M.R., 2018, 'A Multi-Scalar Approach for the Modelling and Fabrication of Free-Form Glue-Laminated Timber Structures' in *Humanizing Digital Reality*, New York, Springer, p.247–257.

Svilans, T., Tamke, M., Thomsen, M.R., Runberger, J., Strehlke, K. and Antemann, M., 2019, 'New Workflows for Digital Timber' in Bianconi, F. and Filippucci, M. (eds.), *Digital Wood Design: Innovative Techniques of Representation in Architectural Design*, New York, Springer, p.93–134.

5 & 6. Production of the physical mockup for Version 3 integrated the glulam modelling toolkit as well as the feedback methods developed during the secondments.

3.3 DESIGN INTEGRATION

Acoustic Wall: Computational and Robotic Design Integration of Four Primary Generators

Isak Worre Foged
Aalborg University
Anke Pasold
Copenhagen School of Design and Technology
Mads Brath Jensen
Aalborg University

Introduction

This study pursues the idea and potential of design-steered convergence processes, using the assembly of a limestone acoustic wall as a 'vehicle' for exploring the integration of computational search methods, pattern expressions, acoustic simulation and collaborative robotics in design and making processes that are then tested and compared in terms of their acoustic performances. The work was initiated from visual and acoustic observations at Piazza San Marco in Venice, Italy, and the Antalya-Demre Limestone Quarry in Turkey.

Venice has an impressive display of articulated limestone, where the combination of colour nuances, geometries, patterns and stone erosion provide the unique characteristics that attract thousands of people to the city every year (fig.1). While it is reputedly the most visited square in the world, Piazza San Marco is also posited to be one of the most quiet, due to the lack of traffic and the acoustic properties of the stone used in the buildings (Horowitz, 2013). In the case of Turkey, upon invitation to the Istanbul Design Biennale, we were brought into direct contact with the Antalya-Demre Limestone Quarry, which provided a unique opportunity to study, explore and identify integrated design processes, including acoustics, limestone, design computation, brick patterns and robotic fabrication processes.

Background

The objective to combine and search design convergence through many aspects and underlying parameters (fig.2), is a common condition in design processes (Dorst and Cross, 2001; Lawson, 2006).

1. Limestone façade at Piazza San Marco in Venice, Italy. Summer 2018. Photo by the authors.

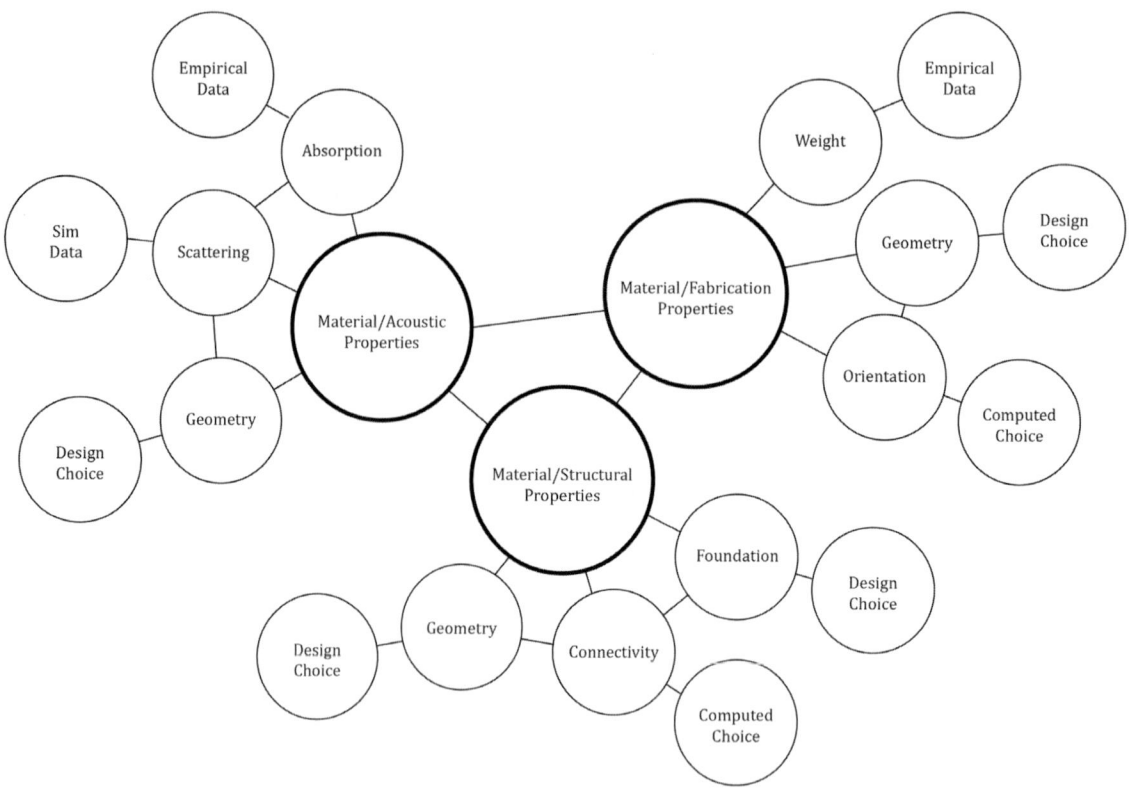

2

Such design conjectures, which aim to form 'wholeness' (Alexander, 2009) may, however, be based on simplified integration if not supported by specific design models which through distinct primary generators, which strategically integrate prioritised aspects (Darke, 1979; Foged, 2018). Consequently, this project attempted to explore collaborative robotics of complex assembled structures, where material properties, acoustics, assembly stability and human–machine interaction were implemented into one explorative design model (fig.2).

By considering the human directly in the computational design and robotic fabrication loop, the project's methods and techniques attempt to support the creative and craft capacities of collaborative processes between systems and humans. Four primary aspects – optics, acoustics, robotics and statics – were, therefore, interwoven into the early design processes to seamlessly connect robotic control with human craft in the computational design model and construction processes, as a way to build novel structures through learning by making.

Previous solutions to collaborative robotics in architecture stem from a growing awareness of humans' influence on design iterations during robotic making, such as the statement 'keeping the 'human in the loop', the intuition and cognition of the operator augmenting the skills of the robot, just as the robot augments those of the designer' (Johns et al., 2014). It becomes necessary to categorise the components of these exercises within a number of directions and motivations which can be related in the field, and to their larger consequences within the architectural discipline. In this chapter, we present a number of approaches to robotic design/fabrication exercises that deal with information, interactivity, and material dynamics.

The project's aim, in relation to fabrication, was to let simple human–robot communication guide the relation between robot and maker, rather than applying complex high-tech visual projections or augmented reality technologies. With this approach, the two making agents – robot and person – relate through intuitive logics of communication, just as technologies are limited to what is needed. In respect to the design model and its logics, the integration of multiple aspects to inform the design of the wall assembly challenges conventional brick bonds. The proposed visual- and acoustic-driven composition of geometrically simple bricks can therefore serve as inspiration and be directly adopted by the creative and manufacturing industries working with masonry structures.

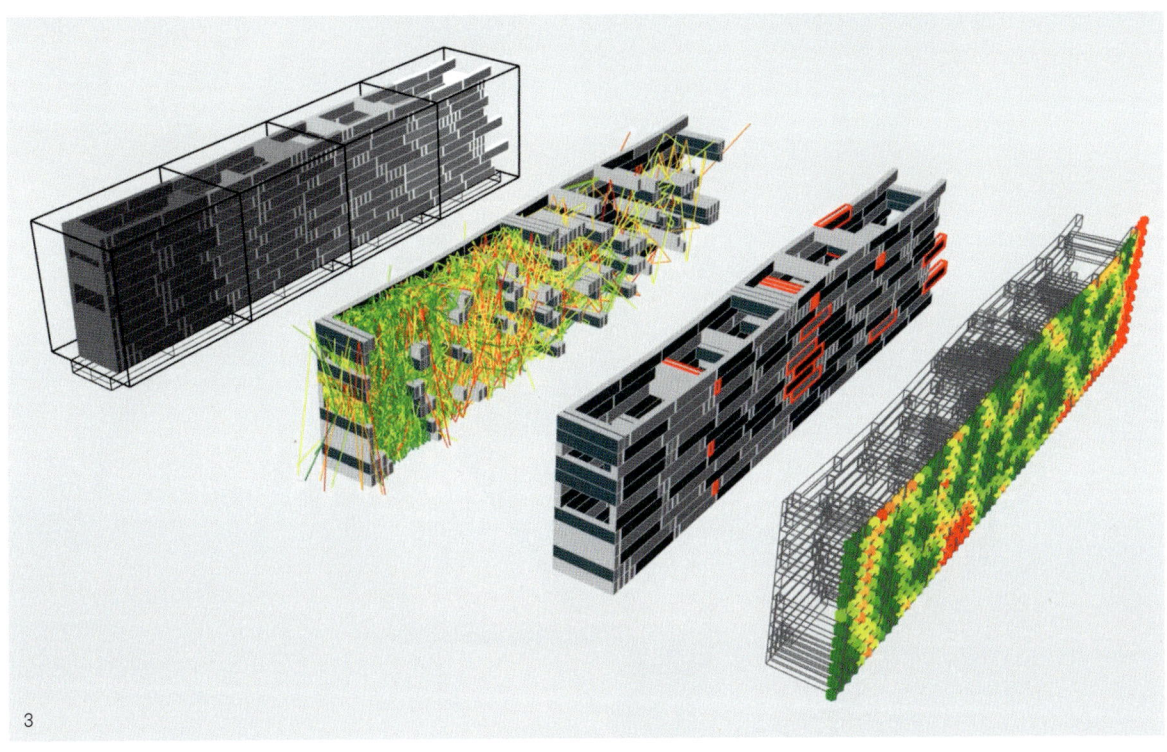

3

The studies in acoustics integration applied the Pachyderm acoustic simulation software into the parametric model, and describe each material element through geometric, material absorption and scattering coefficients. This enables a design search procedure to compute and steer the sound energy that is distributed through each individual double-sided wall and brick-bond iteration (fig.3).

Using this approach, we sought to develop and investigate the combining of multiple primary performance criteria within a computational design model. The model includes craft methods, material properties, local material sourcing, acoustic simulation, fabrication constraints, fabrication control and communication with an onsite production collaborator. The digital ecology established within this computational model was bridged by the robot to a full-scale physical demonstrator utilising limestone bricks measuring 30mm x 60mm x 300mm, which were assembled into a sound-distributing double-layered wall with cross binders. Each limestone brick consisted of one rough side and five smooth sides, which acted as material variables in the search for a limestone wall composition that satisfied project-specific acoustic, structural and expressive characteristics.

2. Diagram of primary integrated aspect and sub-parameters of the computational design model for steered-design search processes. Source: the authors.

3. Computational Design Model, including four primary design generators. From left: a) robot fabrication limitations; b) hybrid-model acoustic simulation; c) local brick support assessment; d) brick bond relations. Image by the authors.

4

The studies present the design model for convergence search, enabled by communication between robot and human collaborator in the making process. A brief description of the computational aspects will be presented here, elaborating on material practice, acoustic simulation, dynamic assessment of instabilities of the bricks as they are layered by the robotic making procedure, and assessment of the full-scale limestone demonstrator.

Methods

The studies were conducted using three methods/models, including development and experimentation with a Computational Design Model; a Collaborative Robotic Model for assembly; and Acoustic Field Measurements for testing the sound transfer.

Computational Design Model
The experimental research was based on the Rhino/Grasshopper computational framework by McNeel Inc., where a series of plugins and bespoke Python-coded components were integrated into a complete integrative design exploration model. These included Kuka I PRC for robotic control, developed by Johannes Braumann; Pachyderm Acoustics, developed by Arthur van der Harten; Goat, developed by Rechenraum; and a set of search conditions and structural instability tests developed by the authors.

Collaborative Robotic Model
The robotic arm used for positioning and gesturing is a Kuka KR20-3, with a modified SMC MLH2-20D pneumatic gripper mounted as end-effector. These technologies were used to illustrate that readily accessible tools and techniques can be applied, and easily converted into industry-oriented projects following this research. A gesturing system, using a Leap Motion sensor, was constructed and used during testing, and a bypass communication system – in the form of a simple push-button – was implemented for communication between robot and human during the making of the brick wall demonstrator.

4. Collaborative robot-based making process with limestone brick bonds composed through a design integration process at the Istanbul Design Biennale 2018. Photos by Efe Gözen and Burcu Bicer Saner.

5. Limestone brick wall, before robot-human built segments are fully connected, composed during the design integration process at the Istanbul Design Biennale 2018. Photo by the authors.

Acoustic Field Measurements

An initial set of acoustic field measurements were taken at Piazza San Marco, using a Class A condenser microphone (i365) with calibrated sound meter software on an iPhone 8, to determine whether the square could be registered as acoustically 'quiet'. Sound pressure measurements were conducted at three different times of day across the square, to cover the relative uniform space and account for variation in occupancy. Following the construction of the limestone wall for the Istanbul Design Biennale, acoustic measurements were conducted to measure the loss of sound energy through the cavity between the two sides of the double-layered wall, and thus to understand the sound transfer properties of the cavity based on material-geometric compositions. Measurements were taken using a Yamaha MSP5 loudspeaker, a Behringer M8000 measurement microphone and RØDETest FuzzMeasure software for sound energy analysis.

Design Experimentation

The intent behind the design experimentation was to explore how a computational design system and collaborative robot-based construction methods could create a novel double-layered acoustic-influenced limestone masonry wall. These design studies aimed to identify and propose ways for more complex assemblies to be defined and designed than single-layered masonry walls. The computational design system's variables include a global form definition and a series of local conditions, where the composition weaves together surface and binder bricks, while maintaining stability across the assembly (also during construction), increasing the sound transfer through the cavity, and modifying the position of the surface and binder bricks, and the orientation of both rough and smooth sides (fig.3). Furthermore, a series of preliminary physical design tests were conducted with scaled bricks to test how the computational, robotic and construction setup could scale to other dimensions, and allowing for an understanding of the system's adaptability to subjective design input.

The study also explored the role of the human co-worker by constructing methods allowing for communication between human and robot during the fabrication process. These experiments also therefore explored the division of labour between human and robot related to the brick stacking and gluing processes. As previously mentioned, hand gestures were used as a method for communication between human and robot, a method that, despite its simple setup (counting of fingers and orientation of the hand), required additional verification to ensure that a recorded hand gesture was indeed the one intended by the human collaborator. This process was necessary for removing the uncertainty involved in delivering the correct command to the robot, although it also protracted the collaborative fabrication process. The verifications were provided by the robot through a single-line LCD display controlled by an Arduino Uno board.

Results and Discussion

The computational design model, based on an ecology of off-the-shelf and bespoke Rhino Grasshopper components, with a two-phase stochastic and deterministic search procedure, was partly able to bring together the primary aspects integrated in this study. However, it was unable to operate or to respond with novel solutions when it encountered undefined conditions or unforeseen uncertainties during a design solution search. One study-specific example of this scenario is the design model positioning of the acoustic source and receiver as variables, which were steered by human intervention and presented significant performance gains that the defined search procedure did not. Hence, when the design model remains open to human steering interventions, possibilities for more novel solutions can be sought, whereas framed searches lead to closed-loop explorations, where human steering is limited to between computational search processes. For this reason, the study indicates that even integrated and advanced computational search processes in design need further abilities for steering in open design processes.

With respect to the collaborative robotic making process, guidance and in-automation steering was provided through simple hand-gesturing. This method, however, was quickly abandoned during the making

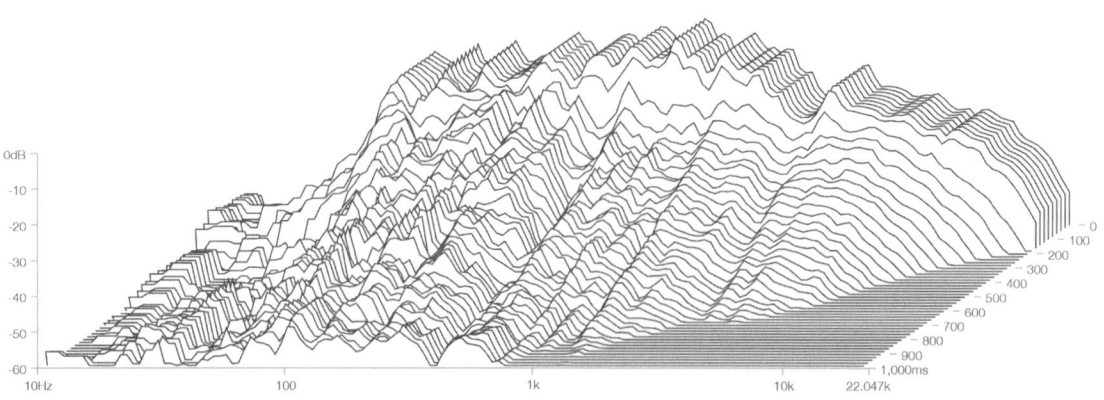

FFT Waterfall (1/12 Octave Smoothing)

of the demonstrator, in favour of the simpler button-actuation command communication. One reason for this appeared to be an insecurity around whether the robot had understood a human gesture or not, and whether the correct robot action would be executed. Lack of confirmation cues between robot and human added unintended uncertainties. These uncertainties slowed down the making process significantly and often influenced the human co-maker to adjust their communication methods.

The study also shows that incorporating robotic fabrication within an undetermined and explorative design process requires a human–robot–material setup where the human co-designer can interact and intervene during the fabrication process and make necessary changes when needed. For example, this could be due to the unaccounted-for dimensional variation of the material elements or, of more interest to this specific study, as a response to a new design intent arising from the human–robot fabrication process itself. Intervening in the robot-driven making process will require a shift away from the predetermined file–to–factory approach and toward new design methods, supporting computational design models that can dynamically respond to design alterations made during fabrication.

The specific design system studies and collaborative robotic making processes described here suggest the need for advancing human–system–robot interfaces. If they are to become integrated agile systems, which operate with and for human creativity and fabrication, their novelty lies in the intelligent interplay between human and system.

Bibliography

Andersen, R.S., Madsen, O., Moeslund, T.B. and Amor, H.B., 2016, 'Projecting Robot Intentions into Human Environments' in *RO-MAN 2016: Proceedings of the 25th IEEE International Symposium on Robot and Human Interactive Communication*, New York. https://doi.org/10.1109/ROMAN.2016.7745145 (accessed 17 December 2019).

Alexander, C., 2009, 'Harmony-Seeking Computations: A science of Non-Classical Dynamics Based on the Progressive Evolution of the Larger Whole' in *International Journal of Unconventional Computing*, p.1–78.

Darke, J., 1979, 'The Primary Generator and the Design Process' in *Design Studies*, Vol. 1, No. 1, p.36–44.

Dorst, K. and Cross, N., 2001, 'Creativity in the Design Process: Co-evolution of problem-solution' in *Design Studies*, Vol. 22, No. 5, p.425–437.

Foged, I., 2018, 'Integrated Design Processes by Sequential Primary Generators' in *Journal of Problem-Based Learning in Higher Education*, Vol. 6, No. 1, p.66–87.

Horowitz, S.S., 2013, *The Universal Sense: How Hearing Shapes the Mind*, London, Bloomsbury Academic.

Johns, R.L., Kilian, A. and Foley, N., 2014, 'Design Approaches through Augmented Materiality and Embodied Computation' in McGee, W. and de Leon, M.P. (eds.), *Robotic Fabrication in Architecture, Art and Design 2014*, New York, Springer, p.319–332.

Lawson, B., 2006, *How Designers Think: The Design Process Demystified*, London, London Architectural Press.

6. Fast Fourier Transformation graph illustrating the acoustic performances from IR measurements of the demonstrator, showing the sound-energy distribution through the wall assembly. Sound energy, according to the measurements, is better maintained and transferred at low frequencies through the structure. Graph by the authors.

3.4 DESIGN INTEGRATION

Coreless Filament Winding: From Academia to Practice

James Solly and Jan Knippers
Institute of Building Structures and Structural Design (ITKE), University of Stuttgart
Moritz Dörstelmann
FibR GmbH

Introduction

This paper presents the case study of Coreless Filament Winding, a digital additive manufacturing technology for architecture that is evolving from the world of academia into a commercial industrial environment. This example is relevant within the Innochain context, as it exemplifies a soft transition whereby links between academic institution and a startup fabrication company have been maintained for mutual benefit.

The Coreless Filament Winding Process

Coreless Filament Winding (CFW) is a fabrication method for the creation of Fibre-Reinforced Polymer (FRP) parts. Since 2011, it has been under active development by the Institute for Computational Design and Construction (ICD) and the Institute of Building Structures and Structural Design (ITKE) at the University of Stuttgart. Details of the process were first published by researchers in relation to the ICD/ITKE Research Pavilion 2012 (Schwinn et al., 2013). CFW may be regarded as a variation on the normal FRP Filament Winding process where continuous fibre bundles are wrapped around a rotating madril (core).

The Filament Winding method is primarily used in industry for its ability to achieve consistent material properties while placing material at high speed. As outlined by Schwinn, the use of a core-based method has limitations for the production of architectural composite parts. Buildings often require many unique parts that require a range of unique cores.

CFW was conceived to address the waste resulting from the large number of cores and the issues associated with the demoulding of core-wound parts. It involves the

1. Coreless Filament Winding. © ICD/ITKE, University of Stuttgart.

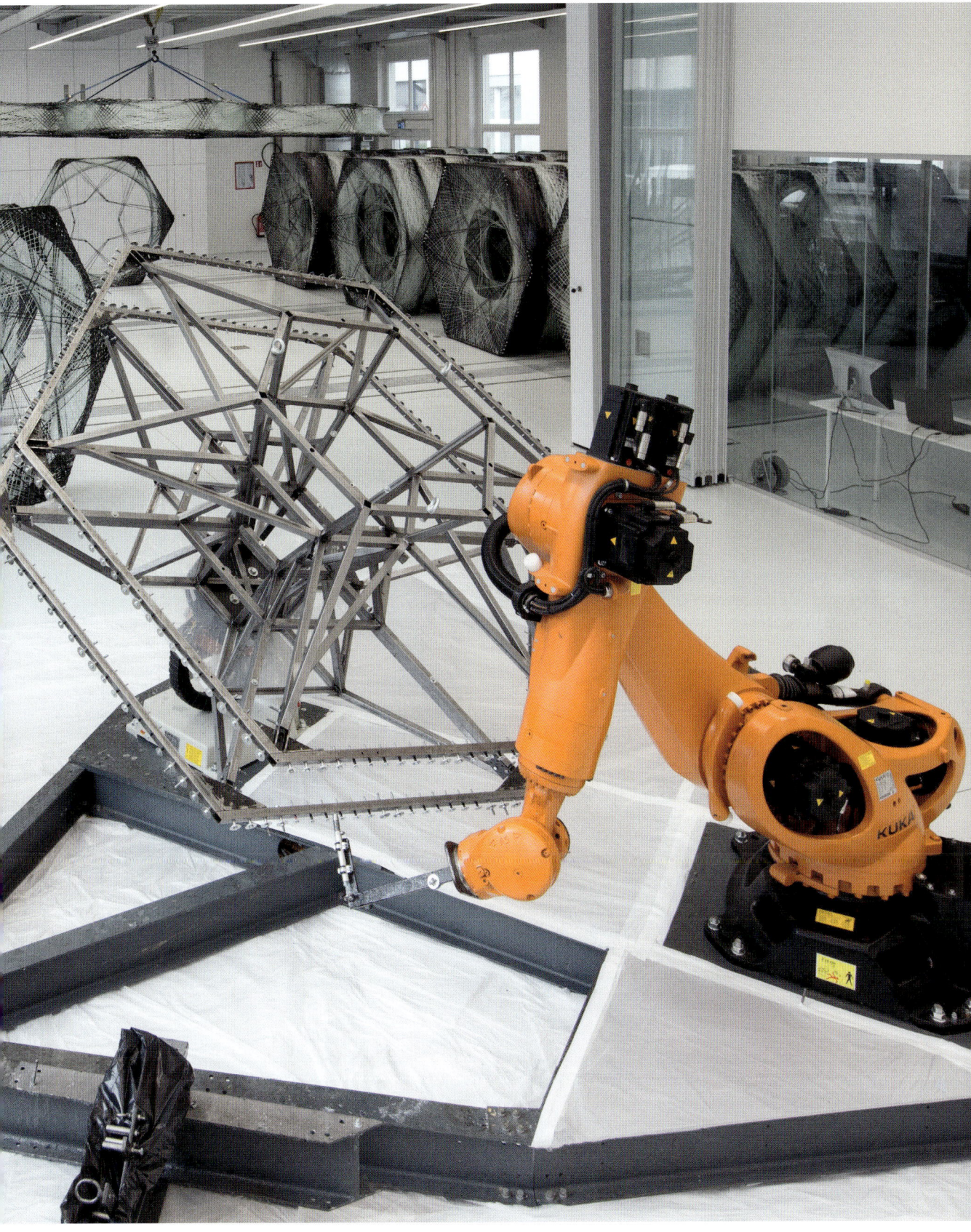

2. Research Pavilion 2016/2017, © ICD/ITKE.

3. Elytra Filament Pavilion under Construction, © NAARO.

4. Slab component, 'Resistant Filigrees' by Jorge Christie.

wrapping of resin-impregnated fibre bundles around spatially-located discrete winding pins. Fibres passing between these pins are sequenced to cross over one another, building up a geometry that emerges from their interaction. As this geometry is a result of both pin location and winding sequence, a single arrangement of pins enables several forms to be created through different sequences. The pins are typically mounted onto skeletal frameworks that can be demoulded and reused following curing (the setting/hardening of the resin) of the FRP component. In some projects, such as the ICD/ITKE Research Pavilion 2013/2014 (Dörstelmann et al., 2015), these frameworks were designed to enable simple adjustment in order to further increase the range of geometries possible from a single winding frame.

The simplicity of the placement method – robotically winding wet fibres around pins – enables high-speed material lay-down especially compared with other additive manufacturing technologies that require the material to harden during fabrication. In CFW, the machine-dependent fabrication stage operates with uncured material, and curing occurs outside the time-critical pathway.

Coreless Filament Winding in Academia

Completed Projects and Research

As the benefits and limitations of CFW have been tested by the University of Stuttgart, several large-scale demonstrator projects have been produced, exploring (and promoting) the potential of the technology. Key projects include:

- ICD/ITKE Research Pavilion 2012: The first pavilion produced using coreless winding, wound to create a single composite structure (Schwinn et al., 2013).
- ICD/ITKE Research Pavilion 2013/2014: Created using CFW modules to allow for offsite fabrication and onsite assembly, creating a structure larger than the reach of the robotic arm (Dörstelmann et al., 2015).
- Elytra Filament Pavilion: Utilising the modular approach from the 2013/2014 pavilion, this structure was the first for a prominent client in a publicly accessible location. It had to conform to local regulations and include interfaces between composites and the typical architectural requirements of cladding and foundations (Koslowski, Solly and Knippers, 2018).
- BUGA Fibre Pavilion 2019: Utilising a new type of modular component, this recent project demonstrated the use of fibres for creating a dome, providing a large increase in scale and satisfying the onerous permit/review process required by the authorities for a structure of this size (ITKE, 2019).

Supporting these larger structures, several smaller CFW prototypes and experiments have been completed, by institute researchers and as part of ITECH Master's thesis projects, such as the 2018 thesis 'Resistant Filigrees' by Jorge Christie.

Beyond Stuttgart, interest in the CFW method has been demonstrated by a number of other academic institutions, highlighting a common interest in this form of material placement – for example, the Cloudmagnet (Wit, 2018) and C-Lith (Wilcox and Trandafirescu, 2015) projects.

3

4

Ongoing Research

As seen in these examples, the possibility for CFW to produce novel geometries and its economical use of carefully aligned material have sparked significant interest in the academic community. While technology for the fabrication of CFW components has progressed significantly during these projects, digital tools for early-stage design and the evaluation of structural safety and integrity lag behind.

For the early design phase, key fabrication constraints must be understood to maintain the simplicity and speed of the CFW method. As geometries emerge from collisions between fibres, without an easily-usable design tool to model this behaviour, projects to date have relied on physical prototypes. The Innochain project 'Virtual Prototyping of FRP' was proposed to address this missing digital tool and the three years of work produced several productive steps plus multiple avenues for further work.

The topics of fabrication-informed design for CFW and evaluation of component structural capacity remain areas of ongoing development with several funded projects due to commence over the coming year.

Academia-Industry Collaboration

The Need for a Fabricator

As shown here, the process of CFW has been well proven for a range of projects, successfully demonstrating the benefits of these composite parts for architectural-scale installations. Given this success, it is unsurprising that private-sector firms have shown an interest and approached the university with requests for projects of their own. This leads to two scenarios in which a commercial fabricator of CFW parts starts to make sense:

1. The client is seeking to implement a novel project and is happy to accept the risks that emerge from incorporating a research element. Here, the development of the project can form part of the ongoing research in the university. However, once a process or methodology has been developed through research, the worth of a university performing a longer-term production role must be considered. Here, an industry fabrication partner becomes useful.
2. The client wishes to purchase a structure that leverages existing technology that has already been successfully trialled in a research project. Typically, this also means they would want a warrantied structure in line with any other building parts purchased in the construction industry. It is extremely complicated for a university to accept such a commission; this is the clear territory of a fabrication company.

During the initial stages of the Innochain project, it was clear that clients existed in both of these categories but there was no experienced fabricator in the market to perform production. While there are companies actively working on the development of CFW-type technologies (e.g. Mercedes Benz and Isotruss Technologies), they do not currently offer services aligned with building-scale production.

To take advantage of this market gap, FibR GmbH was formed in 2016 by ICD Research Associate Moritz Dörstelmann and Textile Technology specialist Philipp Essers. Since its formation, FibR has worked on several projects with the university (outlined below), while additionally performing commercial CFW design and production services for a series of other clients.

First Steps in Collaboration

Since the creation of FibR there have been two key partnerships with the University of Stuttgart that can be considered outstanding examples of academic–industry collaboration. These relationships are of benefit to both parties, as the University gains an immediate addition to the fabrication facilities available to its researchers along with specific fabrication knowledge, while the company (a startup deploying a new and evolving technology) gains access to ongoing research on the fabrication method it is seeking to commercially deploy.

The Innochain Network

In early 2017, FibR GmBH joined the Innochain Network as an Industry Partner of Early-Stage Researcher (ESR), James Solly, at the ITKE. This relationship was not seeking to produce a specific project but was formed for mutual benefit in the ongoing investigation of early-stage design tools. Through this collaboration, two key prototypes were formed: the Optimised Fibre Beam prototype and the Optimised Fibre Façade prototype.

The Fibre Façade prototype utilised a series of tools produced during the three-years of Innochain funding. Form-finding studies determined, for each geometry, which fibres could actually be placed. Optimisation routines iteratively culled fibres from the form to ensure minimum material usage, and winding-path algorithms aided the production of robotic-motion planning. Collaboration with FibR ensured a streamlined workflow from design to engineering to fabrication, and resulted in a detailed fabrication scaffold that can be reused on future projects.

The outcome was a prototype that uses thin carbon-fibre bundles in both tension and compression, resulting in eight structural frames that weigh only 4.2kg in total (the heaviest individual frame weighing just 990g).

5. Fibre façade prototype.

In the Innochain exhibition, these supported 8.75m² of polycarbonate, weighing 90kg, and were designed to carry glass weighing twice this amount.

BUGA Filament Pavilion 2019

Between 2018 and 2019, FibR GmbH partnered with the ICD and ITKE at the University of Stuttgart on the delivery of the BUGA Filament Pavilion. This is an example of a Type 1 project where the pure research elements were performed within the university with input from FibR on some aspects of fabrication. The results of this research phase were then utilised by FibR GmbH for production of the filament components.

Coreless Filament Winding in Industry

Multiple academic papers, some of which are referenced above, have outlined the proposed benefits of CFW for construction. Given these claims, the technology must now be adopted and leveraged by industry to improve the built environment if it is to be considered a success.

It is therefore an exciting time for researchers involved in the development of CFW, as early projects are being produced in a commercial setting by Innochain Partner FibR. Following initial commercial production of furniture-scale items, followed by its aforementioned work on the BUGA project, FibR is currently working on a range of larger-scale commercial projects.

An interesting immediate outcome of working with a range of commercial clients has been an expansion of the material palette used for CFW. While academic research to date has selected materials based on technical performance, other clients are looking for specific aesthetic outcomes.

Conclusion

This chapter has summarised the historic work on CFW performed in academia and highlights the recently-addressed need for a CFW commercial fabricator. Successful academia–industry collaborations are outlined to show the benefit of having both partners working together, and some initial commercial projects are presented. Further large-scale commercial projects are known to be under active development and the first commercially-produced large building components are eagerly awaited. CFW remains a young fabrication process for the AEC industry and, it is hoped that ongoing engagement between academia and industry practice will allow it to finally demonstrate the real-world gains proposed in the research produced since 2013.

Innumerable professors, researchers, students, sponsors and supporters have worked on Coreless Filament Winding and produced the information covered in this chapter. It is not possible to acknowledge every individual here and, while the bibliographical references capture some of them, all those not named are sincerely thanked for their input to this ongoing endeavour.

6

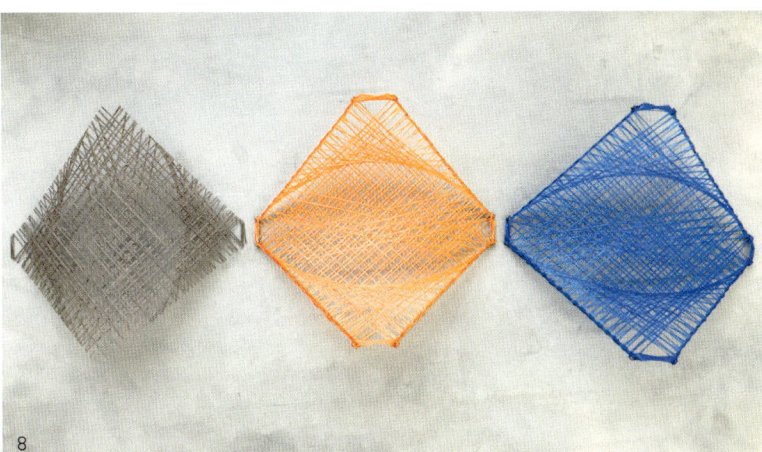

Bibliography

Christie, J., 2018, 'Resistant Filigrees – Shape Optimization-to-Fabrication: Workflow for Coreless Wound CFRP Structures for Spanning Applications', University of Stuttgart: ITECH Master's Studio.

Dörstelmann, M., Knippers, J., Menges, A., Parascho, S., Prado, M., Schwinn, T., 2015, 'ICD/ITKE Research Pavilion 2013-14: Modular Coreless Filament Winding Based on Beetle Elytra' in *Architectural Design*, 85(5), p.54–59.

ITKE (Institute of Building Structures and Structural Design), 2019, BUGA Fibre Pavilion: www.icd.uni-stuttgart.de/projects/buga-fiber-pavilion (accessed 26 February 2020).

Koslowski, V., Solly, J. and Knippers, J., 2017, 'Structural Design Methods of Component-Based Lattice Composites for the Elytra Pavilion' in Bögle, A. and Grohmann, M. (eds.), Proceedings of the IASS Annual Symposium 2017, *Interfaces: architecture. engineering.science*, Hamburg, HafenCity University Hamburg, IASS.

Schwinn, T., La Magna, R., Reichert, S., Waimer, F., Knippers, J., Menges, A., 2013, 'Prototyping Biomimetic Structure for Architecture' in Stacey, M. (ed.), *Prototyping Architecture: The Conference Papers*, London, Building Centre Trust, p.224–244.

Solly, J., Früh, N., Saffarian, S., Aldinger, L., Margariti, G., Knippers, J., 'Structural Design of a Lattice Composite Cantilever' in Structures, Vol. 18, April 2019, Amsterdam, Elsevier, p.1–13.

Wilcox, G., Trandafirescu, A., 2015, 'C-Lith: Carbon Fiber Architectural Units' in *Computational Ecologies: Design in the Anthropocene*, Proceedings of the 35th ACADIA Conference, Cincinnati, p.69–79.

Wit, A.J., 2018, 'Cloudmagnet: A CFRP Framework for Flexible Architectures' in T. Fukuda, T., Huang, W., Janssen, P., Crolla, K., Alhadidi, S. (eds.), *Learning, Adapting and Prototyping*, Proceedings of the 23rd CAADRIA Conference, Beijing, p.49–58.

6. BUGA Fibre Pavilion 2019. © ICD/ITKE, University of Stuttgart.

7 & 8. Fibre furniture and range of winding materials. © FibR GmBH.

3.5 DESIGN INTEGRATION

All That Is Porous: Practising Cross-Disciplinary Design Thinking

Vasily Sitnikov
KTH Royal Institute of Technology, Stockholm

This chapter discusses the material systems commonly employed in the production of precast concrete elements. In particular, it presents an alternative to expanded polystyrene (EPS), a material that is often used in moulding production for complex-shaped concrete elements. Though EPS plays an important role in the production of an energy-efficient built environment, the ecological implications of its growing global use, and inevitably growing waste, raise serious environmental concerns. Putting the industrial policies of EPS use under question, the author proposes the concept of an alternative ice-based material system for concrete manufacturing. This method provides a waste-free, closed-loop recycling manufacturing process. It enables the production of intricate and formally rich structural formations in concrete, for example mesoscale trabecular concrete structures – spatial material organisations that exceed the scale of concrete microstructures, but are much smaller than the design detailing of the concrete elements.

Initially intended to merely eliminate production waste, ice-based concrete manufacturing is a relatively little-explored field in material organisation. This novel opportunity to produce reduced-weight concrete elements with differential local physical properties and expressive formal language is a welcome side-effect of stepping outside standard material practices.

Energy Efficiency

One of the exhibitions that took place at the 2019 Chicago Architecture Biennial was called *All That Is Solid*. The concept was to bring approximately 28m³ of EPS debris from a landfill into the gallery space, reflecting on 'our shifting cultural and economic definitions of waste and worth, resource and refuse' (Li, 2019). EPS is one of the most ubiquitous materials, with the most mismanaged waste culture, but why would an exhibition about architecture criticise a material that is widely associated with disposable cups, tableware and product packaging? The reason is that the EPS we casually encounter in our daily lives is just the tip of the iceberg. Due to its low cost and versatility, EPS has become deeply rooted in the building industry, fulfilling many useful functions, both permanent (e.g. insulation and backfill in landscaping) and temporary (e.g. formwork and moulds for cast concrete). The waste produced in all of these applications is less obvious to the end-user, as it remains obscured from public view. However, recent research suggests that construction materials contribute to the '99% of plastic debris by weight entering the ocean' which are 'more likely to contain chemical additives in greater masses' (De Frond, 2018).

Despite the environmental hazards, the pursuit of an energy-efficient built environment means EPS is widely used as an insulating material. However, EPS has a high embodied energy value – i.e. energy invested during fabrication and transportation. According to data from the Inventory of Carbon and Embodied Energy (Hammond and Jones, 2011), its embodied energy is equal to approximately 88MJ/kg. For comparison, the same amount of energy is needed to heat 1m² of residential space in Norway over a period of 25 years (Minea, 2016). Therefore, a house designed and insulated according to the sustainable concepts of 'passive' or 'zero energy' (a house that uses a lot of EPS insulation) means investing a great amount of energy during the construction stage. In turn, over a period of 80 years, such a house would win merely 7% of energy savings compared to a house with outdated insulation

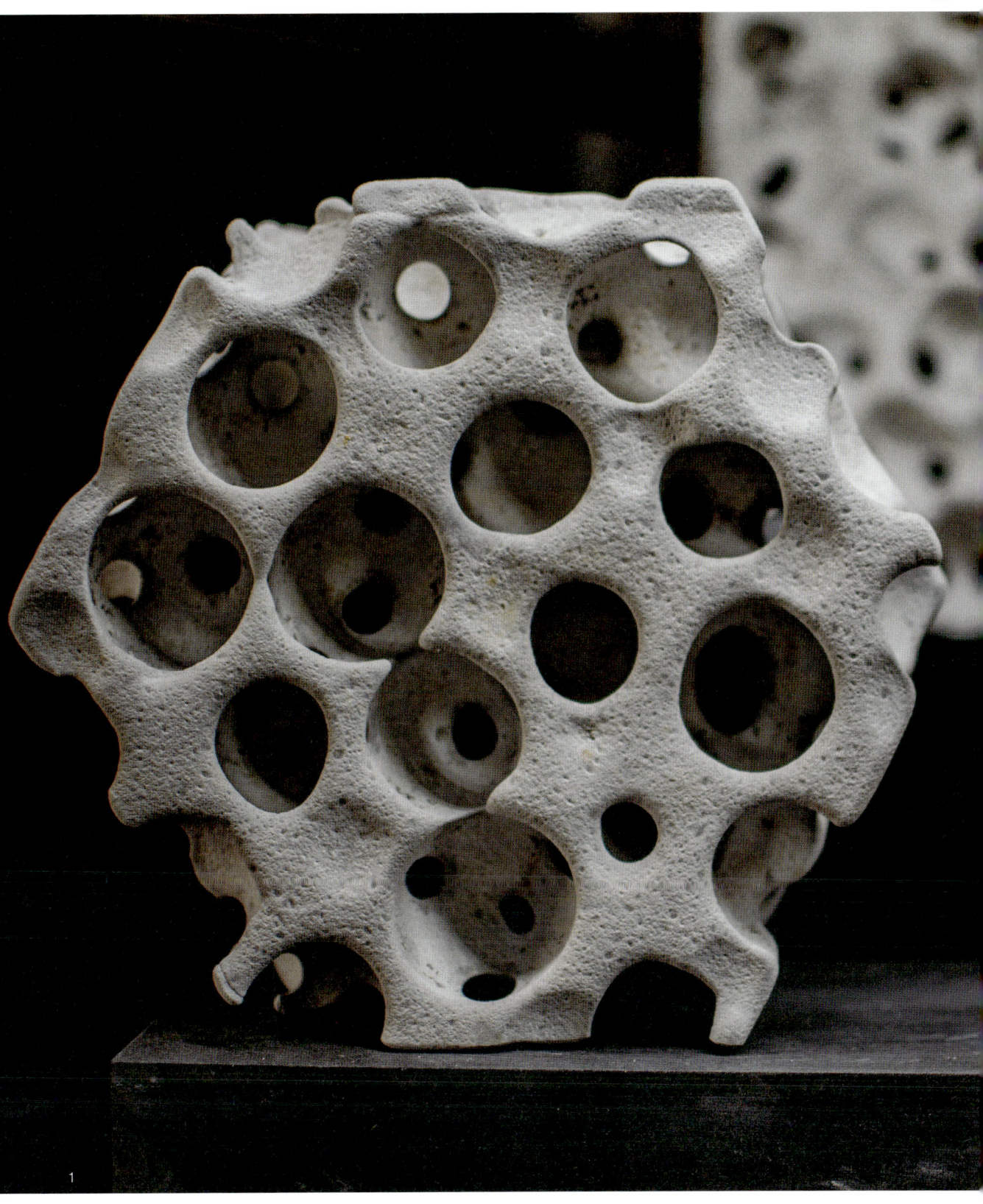

1. A hexagonal prototype of a trabecular HPFRC structure cast using ice aggregate.

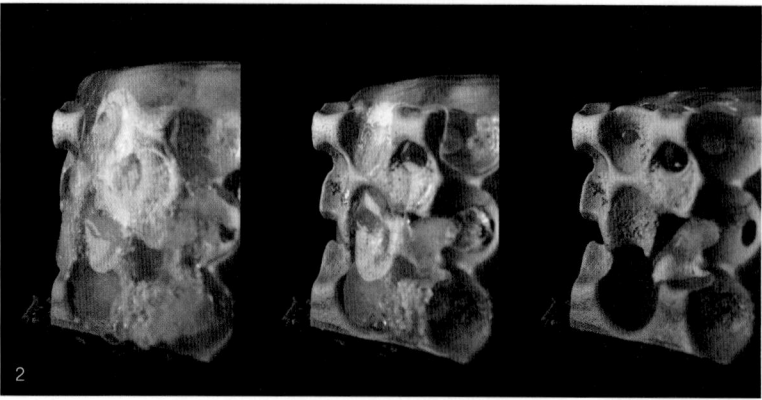

2. Demolding/defrosting of HPFRC hexagon prototype.

3. Detail view of a trabecular HPFRC structure formed with 40mm diameter ice spheres.

standards, as a recent lifecycle assessment analysis shows (Kovacic, 2018). The price of this modest energy saving is increased polystyrene waste, and inevitable eventual contamination of land and the oceans.

Concrete Redefined

When examining concrete's environmental performance, one has to keep in mind that its chemistry, or more precisely chemistry of its constituent, cement, does not significantly differ from that of natural limestone. This means that its exposure to the natural environment is safe, and cannot result in an unforeseen effects, such as long-term chemical contamination. In fact, exposed hydrated cement in concrete constructions has a capacity to capture carbon dioxide from the atmosphere. This means that concrete carbonation, can be utilised to reduce the carbon footprint of concrete's manufacturing and transportation. Just as timber constructions are nowadays seen as carbon deposits, concrete can be redefined according to its capacity to be a carbon-neutral building material.

Furthermore, the embodied energy of concrete is extraordinary low, approximately 0.75MJ/kg. Compared to the previously mentioned 88MJ/kg of EPS, 9-29MJ/kg of steel, or 15MJ/kg of plywood, concrete is a strong choice when it comes to laying the ground for low-energy construction principles. Nevertheless, this has not been the priority for the industry, as the low price of concrete means the need to optimise its use is not pressing. Instead, the industry continues to build excessively thick concrete constructions, since the main function given to concrete is to protect steel reinforcement from corrosion. However, this material configuration is far less sustainable then was originally expected. The long-term exploitation of exposed concrete constructions has shown that diffusion of the atmospheric carbon dioxide in concrete rapidly propagates through its porous microstructures, changing the alkaline level and triggering steel oxidation. To counteract this phenomenon, the thickness of concrete used has gradually increased, resulting in excessively heavy concrete constructions. Concrete is held back from becoming a 'green' building material for reasons rooted in the conservative building codes inherited from preceding epochs. If ferrous reinforcement itself had been replaced with recently developed glass fibre, carbon fibre or other non-ferrous reinforcement, concrete constructions would have lost half of their weight, and the process of carbonation would already have been considered a positive side-effect.

Meanwhile, steel reinforcement is not the only aspect that constrains concrete development. It is commonly known that concrete formwork is one of the most expensive aspects of concrete manufacturing. Usually, the material used in producing the mould is steel, wood, or EPS foam. The more complicated the geometry of a concrete element is, the more difficult it is to reuse the formwork, therefore more formwork material is wasted in the production process. In recent decades it has become common practice to use epoxy-coated EPS formwork for one-off concrete products. As discussed earlier in this piece, EPS waste generated by the construction industry is itself a big issue, but it is not the only issue that this material practice presents. When using steel formwork for manufacturing 1000 concrete panels, only a fraction of 1/1000 of the formwork's embodied energy is added to each cast concrete panel. In the same way, when producing ten concrete elements using wood-based formwork, 0.1 of the wood's embodied energy is added to concrete, which is already a significant increase. However, in case of EPS formwork, concrete products inherit the full embodied energy of the used polystyrene, which drives it from 0.7MJ/kg up to 20MJ/kg (although, depending on the design of the formwork, this value can vary). The main danger of this energy waste is that it is not accounted for by the actors of this production, just as still too few account, for example, that 'every round trip ticket on flights from New York to London costs the Arctic three more square metres of ice' (Wallace-Wells, 2019).

Ice itself presents an alternative to this material practice that has been developed in the author's

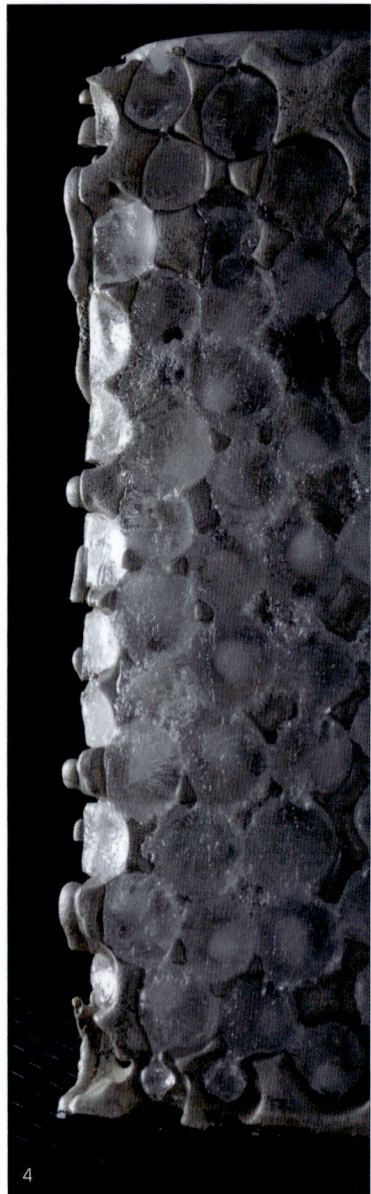

4

5

research into methods of using ice as the formwork material for concrete manufacturing (Sitnikov 2019, Sitnikov et al. 2019). If single-use EPS formwork is substituted with ice formwork, the production of the same concrete element would result in drastically different embodied energy values. Instead of 20MJ/kg of concrete made with EPS, the ice formwork process would add only 10MJ/kg of concrete if, for example, it used an artificial refrigeration system during summer. At the same time ,it will eliminate all solid waste and automate the process, since the ice formwork is self-demoulding and water used in the production of ice can be indefinitely reused.

Mesoscale Trabecular Structured Concrete

The prototypes featured in this chapter showcase spatial patterns that can be imposed on concrete, abandoning any use of petrochemicals in the fabrication process. Breaking away from the 'solid' image of conventional concrete, the technique of using ice as the formwork material enables the production of mesoscale spatial structures in concrete which would be impossible to manufacture with existing formwork materials. While opening doors for new design explorations, such a spatial structure of concrete is, in principle, a new composite material. The concrete used in this cast belongs to the class of high-performance concrete, with compressive strength over 100 MPa and density of 2400kg/m^3. However, when formed into such a structure, its bulk volumetric density drops to 820kg/m^3, maintaining its surface density at very high levels.

The variety of programmable functions for ice formwork is vast, across environmental design, programmable lighting conditions, acoustics, ventilation, insulation and structural-design weight-saving applications. An existing precedent of similar material organisation in architectural design can be found in one of OMA's projects. In 2002, the office was commissioned to design a new Prada retail store in Beverly Hills, LA. The design team crossed disciplinary boundaries and ventured into material programming and physical prototyping, developing an industrial fabrication principle for the foam-like substance: 'a both irregular and regular structure of sponge-like consistency that can be cast in stages from hard to soft and from transparent to opaque' (OMA, 2002). Chemically, the sponge was made of polyurethane cast in silicone moulds to form a random yet carefully-controlled volumetric pattern. The material itself is relatively expensive, so the foam did not enter mass-use. In fact the OMA-FOAM walls of the Prada store are enclosed in glass cases, just like exhibits in a museum, highlighting that this is essentially a full-scale prototype of a building material.

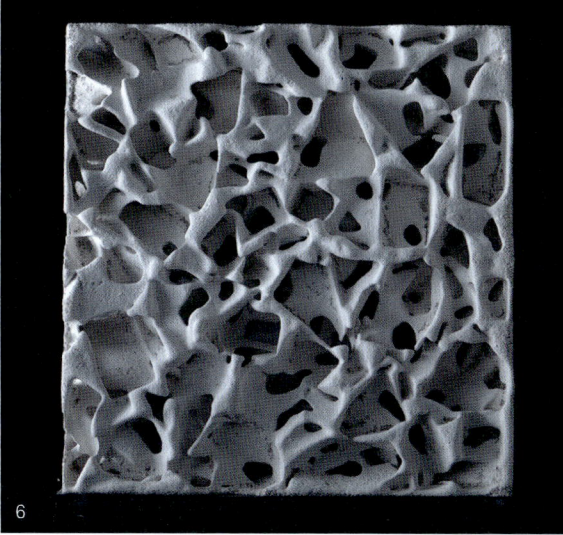 

Yet the material configuration of ice-based concrete casting produces a similar effect at much lower costs. Moreover, borrowing a concept from Sylvia Lavin that refers to a geometrical language translated from one material into another, that is 'wood and wood recollected' (Lavin, 1992), the trabecular concrete structure can be seen as a recollection of OMA-FOAM vision. That is, the phenomenon of OMA-FOAM, once an artificially-synthesised visionary object, today finds a natural way of materialising through a sustainable configuration of concrete and ice. In fact, the method of recollecting synthetic materials in a natural medium could serve as a reliable vehicle on the way toward sustainable living. By taking a step away from the dogmas inherited from an earlier social and economic epochs, and questioning the foundations of material processes, this research investigation has led to potentially rewarding design solutions. It is evident that, at least in architecture, steps like this should be made away from petrochemicals and toward local resources, simplified supply chains and environmentally and socially fair technologies.

4. Demoulding/defrosting of a HPFRC pillar prototype.

5. A prototype of FOAM by OMA at the demoulding stage. Courtesy of OMA, photo: Phil Meech.

6. Light permeability of trabecular concrete structure (irregular crushed ice aggregate sized > 40 mm).

Bibliography

De Frond, H.L., van Sebille, E., Parnis, J.M., Diamond, M.L., Mallos, N., Kingsbury, T. and Rochman, C.M., 2018, 'Estimating the Mass of Chemicals Associated with Ocean Plastic Pollution to Inform Mitigation Efforts' in *Integrated Environmental Assessment & Management*, Vol. 15, No. 4, p.596–606.

Hammond, P.G. and Jones, C., 2011, 'Embodied Carbon: The Inventory of Carbon And Energy (ICE)', *Department of Mechanical Engineering, University of Bath & BSRIA* http://www.circularecology.com/embodied-energy-and-carbon-footprint-database.html#.Xhy-qy2cbzlI (accessed 13 January 2020).

Kovacic, I., Reisinger, J. and Honic, M., 2018, 'Life Cycle Assessment of Embodied and Operational Energy for a Passive Housing Block in Austria' in *Renewable & Sustainable Energy Reviews*, Vol. 82, Part 2, p.1774–1786.

Lavin, S., 1992, *Quatremère de Quincy and the Invention of a Modern Language of Architecture*, Cambridge (MA), MIT Press, p.111.

Li, A., 2019, 'All That Is Solid' (exhibition annotation). https://space-p11.com/all-that-is-solid (accessed 4 October 2019). Minea, V., Chen Y. and Athienitis A.K., 2017, 'Canadian Low-Energy Housing: National Energy Context, and a Case Study of a Demonstration House with Focus on its Ground-Source Heat Pump' in *Science and Technology for the Built Environment*, Vol. 23, No. 4, p.651–668.

OMA, Prada Sponge (project). https://oma.eu/projects/prada-sponge (accessed 4 October 2019).

Wallace-Wells, D., 2019, *The Uninhabitable Earth: Life After Warming*, NYC, Penguin Random House / Tim Duggan Books.

DESIGN INTEGRATION

Research Summary
Bend&Block: A Passive Form-Giving Strategy

Efilena Baseta
Industrial partners: Blumer Lehmann AG, Foster + Partners
Academic Institution: Institute of Architecture, University of Applied Arts Vienna

Adaptable architecture has become a trend in the digital era as a sustainable response to the rapidly changing environment and fluctuating user preferences. Shape-adaptation, in particular, constitutes a key characteristic in 'smart' shading systems, multipurpose spaces and the like. The majority of such systems entail kinetic façades, which change their permeability, or photovoltaic panels, which adapt their orientation. Shape-adaptive systems are, however, limited in scale, despite the sustainable solutions they offer, as they require a lot of energy to perform and are structurally challenging.

This research seeks to identify innovative solutions to develop large-scale, shape-adaptable structures. The research methodology is based on empirical evidence and knowledge, via direct and indirect observations, which lead to the formulation of a hypothesis, verified by existing laws and tested by physical and digital experiments. In this context, the experiment is considered a source of data.

The study of transformable mechanisms of various scales led to the invention of a passive, scalable, bending-active system of controlled deformations. Stiffness change is the key characteristic of the system that was developed, so this structural property was tested through physical experiments with various prototypes. Digital fabrication techniques were employed to create prototypes on a micro-, meso- and macro-scale, while these physical models were used as an analytical tool to verify the functionality of the system. The experimental data that was collected was analysed and compared with the data from digital and physical simulations. The digital models served as an exploratory tool that not only explained the structural performance of the physical models but also generated new ideas for further exploration. Finally, conclusions were drawn regarding the performance of the system, by combining the findings from both the digital and the physical experiments.

Given that this work sought to develop a novel construction system, collaboration with leading-edge industrial partners was crucial. The design and fabrication of a transformable roof structure were carried out, together with Blumer Lehmann AG, using a realistic framework based on academic research. Fabrication was conducted with a Hundegger K3 – an industrial milling machine optimised for the rapid machining of long, straight timber beams. The industrial fabrication of the system indicates its potential to be mass-produced and to find applications in macro-scale (> 10m) structures. A further collaboration, with Foster + Partners, enabled 3D-printed transformable plates in micro-scale (< 1m) to be explored.

The active-bending system of controlled deformations explored in this research is known as Bend&Block. The structural behaviour of this system relies on the joinery details between consecutive layers of multi-layered structural parts. In contrast with traditional, mechanically laminated beams, small transversal gaps are inserted between the layers. These gaps perform the role of a geometrical switch between two states of stiffness. They are opened when the elements are flat, and gradually close during bending. In the flat state, the element is flexible and susceptible to deformations. Once the gaps are closed, the stiffness of the system increases instantaneously and blocks at a specific form. The two-stage stiffness, embedded in the construction details of the system, enables controllable deflections when loads are applied.

To conclude, Bend&Block is a passively-activated form-giving process, with applications in transformable

active-bending gridshells and plates, such as shape-adaptable roofs, bridges and façade elements. The analysis and evaluation of the structural behaviour of various prototypes and demonstrators, at different scales, have proven the functionality of the system. Supplementary physical and digital experiments, however, need to be conducted to scale-up and industrialise the system discussed here.

Acknowledgements

The digital fabrication of the mesoscalar timber prototypes would not have been possible without the support of Angewandte Robotic Lab (Philipp Hornung) and the Wood Technology Laboratory of the University of Applied Arts Vienna, within the framework of the Digital Design and Full-Scale Fabrication seminars 2017 and 2018, led by Andrei Gheorghe.

1. Double-curved gridshell structure which consists of flat fabricated double-layered laths with embedded shear blocks. This system can find application in transformable roofs activated by water/snow loads. Photo: Efilena Baseta

2. A double-layered beam of the Bend&Block system. The graph illustrates the stiffness jump from the flat state to the bend state in relation to the number of layers.

DESIGN INTEGRATION

Research Summary
Adaptive Robotic Carving

Giulio Brugnaro
Industrial Partners: Bjarke Ingels Group, Rippmann Oesterle Knauss GmbH
Academic Institution: The Bartlett School of Architecture, UCL

In recent decades, digital fabrication technologies have become increasingly available, yet manufacturing knowledge is rarely integrated within the established workflows of design practices. Materialisation processes are regarded as the last stage of design-to-manufacturing workflows, where materials are considered passive receivers of a previously-generated ideal form, stored in a digital model. Such linear progression from the design intention to its materialisation necessarily limits the feedback between different stages of the process, forcing designers to engage with only a limited range of standard manufacturing methods and materials, which often leads to wasteful and inefficient solutions.

The complex interaction of non-standard tools, such as chisels and carving gouges, with the heterogeneous properties of timber, cannot be ignored within robotic manufacturing, as it substantially affects the resulting carved geometry. The central challenge addressed in this research was to develop an adaptive simulation model that could bridge the digitally-prescribed design intention and the outcome of the carving process. The research proposed a series of methods to capture, transfer, augment and integrate manufacturing knowledge at an early stage of the design process through the collection of real-world fabrication data, using different sensor devices and machine learning models to achieve an accurate prediction of carving geometries, informed by material behaviours. The acquisition of fabrication data was structured by a series of recording sessions to store, in a library of datasets, the combination of fabrication parameters and respective operation outcomes generated by different material properties (e.g. grain structure, density, direction), wood species and carving tools. The collected datasets can be used to train multiple Artificial Neural Networks (ANNs),

1. Robotic carving process: fabrication stage.

2. Robotically-carved texture, detail.

whose main learning objective is to predict the carved geometry generated by a user-defined robotic toolpath and a series of fabrication parameters.

Collaborations with two industry partners – ROK Architects, Zurich, and BIG, Copenhagen – provided the opportunity to apply the methods we had devised into established workflows and develop a catalogue of design explorations for a wide range of applications, from furniture to building components of larger assemblies. The curation of the training process, by a team of designers, represents the keystone of the design workflow, as the selection of relevant material affordances and fabrication parameters directly determines the range of solutions later available in the digital design exploration. In this way, the trained system represents a package of knowledge that can be integrated within an interface to digitally evaluate multiple, otherwise unavailable, design solutions informed by tools and material properties, before moving to the production stage. Once robotically fabricated, the selected carved geometries are compared in a deviation analysis with the respective simulations, to assess the predictive abilities of the system. The results successfully demonstrate the ability of the trained networks to accurately model the outcome of carving operations, defined in the digital design environment by a series of fabrication parameters.

The impact of the research lies in devising a series of robotic training methods that allow for flexible extension of the range of subtractive manufacturing processes available to designers. Novel design opportunities are explored that support decision-making procedures, based on an accurate simulation of non-standard operations on timber. The integration of manufacturing knowledge at the early design stage allows for a custom design-to-manufacture workflow to be established, informed by continual feedback, that encourages a fruitful dialogue between designers and manufacturers.

DESIGN INTEGRATION

Research Summary
How to Effectively Collaborate at Scale in a Connected Digital Environment

Paul Poinet
Industrial Partners: Buro Happold, Design-To-Production GmbH
Academic Institution: Centre for Information Technology and Architecture (CITA),
The Royal Danish Academy of Fine Arts, Schools of Architecture, Design and Conservation

Managing the design-to-fabrication process of large-scale and complex architectural projects is a significant challenge, despite continual improvements in digital literacy and cost reductions in computational design practices (Deutsch, 2017). It is not enough to be able to model complexity, which must also be managed, shared and co-created in more intuitive ways than it is today within the Architecture, Engineering, Construction (AEC) industry (Scheurer, 2012). The current segregation of design processes and the lack of interoperability result in laborious manual interventions, which often become a daily routine (Van der Heijden, 2015). These drawbacks can be heightened in post-tender phases of large-scale and geometrically complex architectural projects, which bring together multiple trades and companies that need to communicate intricate datasets with each other, from the start of the project until its completion.

The AEC industry, as a whole, has seen a rapid rise in the application of code and scripts on projects – with an increasing number benefiting from, and now relying on, new computational tools and approaches, such as the use of Visual Programming (VP) through Grasshopper for Rhino or Dynamo for Revit. This mass adoption of increasingly powerful and complex computational tools is, however, not without its challenges on projects involving numerous design partners, stakeholders and teams, which, in the most challenging cases, consist of hundreds of individuals. Popular computational tools have natural limitations when scaled across such widespread and diverse teams. The system architecture of much of our industry-standard software and tools, particularly the widely adopted VP environments, do not natively or explicitly encourage collaborative design behaviours, such as co-creation, that are intrinsic to a successful design process. In some cases, the chosen tools, although readily deployed, reinforce bad design practice, encourage unstructured, unsustainable script-creation, or do not support graduated transition from simple computational concepts through to the more advanced solutions in a code environment. It is also difficult to reconcile differences within teams, between VP environments and a more formalised and generalised code environment, and successfully enable advanced computer programmers or software engineers to collaborate meaningfully with less experienced practitioners, in a standard VP environment.

Therefore, to address these challenges, a transparent, extensible and modular design and collaboration system was developed, on both the conceptual and the technical level. The first stage of this project presented the management of non-linear digital workflows and intricate datasets at late stages in the design process of complex architectural projects. The second stage proposed alternative concepts, tools and methodologies to clarify and improve the existing processes used in the AEC industry. These are illustrated in the third stage by means of different empirical experiments grounded in the existing everyday practices of BuroHappold Engineering and Design-to-Production – both industry partners of the Innochain research network and supervisors of the author.

The experiments make use of a diverse range of interdisciplinary concepts borrowed from computer science and data visualisation: schema-based workflows, transaction protocols and inter-scalar search interfaces used to ease and enable the assembly, visualisation and querying of complex datasets at late stages in the design process. These experiments rely on two open source frameworks: the Buildings and Habitats

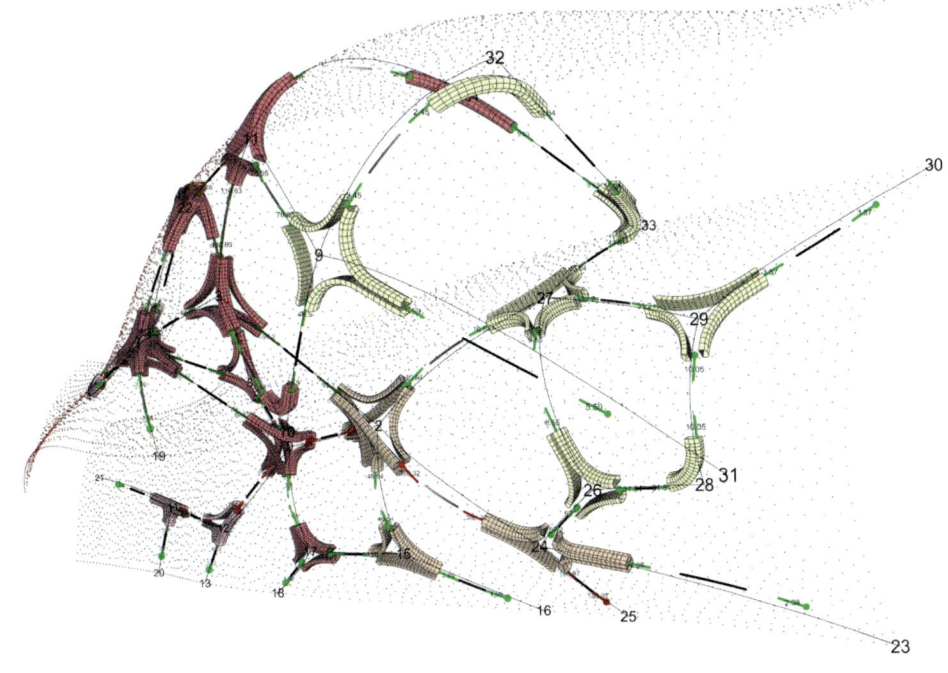

1

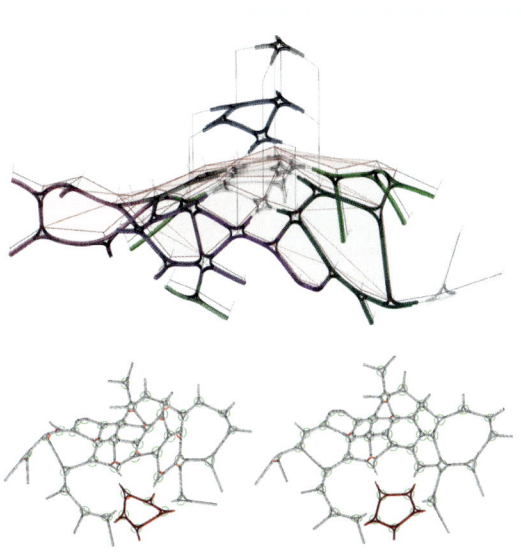

2

object Model (BHoM) – a computational design, interoperability and coding framework for the AEC industry – and Speckle – an extensible design and AEC data-communication protocol and platform, initiated by Dimitrie Stefanescu within the Innochain research network (see also p.62–67 and p.80–81 of this volume). The research concludes by reflecting on the experiments developed so far, extrapolating their potentials and speculating on a broader theoretical framework that enables co-creation and mass participation.

Bibliography

Deutsch, R., 2017, *Convergence: The Redesign of Design (AD Smart)*, Hoboken, NJ, John Wiley & Sons Ltd.

Scheurer, F., 2012, 'From Thinking to Modeling to Building' in Marble, S. (ed.), *Digital Workflows in Architecture: Design-Assembly-Industry*, p.110–131, Basel, Birkhäuser.

Speckle: Open Digital Infrastructure for Designing, Making and Operating the Built Environment, 2018. https://speckle.works (accessed 7 February 2020).

The Buildings and Habitats Object Model: Sustainable Code at Scale, 2018. https://bhom.xyz (accessed 7 February 2020).

van der Heijden, R., Levelle E. and Riese, M., 2015, 'Parametric Building Information Generation for Design and Construction' in *Computational Ecologies: Design in the Anthropocene: Proceedings of the 35th Annual Conference of the Association for Computer Aided Design in Architecture (ACADIA)*, Cincinnati, Ohio. http://papers.cumincad.org/data/works/att/acadia15_417.pdf (accessed 7 February 2020).

1. Topological mapping: spatial branching.

2. Topological mapping: projection-based modelling.

DESIGN INTEGRATION

Research Summary
Ice Formwork: Challenging the Sustainable Production of Non-Regular Geometry in Concrete

Vasily Sitnikov
Industrial Partners: Buro Happold
Academic Institution: Royal Institute of Technology (KTH), Stockholm

The goal of the research is to provide a vision of innovative, environmental and efficient developments for both the design and manufacturing processes of precast cement-based components. A survey of conventional construction technologies, industrial standards, and latest developments in digital fabrication and the material science of concrete provided a list of initial criteria for innovative concrete design.

First, the survey showed that precast concrete production is preferable in comparison to in-situ-cast concrete production. The combination of controlled and equipped environment, skilled labour and the stable logistics associated with precast concrete all contribute to a better use of time, material and energy. Second, the survey identified the potential of recently-developed high-performance concrete (HPC) in reducing the weight of constructions, while providing the same level of structural capacity. Lighter constructions deliver savings on transportation and raw materials (Sitnikov, 2017). Third, the use of non-ferrous fibre reinforcement presented significant benefits over traditional steel rebar. Notably, it is more durable, since it is not subject to corrosion and requires less manual labour.

Design Features

In collaboration with engineers from BuroHappold Engineering in London, the internal structural principle of a fibre-reinforced precast HPC element was researched. If applied as a rain screen on a façade, such an element should span at least 3m to be viable for uses spanning floor-to-floor heights. While aiming at a significantly reduced mass, the target thickness was identified as 3–4cm. Considering the wind load and possible impact, and the absence of rebar reinforcement, the element would require an integrated ribbed grid at the back to maintain its structural continuity. Due to its slender form, such a design would have a very narrow dimensional tolerance and, if cast, would require a two-component formwork: a mould and a counter-mould.

Materials and Process

To maximise the formal potential of this design, the production method needed to be able to cope with a maximum amount of geometric variability and element-uniqueness. One conventional fabrication method, suitable for production of such a design, uses CNC-milled moulds of a solid and low-density material, such as Expanded Polystyrene (EPS). The efficiency and versatility of this approach have been proven in practice, including Neuer Zollhoff by Frank Gehry (Kolarevic, 2003) and Fjordenhus by Studio Other Spaces (Søndergaard and Feringa, 2017). Despite its merits, however, the method results in large volumes of non-recyclable waste and, therefore, requires improvement. With the aim of achieving a more efficient fabrication process, ordinary ice was chosen to replace the EPS.

In the first phase of development, a frost-resistant design of high-performance concrete was created. In collaboration with two research institutes, a concrete blend compatible with Ice Formwork (HPC^{fr}) was designed (Sitnikov and Sitnikov, 2018). In the second phase, numerous experiments were performed to test the CNC-machining of ice, the rheological properties of HPC^{fr}, autonomous demoulding through natural ice-thawing and production of low-defect ice blocks (see Bibliography for video of the process).

The prototypes illustrate the quality of the concrete casts and lend themselves to complex geometry independent from manual labour. Since water can be thawed and frozen an infinite number of times, this production method can function in the form of a closed loop, relying only on electricity supply. Moreover, preliminary assessments have shown that the energy consumption of ice production is outweighed by the overall energy savings (Sitnikov, 2019).

Bibliography

Kolarevic B., 2003, *Architecture in the Digital Age: Design and Manufacturing*, Hoboken, NJ, Taylor & Francis Limited.

KTH School of Architecture, 2018, 'Ice Formwork: An Ice-Based CAM Concept for Precast Concrete'. https://vimeo.com/299240718 (accessed 8 December 2019).

Sitnikov, V., 2017, 'Ice Formwork for Ultra-High Performance Concrete: Simulation of Ice Melting Deformations' in de Rycke, K., Gengnagel, C., Baverel, O., Burry, J., Mueller, C., Nguyen, M.M., Rahm, P. and Thomsen, M.R. (eds.), Humanizing Digital Reality: Design Modelling Symposium, Paris Singapore, Springer, p.395–406.

Sitnikov, V. and Sitnikov, I., 2018, 'Kinetics of UHPC Strength Gain at Subfreezing Temperatures: SP-326 Durability and Sustainability of Concrete Structures', in American Concrete Institute, ACI Special Publication. http://urn.kb.se/resolve?urn=urn:nbn:se:kth:diva-247458 (accessed 8 February 2020).

Sondergaard, A. and Feringa, J., 2017, 'Scaling Architectural Robotics: Construction of the Kirk Kapital Headquarters' in Menges, A., Sheil, B., Glynn, R. and Skavara, M. (eds.), *Fabricate 2017*, London, UCL Press, p.264–271.

1. The back of a large-scale prototype of a lightweight High-Performance Fibre-Reinforced Concrete (HPFRC) rain-screen façade, formed with an ice counter-mould.

2. CNC milling the ice mould using a 6mm ball endmill.

DESIGN INTEGRATION

Research Summary
Virtual Prototyping Tools for a Winding-Based Composite Fabrication Technique

James Solly
Industrial Partners: FIBR GmbH, Foster + Partners, S-FORM GmbH
Academic Institution: Institute for Building Structures and Structural Design (ITKE), University of Stuttgart

As people build higher to provide greater urban density, move to increasingly remote building sites, and endeavour to reduce the material consumption associated with construction, additive-manufacturing processes for high-strength/low-weight materials can offer significant advantages. In this scenario, while extrusion-based 3D-printing methods are limited in deposition rate, as material solidification is required during fabrication, Coreless Filament Winding (CFW) provides a high-speed alternative. In this approach, uncured fibre bundles are sequentially wrapped around reusable, reconfigurable frames, which are then cured. Invented at the University of Stuttgart (Schwinn, et al., 2013), the method is under continual development. In addition, through several built projects, a user-friendly set of winding-simulation tools to assist the design process and enable wider adoption of the method have been developed.

Research Methods

As the project was embedded within a wider ongoing research area at the University of Stuttgart, the research methods employed were informed by a three-year plan involving the development of two large-scale installations fabricated by means of the CFW method. The first major phase of work comprised of a state-of-the-art review, in which research question-formation was delivered through a research-by-fabrication process. Physically realising a project alongside experienced researchers in the field provided access to significant background knowledge on the fabrication system. Furthermore, involvement in the design development and engineering of these projects gave direct experience of specific CFW design problems and the opportunity to consider which ones could be solved using virtual prototyping tools.

1. Fibre façade prototype at the Innochain Exhibition, Copenhagen. Photo: Anders Ingvartsen.

2. Fibre beam prototype created for the Innochain Barcelona Colloquium. Photo: ITKE/FibR.

The development of the digital tools and workflows for CFW virtual prototyping was performed with an experiment-based methodology, where promising ideas that emerged from the initial study phase were tested – first digitally, under simplified conditions, and then physically, during collaborative large-scale projects and research-specific smaller prototypes. This work stage initially focused on using pre-existing, open-access tools and libraries, selecting those with potential relevance to the winding method, then testing them as described. Early on in the work, it became clear that some custom tools would be needed, leading to a series of studies into the fundamentals of physics simulation for thin, fibre-like elements.

Research Partners

The research benefited greatly from both academic and industry partners. Within the University of Stuttgart, the collaborative work on coreless winding at The Institute of Building Structures and Structural Design (ITKE) was performed in partnership with colleagues from the Institute for Computational Design and Construction, led by Professor Achim Menges. The Innochain network brought in three industry partners over the course of the project: Foster + Partners provided the viewpoint of a possible end-user; S-Form provided initial guidance on materials and typical composite-processing techniques; and FibR provided an industrial partner for the fabrication of coreless-wound parts (in collaboration with which the two Innochain prototypes were produced).

Research Outcomes and Applications

Two large-scale filament-wound installations were produced in collaboration with other research projects, alongside two research-specific prototypes. The Elytra Filament Pavilion, a 200m^2 composite canopy, was installed in the V&A Museum, London, in May 2016 (Koslowski et al., 2017); and the ICD/ITKE Research Pavilion 2016/2017 (Solly et al., 2019), a 12m-long composite cantilever, was installed on the University of Stuttgart campus in April 2017.

The Fibre Beam Prototype, a 3.6m-long composite beam, was created to test layout optimisation strategies for a fibre-wound beam, and was exhibited at the Innochain Barcelona Colloquium in 2018. The Fibre Façade Prototype, an installation consisting of eight unique glazing-support frames, wound on a single reconfigurable form, tested several digital design tools created during the research, and was exhibited at the final Innochain exhibition in August 2018.

Through the creation of these physical pieces, a prototype fibre-winding toolchain was developed to support the steps from concept to fabrication. Most of the investigations were made into fibre-winding physics simulation, and this work is being continued to produce a digital design tool for future projects.

2

Bibliography

Schwinn, T., La Magna, R., Reichert, S., Waimer, F., Knippers, J., Menges, A., 2013, 'Prototyping Biomimetic Structure for Architecture' in Stacey, M. (ed.), *Prototyping Architecture: The Conference Papers*, London, Building Centre Trust, p.224–244.

Solly, J., Früh, N., Saffarian, S., Aldinger, L., Margariti, G., Knippers, J., 2019, 'Structural Design of a Lattice Composite Cantilever' in Structures, Vol. 18, Amsterdam, Elsevier, p.1–13.

Koslowski, V., Solly, J. and Knippers, J., 2017, 'Structural Design Methods of Component-Based Lattice Composites for the Elytra Pavilion' in Bögle, A. and Grohmann, M. (eds.), Proceedings of the IASS Annual Symposium 2017, *Interfaces: architecture. engineering.science*, Hamburg, HafenCity University Hamburg, IASS.

DESIGN INTEGRATION

Further Perspectives
Data in Design Practice

Sean Hanna
The Bartlett School of Architecture

For many of the projects discussed in this volume, the most fundamental unit of their design has begun to shift from material or representation to data, and so our emphasis on information and transaction has become increasingly relevant. Architects need data, as our design problems reach unprecedented scales and complexities. As more varieties of data are made available, in exponentially increasing quantities, new and improved methods must be sought to visualise, understand and make adequate use of it. The methods of data processing appropriate to other domains may not be appropriate to architecture, and concern is shifting from the practical and technical problems of how data is processed to the more complex issue of how it fits in with design practice.

Optimisation is a traditional and well-understood use of data, in which a given design is incrementally improved toward a specific goal, and an explicit, quantifiable definition of a problem is essential. It is often given by a parametric model, which expresses the design outcome as a function of specific numerical inputs, and many of the dominant trends in architectural computation of the past decade have been those of parametric design. Design is not all optimisation, however, and much of the discussion surrounding the work at the end of the Innochain project and associated conference has focused on the role data plays in the less clearly-defined aspects of design practice: early-stage design exploration, concept design and definition of the brief.

Part of this shift toward data is occurring due to technological advances, particularly faster computation speed and the algorithmic improvement that accompanies it. Computational fluid dynamics (CFD) methods, such as those developed by Angelos Chronis (figs 1 & 2; see also p.76–77 of this volume), yield faster analyses of design proposals that give the user immediate, real-time feedback on proposed changes. Where analysis was once a distinct activity from the act of design, it is now an integral part. The familiar colour-indexed visualisations that represent CFD, structural simulations and similar analyses have long been used by designers to examine relevant data, but the move to make them a part of early-stage sketch modelling and interaction allows one to see phenomena that are otherwise invisible. The novelty of this expanded sense of vision, coupled with the capacity for machine learning and related technologies in processing the output produced by these methods, underscores the need for a more mature understanding of the designer's use of such data.

Part of the challenge identified can be understood in light of the apparent opposition between intuition and explicit quantitative methods. The former is often how designers work, but is a black box in terms of our lack of understanding and our inability to communicate intuitive thoughts. The latter, in which most data resides, provides the basis for legal requirements, responsibility and describing the project to others. These domains may divide designers collaborating on a project. One obstacle to overcome in design practice is therefore a 'detachment between the higher-level view of the architect [and] the lower-level view of the expert [in a specific domain]', Chronis notes.

Part of the challenge is due to the type of data itself, and its limitations. Traditional means of data-processing assume that we are able to understand what the data represents – the physics behind structural calculations or the volume of traffic – even if there is a large amount of data available. In the age of big data, where both the amount and complexity may be overwhelming and must be mined with pattern recognition and machine learning

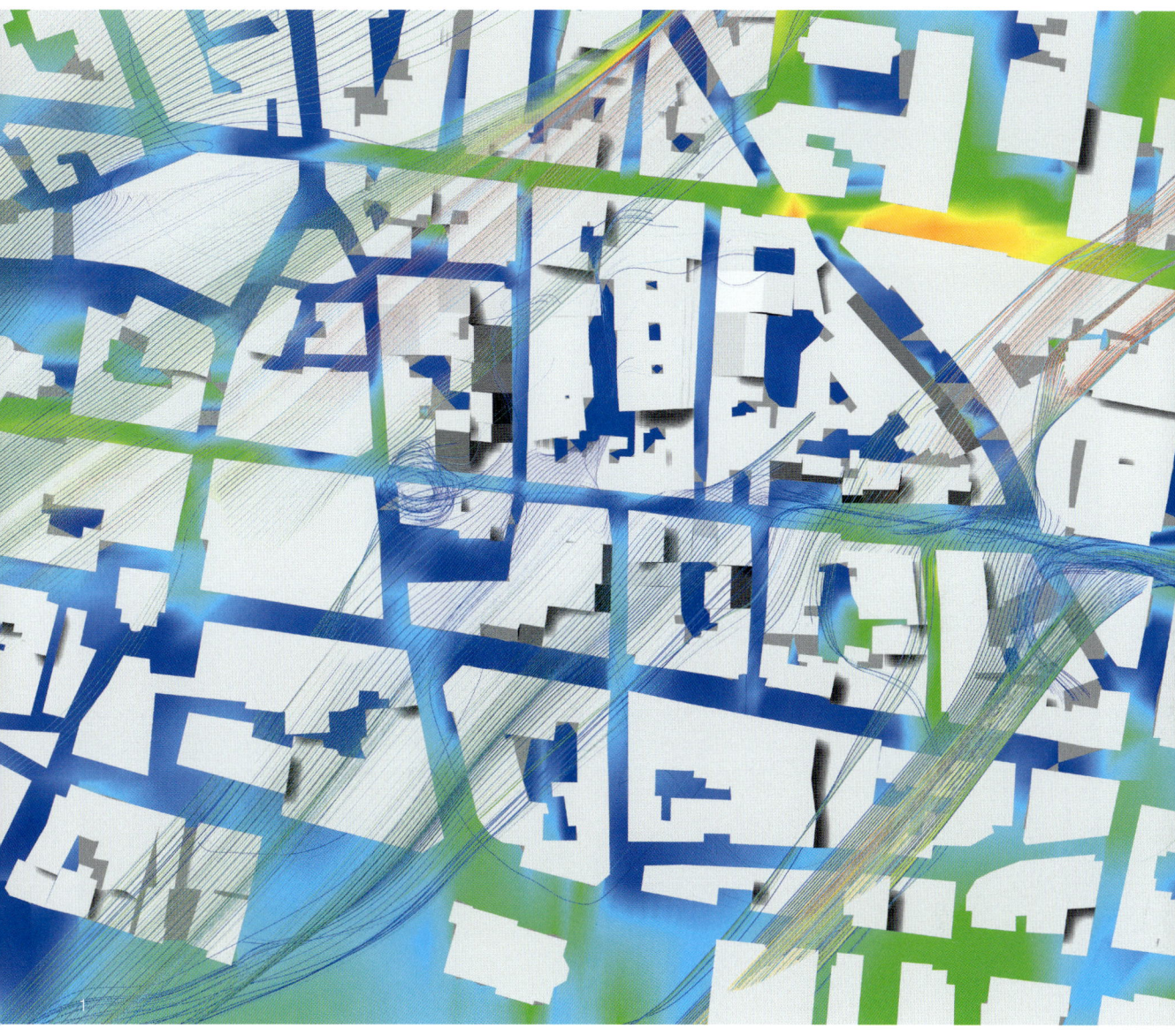

1. Real-time, urban CFD analysis at street level. Angelos Chronis.

algorithms to be useful, the designer may not be able to understand the meaning of the numbers, even in principle. This raises a new kind of question: 'Do we need to?'. 'Does the neural network need to?'

Zeynep Aksöz's research on the Innochain project (summarised in p.50–55 and p.74 of this volume), which incorporated machine learning into structural optimisation and multi-criteria searches, illustrates that there are at least two different strategies for human–computer interaction. The first, in the context of a structural building façade project, uses the designer's own preferences as the data, collected through a process in which the user selects preferred solutions from generated examples based on their own intuition or aesthetic judgement. A support vector machine learns these preferences, and can then stand in for

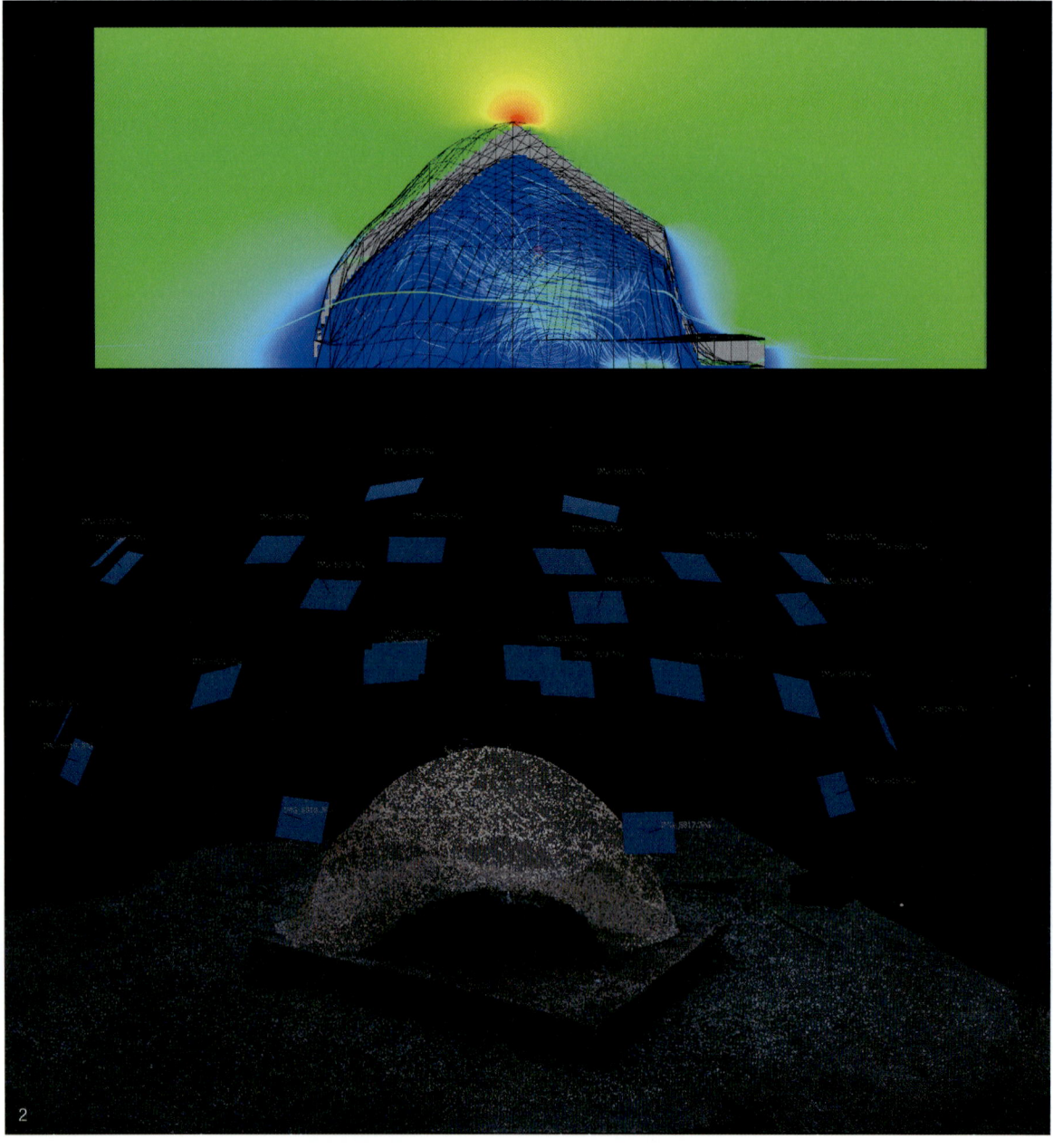

2. Simulation and analysis in the CAD model can be compared with as-built scans of the final construction. Angelos Chronis.

3. CityFunction software, Henrik Malm and Petra Jenning, FOJAB Architects.

3

the designer in further optimisation. A contrasting approach has the designer maintain global control over the project, while the computer makes only local corrections to improve the structural geometry. Both approaches involve collaborative efforts between user and computer, and their use in practice suggests that, at least for early-stage exploration of design options, the architect's overall sense of the project at the highest level is what is valued most. The architect wants a clear picture that can be provided by the machine, and only occasionally to drill down into the details of the data.

In some projects, the obstacle is the limit of the designer's high-level intuition, and data is used to overcome this. Urban planning is a good example of large-scale complexity: the paradigmatic 'wicked problem'. Henrik Malm and Petra Jenning, of FOJAB architects, have presented results from an urban visualisation tool that directly displays the geographical distribution of immediate data, such as population density; time-sensitive sensor data, such as pollution and traffic; and second-order calculations, such as distance to parks and commuting time. Because these sources are numerous, the CityFiction tool presents a combination of raw data in the form of a user-defined fitness function (fig.3). While this has obvious connotations for optimisation, the concerns that have been raised in projects of this scale have less to do with finding an optimum solution than with our level of certainty that the data are stable over long timespans. By visually presenting patterns otherwise spread too far across space or time to be seen, the expert pattern-recognition skills of the designer's brain may effectively be brought to bear. The strategies proposed on the back of such a tool might be of the kind equipped to deal with the city of 2050, its real value being the ability to define different fitness functions, to test multiple scenarios for sensitivity to change and robustness, and so to allow us to comprehend a range of possibilities.

If there is a tentative consensus on the use of data in design practice across the range of projects and methods currently in use, it is that the levels of a project must be handled individually; there is no clear route to optimise a project to a given dataset. In most cases, it is acknowledged that the designer is best positioned to deal with the global direction of a project, while the computer is well suited to handling the details, particularly where these are clearly delimited. The result is that any given project will use a strategy incorporating multiple layers of data, each informing the design via different methods and, ultimately, combining the measurable with the non-measurable.

Novel Strategies for Materialisation

4.1 NOVEL STRATEGIES FOR MATERIALISATION

Rewired Engineering: The Impact of Customisation and Interoperability on Design

Edoardo Tibuzzi
AKT II, London

Once upon a time the conquering of physical or territorial realm was the new frontier. But to conquer sordid, ugly commercialism in this machine age ... this conquest is now 'the new Frontier'. Only by growing a healthy aesthetic in the Soul of our polyglot people can we win this victory.
Frank Lloyd Wright, *When Democracy Builds*

Introduction

The aim of this text is to look under the hood of a practice that has, in one way or another, pioneered the digital transformation of the architecture, engineering and construction (AEC) industry, and to explore how collaboration and use of advanced modelling and analysis tools have changed the design outputs. It also explores the important role of research in practice and academia.

The digital revolution has had a huge impact on most aspects of our society, and, in recent years, it has also begun to invest in the AEC industry. This revolution has brought two main outcomes: a digitalisation of the various aspects of design, and analysing, comparing and finding added value in digitally-collected data. Some 20-odd years ago, in the early days of AKT II structural engineers (still called Adams Kara Taylor back then), the digital revolution was just beginning. Our vision, as structural engineers, was clear: to establish a group able to pioneer change and investigate the potential impact of the artificial, digital 'machine'; and so, *p.art* was created. The singular remit of this cross-disciplinary group – which consisted of engineers, architects, computer scientists and parametric designers – was, and still is, to explore and capitalise on new opportunities via technological and software development, through in-depth research into new

1. Bloomberg Ramp structure during construction, October 2015. Photo: Valerie Bennet, © AKTII.

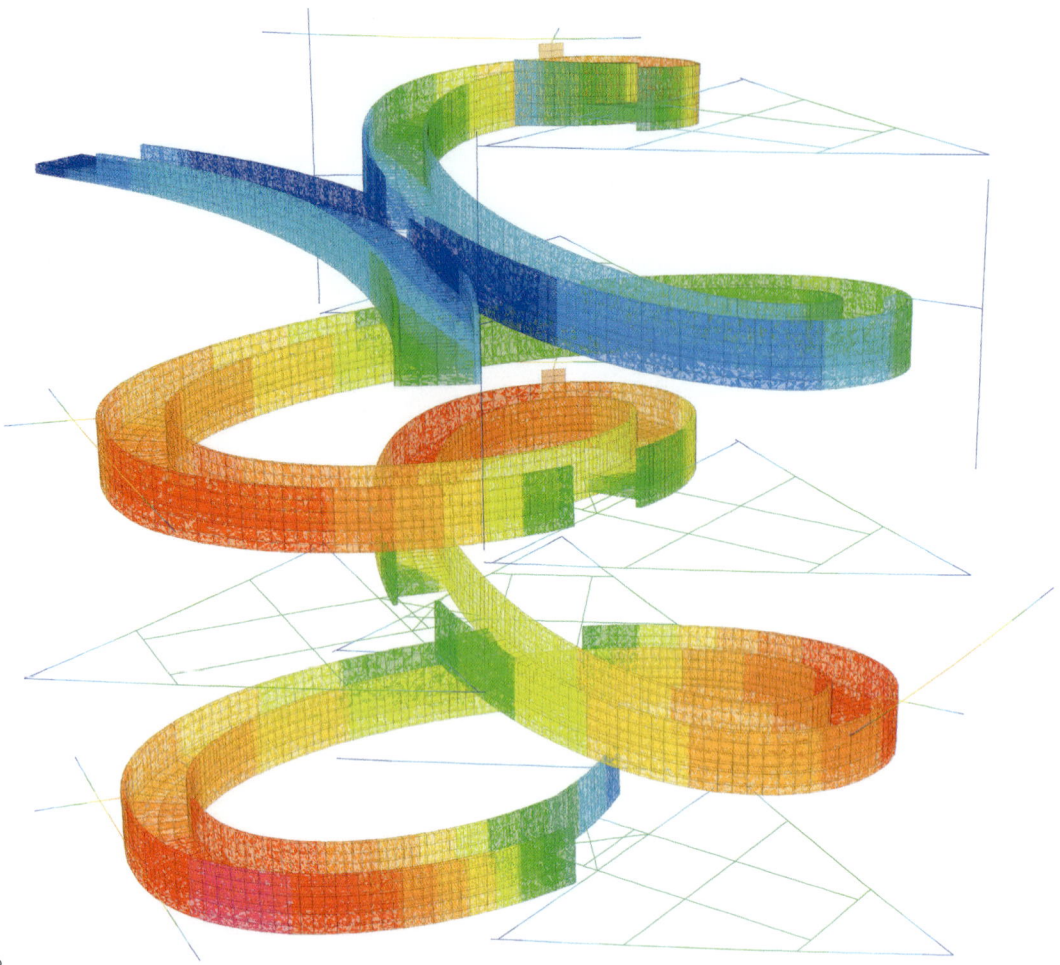

2

materials, construction and fabrication techniques, as well as new digital tool sets and software interfaces that improve coordination between the different partners in design and construction teams.

The technology that we were using at the beginning generated, implicitly or explicitly, all sorts of forms through democratic parameters. The first generation of digital design was born and 'parametric design' was the name used to describe it. Our focus then intensified, looking into how to join up the structural engineer's problem of 'taming gravity' with digital fabrication. This resulted in interoperability problems being addressed in the relationships between engineering and architecture, academia and design, and fabricator and constructor. The problem of enabling interoperability through a software interface is still with us today, the only difference being the brute force of computation that has given us even more ways to break it down. Interestingly, the problem was not to solve collaboration (real or imaginary) with software, but to enable it with caution, the danger being that collaborative design could produce banal and trivial outputs.

2. Finite Element Analysis Model. © AKTII.

Bloomberg Headquarters, London

We had the privilege to collaborate with Foster + Partners on the design of Bloomberg's new European headquarters. Set within the heart of the main office building, there is a unique bronze-clad stepped ramp, a continuous 3D loop that is as much a piece of art as it is a key aspect of movement through the building. All arrivals are taken by lift to the 'Pantry' – a double-height entrance space on the sixth floor – from which they use the ramp to filter down to their floors. The ramp has been designed and proportioned as a place of meeting and connection, allowing people to have impromptu conversations with colleagues, while not impeding the flow of people. On plan, the ramp is hypotrochoidal, meaning that it follows a line traced by a fixed point within a circle, as the circle rotates within another circle. Rising from level two to eight, the ramp is 1.8m wide between balustrades and spans up to 30m between floors; the elliptical oculus within the surrounding floor plates rotates 120° on each floor to follow the curve of the ramp and form connections. Constructed as a structural monocoque, where the chassis is integral with the body, rather like a ship's hull or a bridge, the ramp was prefabricated in large interlocking segments, staggered and bolted as a kit of parts, but ultimately forming a smooth continuous structure. The floor at level seven is cut out to create the double-height Pantry volume which sits between levels six and eight; this means that the ramp is not connected to the floor plate here as it is on other levels. Access was resolved by inserting a sloping link-bridge that connects to the ramp and floor edge. Both ramp and link-bridge are structurally coupled and act as twin structures supported by two of the main central columns that terminate at this interface. The structural performance of the ramp was assessed for a series of combinations of design parameters.

At the design stage, Foster + Partners and AKT II shared a unique parametric Grasshopper model. The whole design was controlled through a singular algorithm, interfacing with the different design and simulation packages, which allowed for an extensive assessment of the various forces driving the geometry and material. As we were pushing steel to its structural limit, we needed a more in-depth analysis of the impact of human-induced vibration. The analysis results were launched and retrieved from the same algorithm, allowing us to inform the architectural design and shape the ramp to improve problematic areas or to save material, where possible.

Design is largely collaborative, and without a clear definition of targets, it can result in homogenisation of an output where all disciplines are equal. From parametric design of the early stages to post-digital and beyond, we are asking ourselves: 'Where are we now?' and 'What do we do with this power enabled by computation?'

Systems found in the natural world can perform computations up to a maximal ('universal') level of computational power, and most systems do, in fact, attain this maximal level of computational power. Consequently, most systems are computationally equivalent. For example, the workings of the human brain or the evolution of weather systems can, in principle, compute the same things as a computer. Computation is therefore simply a question of translating inputs and outputs from one system to another (Wolfram, 2002).

Essentially, whenever one sees behaviour that is not obviously simple, in any system, it can be thought of as corresponding to a computation of equivalent sophistication.

Swedish philosopher Nick Bostrom argues that at least one of the following propositions is true: 1. The human species is very likely to become extinct before reaching a 'posthuman' stage; 2. Any posthuman civilisation is extremely unlikely to run a significant number of simulations of its evolutionary history (or variations thereof); 3. We are almost certainly living in a computer simulation. It follows that the belief that there is a significant chance that we shall one day become posthumans who run ancestor-simulations is false, unless we are currently living in a simulation (Bostrom, 2003).

The two theories from Wolfram and Bostrom are reaffirming the role and power of computational design, in both the real and the simulated realms, but it is important to remember that a conflict remains between aesthetic, structural and technological efficiency and value. So, for a practice like us, it is imperative to acknowledge that technology is driving us to a position that is binary. Without soul, tools only give a sterile answer, and if the question is wrong, so too will be the answer.

The thought that technology as truth absolves moral responsibility is also dangerous. It removes the need for agency and accountability, and, most of all, puts creativity in danger of extinction. Tools are not innocent, and pervasive analytics can create dysfunctionality, as people act on such insights because they are beautifully presented, but they can be entirely misinterpreted or, even worse, maliciously biased. With this in mind, we have developed an integrated interface to use in the design stages, to bridge digital tools, allowing our designers to take control and provide the added value needed. This interface was used in the following project.

The Serpentine Pavilion, London

For The Serpentine Galleries' annual event in London's Kensington Gardens, we provided structural engineering services for the design of the superstructure of BIG's 2016 Pavilion, envisioned as an 'unzipped' wall of glass-fibre-reinforced plastic (GFRP). The superstructure

3

comprised two surfaces, which began as separate curved sinusoidal walls at ground level and rose to merge as a straight, horizontal line at an elevation of 14m above ground. The surfaces were formed from a series of boxes, each measuring 500mm x 400mm. The length of each box was such that they overlapped their neighbours sufficiently to create an enclosure, while there was also adequate connection length between adjacent boxes for structural purposes. The transition from two separate halves to a single surface at the apex was achieved by arranging the boxes in alternate chequerboard patterns on either side of the wall, allowing them to merge seamlessly. Fiberline in Denmark manufactured the GFRP boxes using a new improved mixture to enhance the material's rigidity; these were then joined by aluminium connectors and bolts. The bending, compression and shear forces generated by the arching action of the pavilion were transferred between the bricks by push–pull forces in the connecting bolts, along the overlapping edges of the boxes. In the longitudinal direction, horizontal wind loads were transferred through a combination of shell and Vierendeel action. The boxes were stepped such that people could sit or climb on the lowest rows, which was considered in the loading.

To realise such a large and structurally complex building, it was necessary to go from concept design to fully coordinated production information in less than three months. In addition to these time pressures, budgetary constraints required material quantities to be reduced, as far as possible, without compromising the ambition of the design. For these reasons, the BIG and AKT II design teams chose to generate the entire geometry through parametric-design processes. This enabled the rapid evaluation of different options for the underlying grid early on, testing the relative merits of rectangular and square grids at different scales, as well as more complicated pin-wheel and reciprocal arrangements for the boxes. For each option, the design team could refine an array of parameters – from micro values such as the individual box height and width, to macro dimensions such as the minimum 'offset' between adjacent boxes, overall wall heights, lengths and sine wave proportions – and interrogate the resulting forms to extract quantities for material volume, number of fixings and so on. At every iteration, these metrics were passed along to fabricators to establish cost and timeframes for production and assembly.

In conclusion, our industry is preparing to face an important shift in the controlling forces of design, where data will play a fundamental role in rewriting codified approaches and performance-based choices. New roles and skills will, therefore, become fundamental in the design process to maintain a balance between optimal and functional, optimised and harmonic, robotic and human.

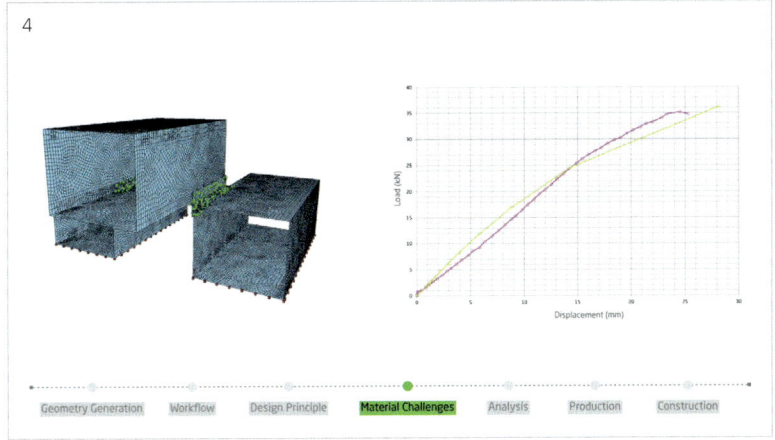

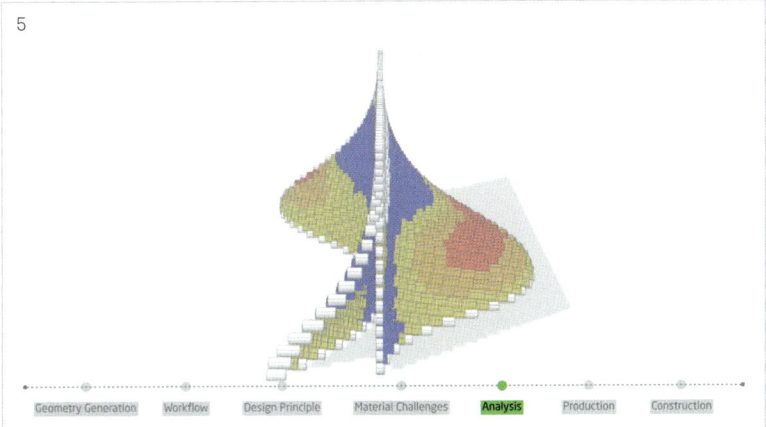

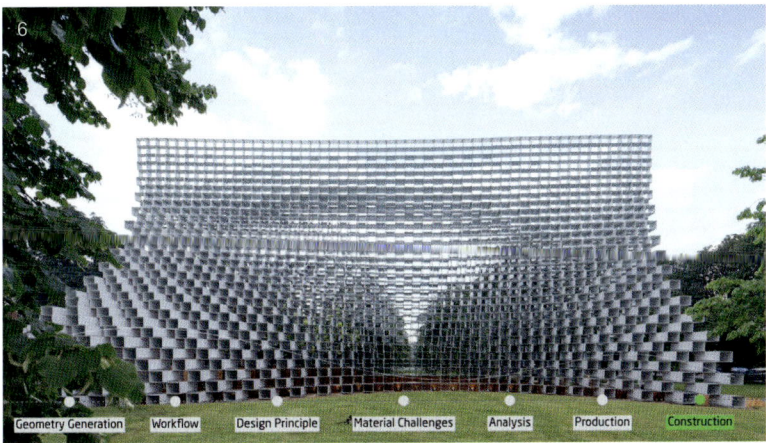

3. Drone photo of completed BIG Serpentine Pavilion. © AKTII.

4. Load/deformation comparison between FEA Model and Physical test. © AKTII.

5. Visualisation of forces acting on box components. © AKTII.

6. Front photo of completed pavillion. © AKTII.

Bibliography

Bostrom, N., 2003, 'Are You Living in a Computer Simulation?' in *Philosophical Quarterly*, Vol. 53, No. 211, p.243–255.

Kara, H. and Bosia, D., 2016, *Design Engineering Refocused*, London, John Wiley & Sons, p.214–233.

Kingman, J., Dudley, J. and Baptista, R., 2017, 'The 2016 Serpentine Pavilion. A case Study in Large-Scale GFRP Structural Design and Assembly' in Menges, A., Sheil, B., Glynn, R. and Skavara, M. (eds.), *Fabricate: Rethinking Design and Construction*, London, UCL Press, p.138–145.

Rabagliati, J., Janssen, J., Tibuzzi, E., De Paoli, F., Casson, P. and Maddock, R., 2018, 'Bloomberg Ramp: Collaborative Workflows, Sharing Data and Design Logics' in De Rycke, K., Gengnagel, C., Baverel, O., Burry, J., Mueller, C., Man Nguyen, M., Rahm, P. and Thomsen, M.R. (eds.), *Humanizing Digital Reality, Design Modelling Symposium Paris 2017*, Singapore, Springer Nature Singapore Pte Ltd., p.153–166.

Wolfram, S., 2002, *A New Kind of Science*, Cambridge, UK, Wolfram Media.

Wright, FL., 1945, *When Democracy Builds*, Chicago, University of Chicago Press.

4.2 NOVEL STRATEGIES FOR MATERIALISATION

Drone Spraying on Light Formwork for Mud Shells

Stephanie Chaltiel
MuDD Architects
Maite Bravo
BCIT Vancouver
Diederik Veenendaal
Summum Engineering
Gavin Sayers
AKT II

Introduction

Recent developments in robotic fabrication have led to the rapid emergence of novel methods of additive manufacturing, using either extrusion or spraying of wet and dry concrete mixes, also known as 'shotcrete' which has a long history (US Army Corps, 1993) and is widely used today in diverse construction applications, with a variety of formworks.

'Bioshotcrete' refers to experimental construction techniques that combine additive manufacturing with mortars made of natural materials instead of concrete, facilitating the construction of architectural envelopes and vaulted structures referred-to as mud shells. These techniques involve the drone spraying of raw clay, sand and fibre mixes (i.e. 'biomortars') and are currently under development by a multidisciplinary team of engineers and architects. A drone is fitted with a hose that sprays successive depositions of biomortars over light formwork (Bravo and Chaltiel, 2017).

Some of the many advantages of using bioshotcrete include: avoiding the use of heavy machinery onsite; reducing the necessity for labour-intensive bespoke scaffoldings; and saving time in setup and fabrication.

In this text, a brief history of the emergence and development of bioshotcrete is presented. Two case studies are then discussed in terms of the fabrication required for different types of light formwork, ranging from prefabricated to customised elements, as well as the careful formulation of biomortars and their correct deposition sequencing. Finally, possible future scenarios for the implementation of this technique are outlined.

1. Terramia project built during Milan Design Week 2019. Photo: Studio Naaro.

Development of Bioshotcrete

The proposed technique for the fabrication of monolithic earthen shells with drone spraying is based on a precise protocol.

The process starts with material formulation, preparation and sequencing (Bravo and Chaltiel, 2017), including the selection of suitable material mixes. The material has been under development since 2012, in collaboration with the CRAterre laboratory and Wilfredo Carazas, a leading expert in raw earth construction.

For drone depositions, ongoing experiments started in December 2017 conducted with RcTakeOff, which developed a bespoke drone for bioshotcrete. These experiments yielded an improved system whereby the drone was fitted with an Euromair hose, connected to a powerful pump on the ground.

Light Formwork

Several types of lightweight formworks, suitable for drone spraying, have been explored in built projects since 2018:
- an inflatable formwork for a dome, inspired by the Bini-dome system and other pneumatic formworks (Van Hennik and Houtman, 2008),
- a geodesic frame with dry jute bags attached, inspired by the Concrete Canvas product (Chen et al., 2016), and
- a set of bamboo arches with fabric stretched across, inspired by the Ctesiphon system by James Waller and other fabric formworks (Veenendaal, 2016).

Initial tests at the Barcelona Drone Center explored the possibility of using a drone to undertake several trips to coat a large inflatable dome (fig.2), but encountered challenges in terms of process-related inaccuracies relating to the reference geometry and thickness of the final structure (Šamec et al., 2018) and, especially, stability (Bravo and Chaltiel, 2018).

To address these issues, two possible solutions were identified for formwork: a prefabricated geodesic wood frame fitted with jute bags filled with straw (fig.3), and vaulted structures using pre-bent bamboo arches with stretched fabric (figs. 1 & 6).

Case Studies

Two case studies implemented distinctive techniques allowing fast, onsite formwork assembly and an easy drone-spraying process using wet and dry biomortars.

Mud Shell, the first case study, is a dome with a 4m diameter. It investigated drone spraying with various layers of biomortars on dry, prefabricated insulation modules secured onto a geodesic frame. Terramia, the second case study, is composed of three vaulted structures measuring 3.5m–5.5m in height. It investigated drone spraying of locally sourced biomortars with different wet and dry layers onto bespoke fabric tensioned across pre-bent bamboo arches.

Mud Shell London Design Festival 2018

The Mud Shell project by MuDD Architects was built for the London Design Festival 2018 on the South Bank,

2. Drone depositing a coat over a large inflatable dome. Barcelona Drone Center, 2018. Photo: Frederic Carmona.

3. Mud shell geodesic design where the entrance is reinforced with two poles. The five top triangles of the geodesic dome are made of plastic sheets to protect the structure from the rain.

where the drone spray sessions were organised as live demonstrations for the public.

The construction process started with the assembly of a pre-made geodesic wooden frame composed of 35 triangles with 3D-printed PLA connectors complete with locking caps fitted on the inner side for reinforcement. Some 1,750 prefabricated, light-insulating, 15cm x 20cm jute fabric modules were secured to act as lost formwork, filled with 3cm straws positioned in rows with a 5cm minimum overlap.

The spray phase featured a drone, fitted with a 20m hose connected to a Euromair pump, which allowed the pilot and co-pilot to coat the structure in a uniform way without repositioning any of the machines or tools, as the hose was flexible enough to turn around the structure. The construction process was undertaken within a meshed space so that it could be classified as an indoor project which only requires health and safety approval and avoids long delays with aviation law compliance. The drone was, therefore, spraying inside a restricted area, which required it to tilt and rotate at angles of between 0 and 70 degrees, so as to coat the entire surface of the dome. The 40-amp Euromair Pump allowed the water ratio to be electronically input, providing a consistently homogeneous mortar and material grains not exceeding 5mm. A 5mm-diameter nozzle was used for the first layer, and a 1cm-diameter nozzle for the final layers, at fluctuating distances of between 10cm and 100cm from the surface. The speeds of deposition were between 50cm and 100cm per second, allowing a flow of matter of 8 litres per second. The materials used for the mortar spray included Claytec earth and linen-fibre ready-mixes and aerial lime powder. A series of drone depositions – six layers of 1cm – completed the process. Due to windy and wet weather conditions, the drying time in-between each drone spray session was about three hours. Stirring time, drone speed and type of nozzle were all crucial factors in obtaining the correct adhesion and finish.

The shell was based on an earlier built prototype of similar characteristics and size that the same fabrication team built at the Domaine de Boisbuchet in August 2018. This helped to refine the design to avoid damage from rain exposure by covering the top five isosceles triangles with waterproofed transparent sheets and by reinforcing the entry with two inclined poles, defining a smaller open area (fig.3).

The prefabricated dry modules (1m side triangular frames fitted with 50 jute bags filled with straw for insulation) proved efficient in terms of acoustics and wind protection and allowed a fast assembly onsite. The filling of each jute bag by hand proved to be labour-intensive, however, and they would need to be produced in an industrial manner if implemented at a larger scale.

Terramia Milan Design Week, 2019

Terramia was designed and built by MuDD Architects with Summum engineering and AKT II in collaboration with CanyaViva, at the Regione Lombardia government headquarters.

This project proposes the construction of vaulted structures with lightweight, stay-in-place formwork composed of bamboo arches and a tailored fabric surface, which is later drone-sprayed with clay mortar. The initial form-finding sought to rationalise and optimise the competition-winning forms into geometries

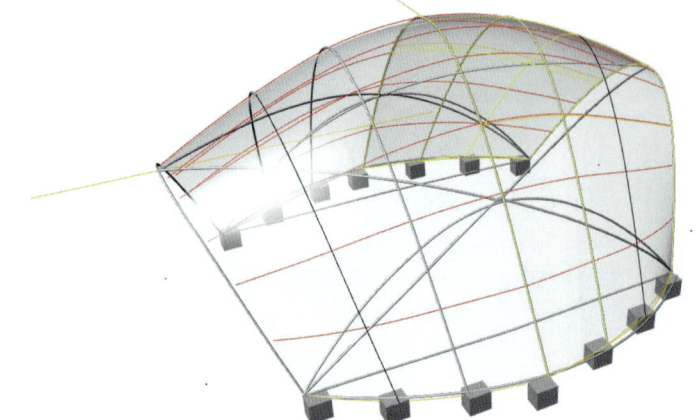

4

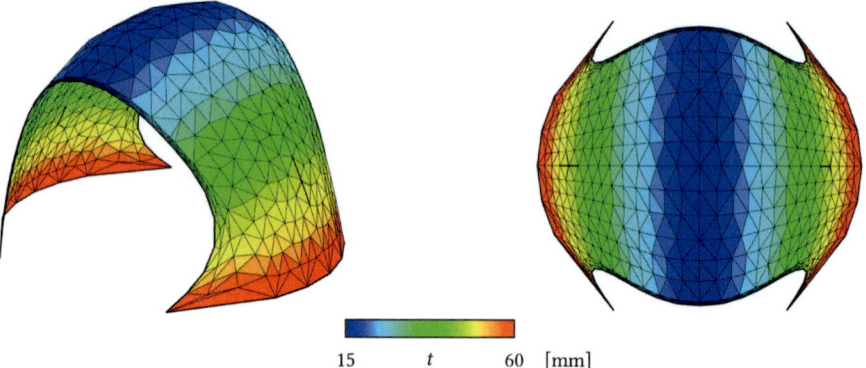

5

that could be realised within a limited number of arches in the short onsite construction schedule of four days. Eventually, a strategy using parallel parabolic arches was chosen. A number of structural typologies were investigated, each steered by the practical experience of the fabricator. The minimum radius of curvature of each arch was based on practical experience as well as the anticipated bending stresses induced in the bamboo when curved into shape. In analysing the radii of curvature, several factors were taken into account: bamboo species, moisture content, number of stems per arch, and their diameter and wall thickness as they varied along the arch. This meant stresses were checked against a varying bending strength of between 61 and 78 megapascals.

    The bamboo (*phyllostachys edulis* or *moso bamboo*), harvested on the outskirts of Milan, was cut to 8m or less for transportation, with an estimated diameter of around 5mm at the tip, and 90mm–120mm around the 8m mark, with a wall thickness of about 10% of the diameter. The bamboo stems were combined to form arches of between 7m and 13.5m in length. These in turn were assembled into lightweight, flexible formworks to

4. Geometry exploration of bamboo arches with optimisation of the arrangements to minimise the number of thin arches.

5. Simulation of the mortar deposition thickness evaluation.

6. Drone blowing onto wet mortar. Photo: Studio Naaro.

6

produce the final shell structures, which were 3.5m–5.5m tall.

The cladding was a tailor-made jute fabric, with double stitching of the circular flexible PVC windows. A drone was used to fit the 175m fabric cover for the larger shell onto the bamboo arches. The fabric weighs 50kg but the drone can only carry 25kg, so the strategy was to have six people onsite working alongside the drone to haul the weight and help bring the fabric along the arches, which was successfully completed in ten minutes.

For the deposition, a 2m-wide drone with 50cm legs and 20 minutes of flight autonomy enabled tools to be connected underneath which provided safe landing. Two pump machines were used for the dry and wet layers (with a 20m-long hose) respectively. The two types of biomortar were: a wet viscous layer of local clay, with a grain size less than 1mm, and a grey and yellow colour (1 unit of sand + 1 unit of clay + 1 unit of fibres + 2 units of water); and a dry layer of rice husks. The deposition technique included one wet layer of about 1cm thickness (50 square metres from 20 x 8-litre buckets) and one coat of fibres drone-blown onto the freshly-coated surface, to achieve an overall thickness of 1.2cm on each shell.

Conclusion

The experimental stages and construction prototypes have resulted in key outcomes, such as assessing the impact of using local materials and the added drone-lifting capabilities of textile formwork over tall arches, including onsite collaborative work between drones and fabricators. Regarding the untested, raw, local biomortars inspired by earthen architecture mixes consisting of clay sands and rice husks, the challenge was to calibrate the spray tool with nozzle type, pressure and flight speed to achieve a homogeneous coating while keeping grain and fibre size within the range of the pump machine's capabilities. In large-scale construction, Terramia revealed that using the drone-blown dry insulation material over wet mortar was more effective than using the prefabricated jute bags in the Mud Shell project, as it does not require prefabrication or initial 3D scanning for added insulation.

Future Work

While drone spraying has been found to ease the deposition of mortars, which favours their use their use in high or difficult-to-reach areas, including extreme geographies such as cliffs, it could also include drone sensing and monitoring.

In terms of drone sensing, 3D scans and temperature maps are an exciting development in automated or remotely piloted drones, as well as for crack recognition, temperature mapping and variable thickness control. In terms of monitoring, an automated process would not require highly skilled fabricators onsite, resulting in significant cost savings. It can also include an AI system to interpret the images and process all the sensor data.

Additional adapted technologies for future projects include having the drone undertake various trips while fitted with batteries and a mortar container going back to the feeding station after each spraying phase. These non-tethered scenarios would be particularly relevant for fast-hardening concrete that can be sprayed in very thin layers and would benefit from the high-speed deposition performed by the drone spray. Furthermore, as fast-setting concrete is toxic, the drone spray would ease this laborious and dangerous task for the builders. The system can also be tethered, which means not only

that the drone is fitted with the spraying hose attached to the pump on the ground, but also that it is constantly supplied with electricity by a power cable attached along the hose. The use of tethered and non-tethered scenarios should be explored depending on the objectives of each project.

An important development of the drone-aided construction the authors are proposing for future projects involves façade refurbishment performed behind a light mesh for international drone flight compliance with drone spraying in dense city centres. These large-scale fabrication strategies using locally-sourced mortars and light equipment onsite (the drone fits into two items of luggage) enable affordable and high-quality finishing of the façade including large-scale ornamentation using a stencil CNC cut to fit the façade to be refurbished.

Such future innovations will enable the shotcrete industry to include lighter machines and greener matter while offering bespoke freeform architectural envelopes.

7. Aerial view of the completed shells with very thin coats of drone-sprayed wet and dry raw mortars.

Bibliography

Bravo, M. and Chaltiel, S., 2017, *Monolithic Earthen Shells Digital Fabrication: Hybrid Workflow. The Design Modelling Symposium*, Paris, Springer.

Bravo, M. and Chaltiel, S., 2017, 'Paste Matter 3D Printing in Monolithic Shells Fabrication Methods' in Joao de Oliveira, M. and Crespo, F (eds.), *Kine[SIS]tem International Conference Proceedings: From Nature to Architectural Matter*, June 19th–20th, 2017, Lisbon, Portugal, p.10–18.

Bravo, M., Chaltiel, S. and Carazas, W., 2018, 'Matter– Robotic Calibration for Bioshotcrete' in *Temes de Disseny*, No. 34, p.80–91.

Chaltiel, S. and Bravo, M., 2017, DISCIPLINES & DISRUPTION, Proceedings of the 37th Annual Conference of the Association for Computer Aided Design in Architecture (ACADIA), Cambridge, MA 2–4 November, 2017, p.94–99 'Monolithic Earthen Shells Robotic Fabrication'.

Chaltiel, S., Bravo, M., Goessens, S., Latteur, P., Mansouri, M. and Ahmad, I., 2018, 'Dry and Liquid Clay Mix Drone Spraying for Bioshotcrete' in 'Creativity in Structural Design' in *Proceedings of International Association for Shell Structures, Form and Force Conference*, Boston, July, 2018. https://dial.uclouvain.be/pr/boreal/object/boreal%3A213917 (accessed 10 February 2020)

Hui, L., Chen, H., Liu, L., Zhang, F., Han, F., Lv, T., Zhang, W. and Yang, Y., 2016, 'Application Design of Concrete Canvas (CC) in Soil Reinforced Structure' in *Geotextiles and Geomembranes*, Vol. 44, No. 4, p.557–567.

Kromoser, B. and Huber, P., 2016, 'Pneumatic Formwork Systems in Structural Engineering', in *Advances in Material Science and Engineering*, special edition, article ID 4724036.

Šamec, E., Srivastava, A. and Chaltiel, S., 2019, 'Light Formwork for Earthen Monolithic Shells'. *Proceedings of the International Conference on Sustainable Materials, Systems and Structures (SMSS2019): Challenges in Design and Management of Structures* (conference paper), Rovinj, Croatia.

Tibuzzi, E. and Dayan, M., 2017, *Multi-Performative Skins. Fabricate Conference Proceedings*, London, UCL Press, p.280–285.

US Army Corps of Engineers, 1993, 'Standard Practice for Shotcrete' in Gedeon, Gilbert, *Introduction to Shotcrete Applications*, New York, CED Engineering. Online course documentation. https://www.cedengineering.com/courses/introduction-to-shotcrete-applications (accessed 10 February 2020)

Van Hennik, P. and Houtman, R., 2008, 'Pneumatic Formwork for Irregular Curved Thin Shells' in Onate, B. and Kröplin, H. (eds.), *Textiles, Composites and Inflatables 2*, Dordrecht, The Netherlands, Springer, p.99–116.

Veenendaal, D., 2017, 'Design and Form Finding of Flexibly Formed Shell Structures' *ETH Zurich*, p.105–159.

4.3 NOVEL STRATEGIES FOR MATERIALISATION

Industrialising Concrete 3D Printing: Three Case Studies

Nadja Gaudillière
XtreeE, Rungis and Laboratoire GSA, École Nationale Supérieure d'Architecture Paris
Justin Dirrenberger
XtreeE, Rungis and Laboratoire PIMM, Arts et Métiers-ParisTech
Romain Duballet
XtreeE, Rungis and Laboratoire Navier, Champs-sur-Marne
Charles Bouyssou, Alban Mallet, Philippe Roux and Mahriz Zakeri
XtreeE, Rungis

Introduction

Experimentation with 3D-printed concrete in architecture has flourished over the past decade and, consequently, so too has the development of industrial-grade manufacturing processes. 3D printing is part of a wave of robotic construction technologies developed with the 'digital turn' in architecture (Carpo, 2012) and, with it, the exploration of the possibilities offered by digital fabrication tools (Gramazio et al., 2015). Robotic technologies for construction sites have been designed since since the mid-20th century, but essentially consisted in the beginning of specialised machines accomplishing a single, repetitive task. Recent research has focused on more versatile machines, such as six-axis robotic arms, to perform a great diversity of tasks. This new approach to robotic construction processes, as well as the 'digital and informational turn' accompanying it, makes way for a potentially drastic renewal of the construction industry and its methods.

The introduction of these new robotic manufacturing technologies into the construction industry is still in the early stages, with numerous challenges needing to be overcome to reach full integration. These challenges must be studied in light of the potentialities of concrete 3D printing and other robotic fabrication processes, to ensure implementation in the construction industry in the most relevant way.

This paper gives a brief analysis of the current advancement of concrete 3D-printing technologies and the challenges facing researchers and companies, alongside three case studies of applications of concrete 3D printing developed by XtreeE. These applications have been developed in partnership with various significant players in the French construction industry,

1. 3D printing the artificial reef.

and have led to the manufacturing of several products as part of completed construction projects. Given the practical dimension of these case studies, they provide complementary information to academic research that can be used for further reflection on the industrialisation of such technologies.

Current Advancements in Concrete 3D-Printing Processes

Practical Aspects

The first manufacturing systems developed for concrete 3D printing – by precursors such as J. Pegna (Pegna, 1997); Contour Crafting (Khoshnevis, 2004); Loughborough University (Buswell et al., 2007); and D-Shape (Cesaretti et al., 2014) – are based on a variety of manufacturing systems, for both the printing nozzle and the motion system. A review of the various 3D-printing manufacturing systems developed so far can be found in Duballet et al., 2017.

Although the technologies discussed in this paper are often referred to as 'concrete 3D printing', a more accurate description is 'cementitious materials 3D printing'. The development of various cementitious material formulations has accompanied the development of the first 3D-printing manufacturing systems, with each research group developing a specific formulation tailored to its needs and system characteristics. In recent years, as cement manufacturers have become interested in the topic, several ready-to-use 3D concrete printing (3DCP) mixes have been developed and are now marketed. Various 3DCP mixes are available, but the materials used all have the same general rheological properties. A review of existing mixes and rheological properties can be found in Roussel (2018) and Buswell et al. (2018).

With the development of 3DCP manufacturing systems and adequate mixes, numerous applications have also been studied and developed. 3D printing has been experimented with at the scale of large buildings and architectonic elements such as columns, stairs and floors (Gaudillière et al., 2018 and Rippmann et al., 2017). Products developed vary in use, including items for public works, indoor and urban furniture, and building components, amongst others. Research has focused both on product design and new structural possibilities. A detailed review of possible building systems and of existing prototypes can be found in Duballet et al., 2017.

Challenges

Prototypes and projects built over the past few years have demonstrated both the viability and potential of 3DCP technologies. Several of these examples have been built by 3D-printing companies in partnership with both cement manufacturers and construction companies, demonstrating the active interest of the construction industry in these processes. Nevertheless, both ongoing and published research on 3DCP processes and the conditions of production of projects points to challenges that must be tackled for industrial-grade 3DCP to fully mature and develop.

Beyond existing technical challenges, a review of which can be found in Buswell et al., 2018, the issues still to be confronted are, in the main, linked to long-established habits in the construction industry and the inertia that can be encountered in large industries. Despite the pervasion of new technologies, most of these digital tools have been adopted for the design stage and management of building sites. The 'digital turn' is based on the notion of 'non-standard production' (Cache, 1998), whereas the construction industry relies on 'standard production'. A major paradigmatic shift must, therefore, happen for robotic construction processes to be fully adopted. While this change is under way – as the construction industry is, in part, divided up into many small business structures – it has not yet been fully assimilated. Furthermore, this evolution must be accompanied by the creation of new (currently non-existent) regulations, particularly for 3DCP. Such regulations will facilitate the adoption of digital technologies by all stakeholders in the industry, including insurance providers.

Where existing research has demonstrated the usefulness of 3DCP in areas such as material savings (Rippmann et al., 2017 and Duballet et al., 2018) and its potential to reduce the environmental cost of building methods, the assessment of the impact of robotic technologies remains a major challenge. Confronting these challenges will enable 3DCP potentials to blossom. Industrial developments by prominent companies hint at the potential for greater productivity in the construction industry, which has been a notoriously problematic issue in recent decades. Finally, beyond the possibility of dealing with current construction and environmental challenges, experimenting with the use of 3D printing in architectural design could lead to the development of new formal and structural languages in the discipline.

XtreeE Case Studies

The XtreeE Printing System

The printing system developed by XtreeE, with which the case studies presented in this chapter were produced, is composed of four distinct parts: a computer supervising the 3D model and toolpath; a mixing unit for the 3DCP mix; a monitoring system for the dosage of the mix and additives; and the printing head developed by XtreeE, mounted on a six-axis robotic arm. Further details on the process and system can be found in Gosselin et al., 2016.

Maritime Engineering: Artificial Reef

The first case study focuses on design and fabrication methods employed by a multidisciplinary team, involving architects, additive manufacturing specialists, generative designers and marine engineers to produce a 1m³ artificial reef, shown in fig.2. In February 2018, the reef was immersed in the Calanques National Park in France, as part of the REXCOR research project. The aim of REXCOR is the restoration of the rocky shoals of the Cortiou cove, into which Marseille city sewage has been discharged since 1896, impacting on the marine environment.

With the aim of restoring a lost ecological habitat, this biomimetic, porous reef mimics one of the richest environments in the Mediterranean Sea,

2. The artificial reef just after immersion.

3. Stormwater collector installation.

the Coralligenous habitat. This marine habitat – made of a structurally complex and dense biogenic substrate – took hundreds of years to form and is known to be a shelter for thousands of species, including fish, crustacea, coral, algae, molluscs, etc. Artificial concrete reefs are traditionally produced by assembling concrete slabs, drastically reducing the complexity of the available shapes and, with it, marine life development. 3D printing allows for greater possibilities, enabling marine engineers to design complex, tailor-made reefs. It also allows for multiple-scale cavities, unachievable through other processes but critical to the redevelopment of marine life in the targeted area.

A specific design method for the reef was developed, with the printing system's constraints – including a maximal slope angle and the continuous flow of concrete – and the biomimetic constraints – originating from the targeted ecological habitat – in mind. The prototype was printed sideways and consisted of a continuous, intersecting sheet of concrete, which considered the constraints while maximising the diversity of sizes and shapes for the cavities. On this occasion, an innovative workflow had been implemented between the members of the team, with their differing areas of expertise needing to be put together to create the final geometry of the reef.

Although the immersion of the artificial reef presented here is recent, with regard to marine colonisation, traces of adoption by several species from the area can already be observed, confirming the potential of 3DCP technologies for future ecological engineering and restoration projects.

Public Works: Stormwater Collectors
The second case study is a series of 3D-printed stormwater collectors for the cities of Lille and Roubaix in France in 2017 and 2018 (fig.3). These collectors are part of a larger series of prototypes produced by XtreeE and installed onsite, addressing specific public works' needs. The idea for the collectors originated in a workshop that brought together public-works company Point.P TP and XtreeE to study the potentials of 3DCP. This series of prototypes and their use in real-life situations has underlined the potential of 3DCP in public works.

The first collector prototype was 3D printed and installed in partnership with Point.P TP, followed by three more, built according to the same manufacturing method. The first collector was designated to a part of the subterranean water network, situated under a busy road. The recourse to 3D printing enabled a drastic reduction in onsite intervention – two days, instead of the usual two weeks – thus reducing inconvenience and traffic disruption. The initial design was improved upon the following three collectors, with the development of a lifting system that consumed less material. The device developed for this was also used to protect the existing subterranean grid made of ancient brick vaults. As these were susceptible to damage by a standard intervention, the use of 3D printing enabled a connection detail to be manufactured that preserved the vaults, despite their structural weakness.

These prototypes provided an opportunity to develop a workflow integrating several design teams and building sites. The collectors themselves represent an interesting experiment that integrates 3D concrete printing into standard industrial workflows and methods; for the fabrication of the collectors, the team applied a mixed manufacturing technique based on a cast and printed reinforced concrete slab. Further description of the project and the mixed manufacturing technique can be found in Gaudillière et al., 2019a.

Architectonic Elements: Freeform Truss Pillar
The production of architectonic elements raises many issues regarding 3DCP processes. Several research teams and companies are developing technologies with the goal of increasing the scale of the printing area, in order to produce increasingly larger buildings in a single print. Others favour prefabrication, often onsite, as is the case in the pillar presented here. Although advocates of the use of 3D printing in construction often highlight the idea that it could lead to the disappearance of connections for building parts, this may be a questionable outlook. The development of combinations of 3DCP and other manufacturing methods appears to be essential for assimilation into the construction industry, whereas advocating for continuous, very large-scale 3D printing might prevent this. Developing smaller-scale architectonic elements, therefore, is perhaps the optimal way to mix methods, both for the fabrication of the elements and buildings themselves.

The pillar (fig.4) is a 4m-high column, made of an integrated 3D-printed formwork filled with cast concrete. The decision to cast concrete was made following the absence of regulations for 3DCP in construction at the time. This resulted, as shown in Table 1, in an augmentation of the amount of matter used in the pillar. A detailed description of the manufacturing method is available in Gaudillière et al., 2018, and in Buswell et al., 2018. The workflow was similar to those in building projects and was, therefore, much more linear. The decision to resort to 3D printing was made much later than in the two other case studies presented here.

4. Krypton Pillar, Aix-en-Provence.
Photo © Lisa Ricciotti.

Project	Production Time (%)	Material Consumption (%)
Artificial Reef	33	33
Collectors	66	33
Pillar	21.6	-29
Urban Furniture	62.5	59.2
Average	45.8	24.05

Table 1. Production time and matter consumption for projects in comparison to traditional production methods.

Production Times and Material Consumption

A study has been conducted to compare production time and material consumption for 3D-printed objects and for traditionally-built equivalents. Objects compared include the three case studies presented in this chapter, as well as prototypes for urban furniture. Details can be found in Gaudillière et al., 2019b, while results are given in Table 1.

Conclusion

This paper presents three projects developed by the company XtreeE, in different contexts, as well as information on the different participants involved, manufacturing techniques employed, production time and material consumption. Through the description of these three case studies, this paper attempts to relate the experience in the field to existing research and challenges identified in the development of 3DCP, for a better understanding of possible industrialisation routes.

Case studies, such as the ones presented in this paper, highlight several important factors for the development of environmental design guidelines. Case studies stress the need for regulation and for a fine-tuned control of optimisation processes, accompanied by said design guidelines. The workflows presented here advocate for the combination of 3DCP to already pre-existing techniques and for close collaboration between traditional stakeholders and new players, prompted by the development of 3D printing.

By combining the expertise of stakeholders in the industry and the mastery of robotic technologies developed by researchers, such as 3DCP, design guidelines could be established that minimise the negative impact of construction activities. New levels of productivity and efficiency could be reached, alongside significant improvements in the quality of the built environment.

Acknowledgements

The XtreeE team would like to thank the partners that have helped make the projects presented in this paper possible and that have contributed to them, including:
Stormwater collectors: Point.P TP, La Sade.
Artificial reef: Seaboost.
Krypton pillar: EZCT Architecture & Design Research, Marc Dalibard Architecte, LafargeHolcim, Fehr Architectural, Artelia, AD Concept.

Bibliography

Buswell, R.A., Soar, R., Gibb, A. and Thorpe, A., 2007, 'Freeform Construction: Mega-Scale Rapid Manufacturing for Construction' in *Automation in Construction*, Vol. 16, p.224–231.

Buswell, R.A., Leal de Silva, W.Z., Jones, S.Z. and Dirrenberger, J., 2018, '3D Printing Using Concrete Extrusion: A Roadmap for Research' in *Cement and Concrete Research*, Vol. 107 (May 2018).

Cache, B., 1998, 'Objectile: Poursuite de la Philosophie par d'autres Moyens?' in *Rue Descartes*, No. 20, p.149–157.

Carpo, M. (ed.), 2012, *The Digital Turn in Architecture 1992–2012: AD Reader*, Hoboken, NJ, John Wiley & Sons.

Cesaretti, G., Dini, E., Kestelier, X.D., Colla, V. and Pambaguian, L., 2014, 'Building Components for an Outpost on the Lunar Soil by Means of a Novel 3D Printing Technology' in *Acta Astronaut*, Vol. 93, p.430–450.

Duballet, R., Baverel, O. and Dirrenberger, J., 2017, 'Classification of Building Systems for Concrete 3D Printing' in *Automation in Construction*, Vol. 83, p.247–258.

Duballet, R., Baverel, O. and Dirrenberger, J., 2018, 'Space Truss Masonry Walls with Robotic Mortar Extrusion' in *Structures*, Vol. 18, p.41–47.

Gaudillière, N., Duballet, R., Bouyssou, C., Mallet, A., Roux, P., Zakeri, M. and Dirrenberger, J., 2018, 'Large-Scale Additive Manufacturing of Ultra-High-Performance Concrete of Integrated Formwork for Truss-Shaped Pillars' in Willmann, J., Block, P., Hutter, M., Byrne, K. and Schork, T. (eds.). *Robotic Fabrication in Architecture, Art and Design 2018*, Cham, Switzerland, Springer, p.459–472.

Gaudillière, N., Duballet, R., Bouyssou, C., Mallet, A., Roux, P., Zakeri, M., Dirrenberger, J., 2019a, 'Building Applications Using Lost Formworks Obtained through Large-Scale Additive Manufacturing of Ultra-High-Performance Concrete' in Sanjayan, J.G., Nazari, A. and Nematollahi, B. (eds.), *3D Concrete Printing Technology*, Oxford, Butterworth-Heinemann, p.37–58.

Gaudillière, N., Duballet, R., Bouyssou, C., Mallet, A., Roux, Ph., Zakeri, M. and Dirrenberger, J., 2019b, 'Bénéfices temps et matière dans le recours au processus d'impression 3D béton pour des applications dans le domaine de la construction' (conference paper from DiXite3dPrint: Fabrication Additive pour la Construction. Quelle Actualité Nationale? 17–18 January 2019, Champs-sur-Marne, France).

Gosselin, C., Duballet, R., Roux, P., Gaudillière, N., Dirrenberger, J. and Morel, P., 2016, 'Large-Scale 3D Printing of Ultra-High-Performance Concrete: A New Processing Route for Architects and Builders' in *Materials and Design*, Vol. 100, p.102–109.

Gramazio, F., Kohler, M. and Willman, J., 2015, *The Robotic Touch: How Robots Change Architecture*, Zurich, Switzerland, Park Books.

Khoshnevis, B., 2004, 'Automated Construction by Contour Crafting-Related Robotics and Information Technologies' in *Automation in Construction*, Vol. 13, p.5–19.

Pegna, J., 1997, Exploratory Investigation of Solid Freeform Construction' in *Automation in Construction*, Vol. 5, No. 5, p.427–437.

Rippmann, M., Liew, A. and Block, P., 2017, 'Structural 3D Printed Floor' in Yuan, P.F., Menges, A. and Leach, N. (eds.), *Digital Fabrication*, Shanghai, Tongji University Press.

Roussel, N., 2018, 'Rheological Requirements for Printable Concretes' in *Cement and Concrete Research*, Vol. 107, p.76–85.

4.4 NOVEL STRATEGIES FOR MATERIALISATION

Integration of Material and Fabrication Affordances within the Design Workflow

Giulio Brugnaro, Sean Hanna, Peter Scully and Bob Sheil
The Bartlett School of Architecture, UCL
Silvan Oesterle
Rippmann Oesterle Knauss GmbH (ROK)

Introduction

In current design practices, the lack of feedback between the different steps of linear design processes forces designers to engage with only a limited range of standard materials and manufacturing techniques, leading to wasteful and inefficient solutions. Focusing on robotic carving with timber, this paper investigates the extent to which the early-stage integration of material knowledge as part of design-to-manufacture workflows makes it possible to explore novel, previously unavailable, design solutions informed by the fabrication process.

Background

The integration of digital fabrication technologies within design practices is challenging the separation between designing and making in current production workflows (Koralevic, 2008; Carpo, 2011). A novel sensibility toward materials and tool technologies has become a central part of the architectural discourse (DeLanda, 2002; Menges, 2015), where designers are asked to envision performance-driven processes bridging the digital and physical realms, rather than focusing on the creation of static forms (Gramazio and Kohler, 2008). Simulation tools and robotic fabrication technologies are regarded as enabling frameworks to establish feedback loops driving the design and making of artefacts (Maxwell and Pigram, 2012).

The development of sensor devices to record and reconstruct manufacturing tasks has made it possible to adopt machine learning models, such as Artificial Neural Networks (ANNs), that are able to synthesise and integrate knowledge to support decision-making, based on the live material and process data (Lu, 1990;

1. Robotic carving operations: fabrication stage.

van Luttervelt et al., 1998). The identification of complex non-linear patterns in data enables individual fabrication parameters to be optimised in relation to the physical output of the task, increasing the overall efficiency of the production process (Tsai et al., 1999). The encapsulation of such knowledge into a transferable package offers the opportunity to integrate with a design interface, allowing for exploration of design opportunities based on fabrication and material considerations (Hanna, 2007; Tamke et al., 2018).

Methods

This research used real-world fabrication data, collected by human experts and autonomous robotic sessions, to derive a more accurate geometrical prediction of carving operations on timber. To achieve this, the methods developed present a series of training procedures for a robotic fabrication system, where the instrumental and material knowledge of skilled human craftspeople is captured, transferred, robotically augmented and finally integrated into an interface that makes this knowledge available to designers.

The training process is based on a cycle of three main stages:

1. **Recording:** The acquisition of fabrication data is structured around a series of carving sessions to collect into a dataset the combination of fabrication parameters driving the carving operation (i.e. tool/surface angle, tool/grain direction angle, force feedback, input cut length, input cut depth) and pair them with their respective outcomes measured as 'actual length', 'width', 'depth of the cut' and 'total removal volume'. Such information is captured, in real-time and retrospectively, using an array of motion capture (MOCAP) cameras to track the position and orientation of the carving tools and 3D-photogrammetric techniques to reconstruct in a highly detailed mesh geometry the result of the carving operations.
2. **Learning:** The collected datasets are used to train a supervised machine learning model, or ANN, whose main learning objective is to predict the geometric outcome of a subtractive operation from a user-defined toolpath and the series of fabrication parameters described above, as well as generating a robotic toolpath out of a digitally-carved geometry. Each robotic toolpath is a sequence of target frames, which define the position and orientation of the carving gouge along the cut. Given a sequence of target frames, the trained ANN predicts, at each frame, the geometric output parameters of the cut (length, width, depth), considering the influence of material properties determined by the wood species (i.e. grain arrangement and density) and the resulting angle of the carving operation in relation to the grain direction.
3. **Fabrication:** The trained ANN represents a package of instrumental knowledge that can be transferred, reused, extended and, most importantly, integrated within an interface to digitally evaluate multiple design solutions informed by tools and material properties before moving to the production stage.

The training workflow should not be considered a linear progression from the recording to the fabrication stage but rather as a knowledge platform that can be remodelled over several cycles with new fabrication data, trained to improve its prediction performance and applied to various design tasks.

Industry Experiments

Collaborations with two industry partners – ROK Architects and BIG – provided the opportunity to apply these methods into established workflows and develop a catalogue of design explorations for a wide range of applications, from furniture to building components of larger assemblies.

The secondment at BIG took place concurrently with the installation of two industrial robotic arms in the office space. This enabled the team of designers to directly engage with the training workflow for robotic carving operations through an extensive series of experiments exploring the potential of integrating fabrication and material aspects at an early stage of the design process.

During the training, designers started by selecting three substantially different wood species (Lime, Tulip and Oak) for both their aesthetic qualities and mechanical properties. The second focus of the investigation was on the interaction of a set of different carving tools with the material properties, such as grain density and directionality of the selected wood species. Each wood species dataset counted between 430 and 460 robotic carving operations. Each training board (300mm x 400 mm) counted between 32 and 36 cuts and took an average of 15 minutes to be produced, with the setup – positioning, fixing and calibrating – being the most time-consuming part.

The trained system, based on sensor data collected during the recording sessions, was integrated into a design interface already in use at the firm (Rhino3D/Grasshopper), to provide an accurate prediction of the carving operations and explore multiple material solutions in terms of patterns and texture marks, before moving to the production stage.

For each fabricated panel, several digital designs were explored through the ANN-based simulation of the outcome geometry. The tree-like structure of the investigations allowed the design to advance through a sequence of 'what-if' scenarios (Vaneker and Van

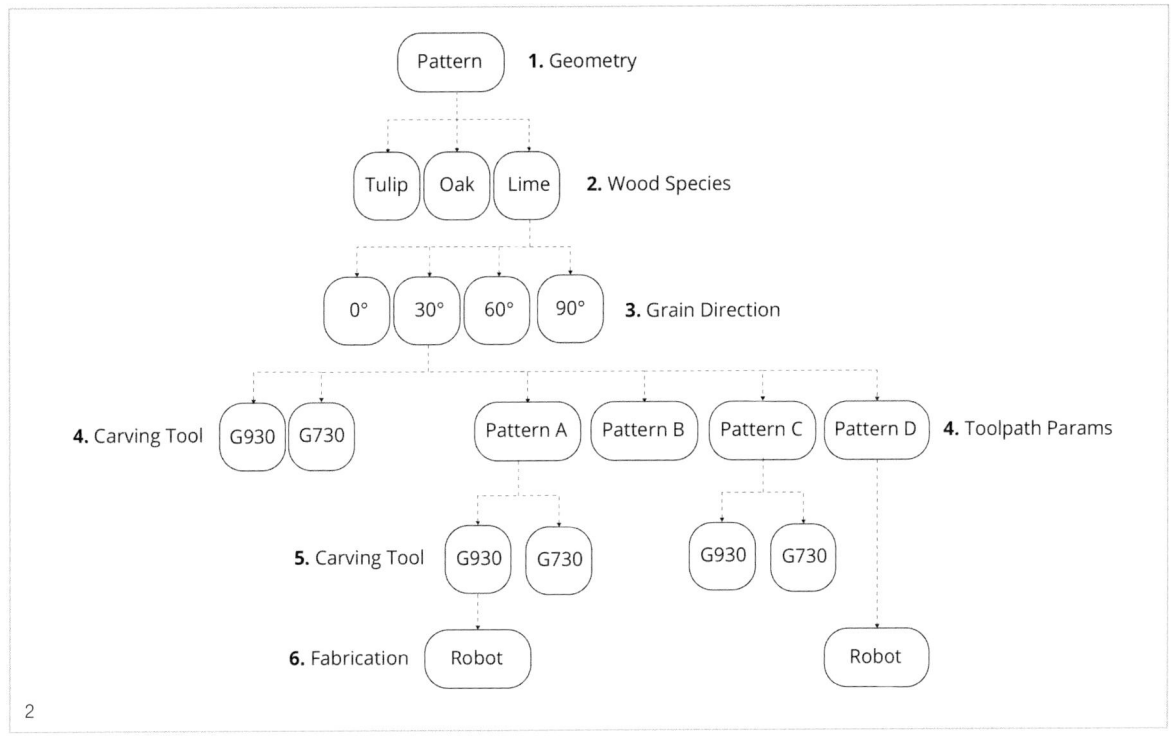

2. An example of the 'what-if' scenarios analysed during the design of carved panels through the comparison of the variance introduced by fabrication and material choices.

Houten, 2006) presenting, at each stage, a comparison of the effect generated by a specific fabrication or material parameter on the overall design as inherited from the previous stage (fig.2). Such explorations entail the analysis of geometric pattern variations, wood species and density (fig.3), grain directions, carving tools and specific fabrication parameters (e.g. tool/surface angle) which would significantly affect the resulting length, depth and width of the cuts composing the overall pattern.

Once robotically fabricated, the selected carved geometries were compared using a deviation analysis with the respective simulation to assess the predictive abilities of the system (fig.4).

The secondment at ROK set out to further test the machine learning-based design tool, the associated workflow and the robotic-carving process (fig.5) through the design of a piece of furniture for a gallery space, where a composition of carved boards created a series of platforms to display small items (fig.6).

The demonstrator was used to address challenges such as the balance between top-down decisions and features emerging bottom-up from properties of the material, using the simulation framework to visualise unexpected results and to adjust the fabrication parameters to match the prescribed design intentions and requirements. The ANN networks necessary for the simulation were trained using Lime – a light-coloured wood species – and a set of two different carving tools. For each of these fabrication steps, the trained ANN

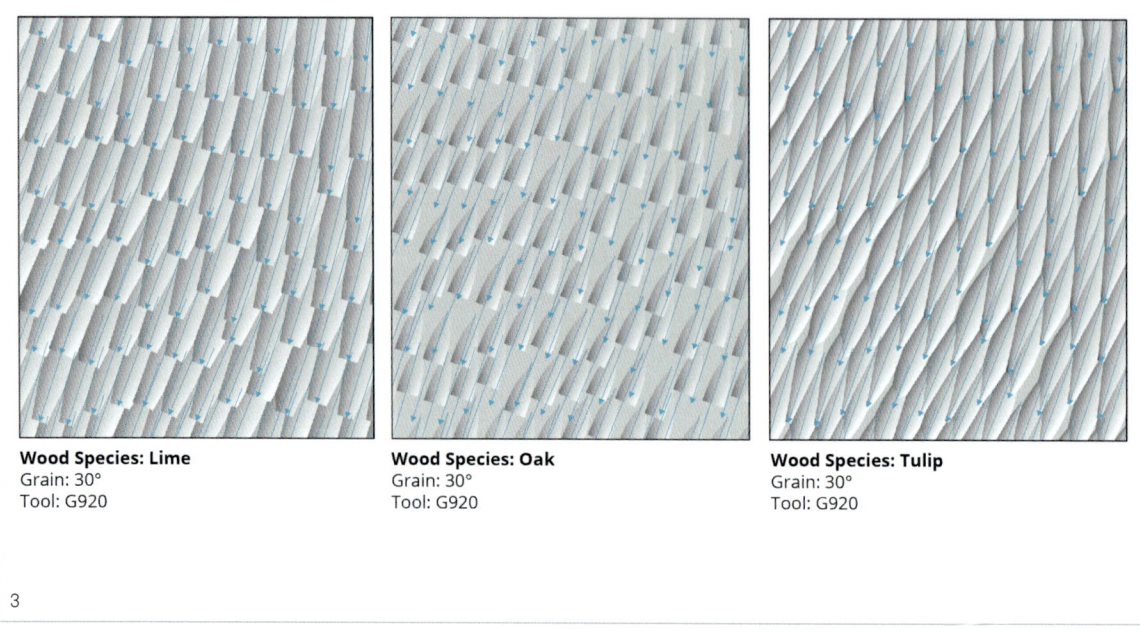

Wood Species: Lime
Grain: 30°
Tool: G920

Wood Species: Oak
Grain: 30°
Tool: G920

Wood Species: Tulip
Grain: 30°
Tool: G920

3

generated a simulation of the carving outcome that evaluated, at each step, the impact of the design choices before production. Each carved board, while following a similar design logic, presented local individual features and variations in the pattern arrangements of parallel flutes due to the wood grain behaviour on the control of input design parameters. As in the previous case study, each carved board was reconstructed digitally post-fabrication using photogrammetry and compared to the ANN-based prediction, generating a gradient-based mapping of the deviation between the two. This made it possible to validate the tool and assess the impact of its application as core elements of the digital design process (fig.7).

Results

The catalogue of material evidence and digital experiments, performed during the secondments, suggests that the curation of the training process represents the keystone of the entire design workflow. Following the selection of wood species, the search domain defined, at an early stage, relevant material properties, carving tools and fabrication parameters that directly determined the range of solutions available in the later digital design stage.

The exploration of 'what-if' scenarios, driven by tools and material properties, would not be possible using purely digital geometric considerations, rather than a collection of real-world fabrication data. The evaluation of the impact of choices, such as the selection of a specific wood species, therefore, allows a series of otherwise unavailable design opportunities to be unlocked and supports a better-informed decision-making process.

While the prediction of single carving operations is accurate to within a fraction of millimetres, the analysis of complex fabricated patterns shows a higher deviation between the ANN-based prediction and the photogrammetric reconstruction of the carved board. The main reason for this is, likely, due to the combined effect of overlapping cuts whereby mechanical conditions are generated that are not present in the single-cut configuration. Nevertheless, the ANN-based simulation showed an overall high level of accuracy in its predictions, proving its ability to correctly model the impact of different materials and fabrication affordances on the geometric outcome of carving operations.

The final fabrication stage of a specific 'what-if' scenario does not represent, necessarily, the end of the design process but, rather, becomes the starting point for another set of digital explorations, which can build upon the initial fabricated evidence. Following a tree-like structure, the design-to-fabrication process is rarely linear, and choices made at an early stage can always be revised, especially if new material evidence is included.

The simulation allows the designer to easily explore material-aware solutions ahead of the fabrication stage; however, this needs to be carefully balanced with the more conventional top-down, geometry-driven design approach. The tools developed here allow the original design intention to be achieved through the optimisation of individual fabrication parameters or, alternatively, a more open-ended trajectory where material and fabrication affordances act as design drivers.

3. Comparison of the influence of three different wood species (Lime, Oak, Tulip) on the same digital input geometry.

4. Deviation analysis between a portion of the fabricated carved panel and its ANN-based simulation.

5. The robotically-carved boards follow a pattern made of parallel flutes presenting local variations given both by input design parameters and material behaviours.

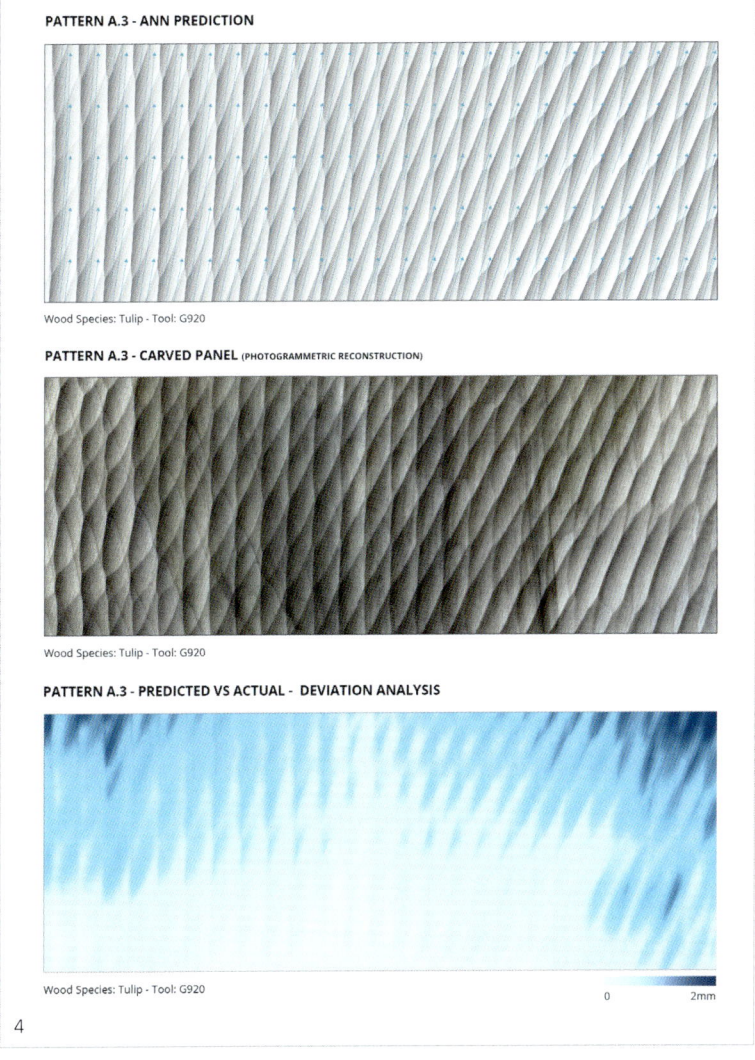

6

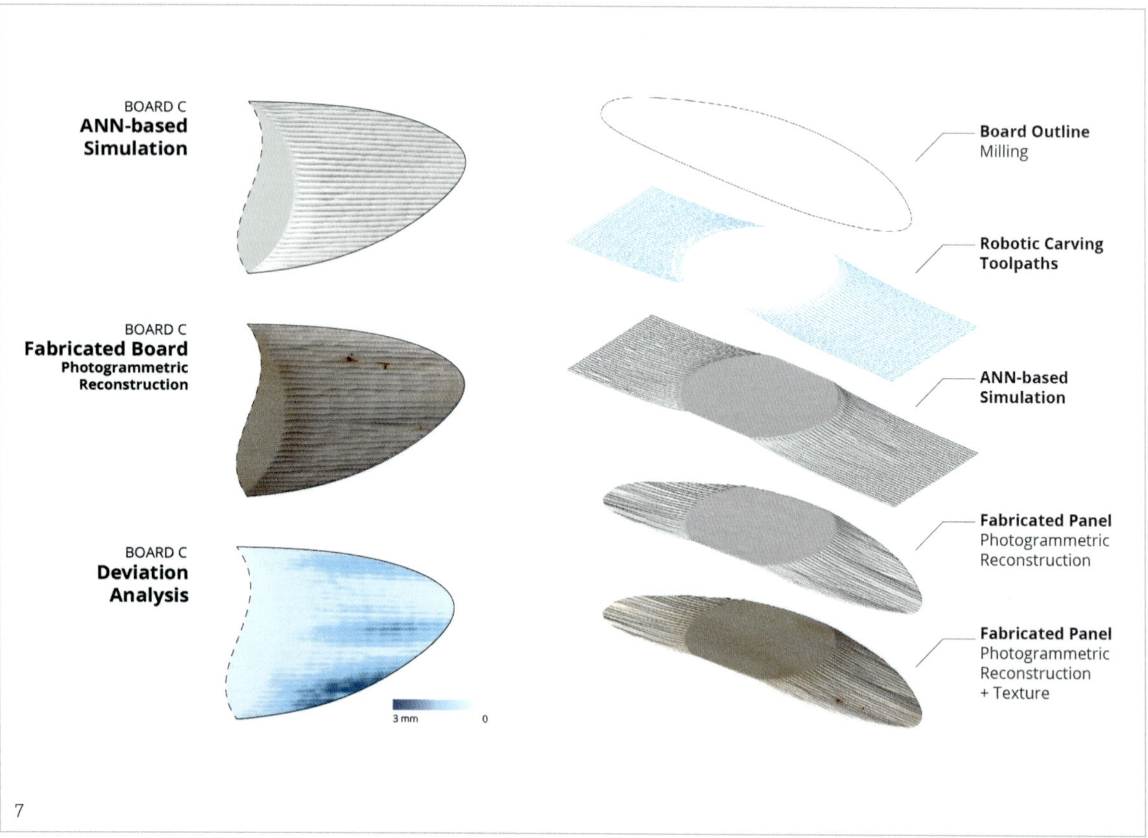

BOARD C **ANN-based Simulation**		Board Outline — Milling
		Robotic Carving Toolpaths
BOARD C **Fabricated Board** Photogrammetric Reconstruction		ANN-based Simulation
		Fabricated Panel Photogrammetric Reconstruction
BOARD C **Deviation Analysis**	3 mm — 0	Fabricated Panel Photogrammetric Reconstruction + Texture

7

Conclusions

The main contribution of this research is to the field of applied machine learning strategies, bridging robotic-manufacturing environments and digital-design interfaces. Although the research strategically focused on one very specific application – robotic carving with timber – the methods developed have the potential to be applied to a wider variety of non-trivial robotic manufacturing tasks that require dexterity and a high-level understanding of the process.

Previous research has explored machine learning models being applied to optimise robotic tasks within an industrial context. The novelty of this research lies in applying similar established methods within the workflow of creative practices to augment and support the abilities of designers.

The successful development of a series of methods to collect, process and encapsulate manufacturing knowledge and its application within a design environment demonstrates the benefits of interacting with fabrication tools and material affordances early on, to make better-informed design decisions.

From the perspective of designers, the access to packages of instrumental knowledge enables manufacturing techniques to be extended, as the trained networks significantly increase accuracy in the prediction and simulation of non-standard processes. Designers willing to engage with the curation of the training process have the opportunity to create custom-designed manufacturing workflows, validated by feedback data and statistical models. For companies, the research demonstrates the advantages of packaging knowledge, making it available to all the stakeholders involved in the design-to-manufacturing workflow, to ensure fruitful communication from the outset and help avoid costly mistakes at a later stage.

6. The demonstrator, named Kizamu (Japanese for 'carving'), is composed of a series of boards used to display small objects in a gallery.

7. The ANN-based simulation illustrates the impact of design decisions, in relation to the properties of the wood, and informs the robotic fabrication accordingly.

Bibliography

Carpo, M., 2011, *The Alphabet and the Algorithm*, Cambridge, MA, MIT Press.

DeLanda, M., 2002, 'Philosophies of Design: The Case of Modelling Software' in Salazar, J. (ed.), *Verb 1 (Architecture Boogazine): Authorship and Information*, Madrid, Actar Press.

Gramazio, F. and Kohler, M., 2008, *Digital Materiality in Architecture*, Baden, Switzerland, Lars Müller Publishers.

Hanna, S., 2007, 'Inductive Machine Learning of Optimal Modular Structures: Estimating Solutions Using Support Vector Machines' in *Artificial Intelligence for Engineering Design, Analysis and Manufacturing*, Vol. 21, No. 1, p.351–366.

Kolarevic, B. and Klinger, K.R., 2008, *Manufacturing Material Effects: Rethinking Design and Making in Architecture*, New York, Routledge.

Lu, S. C.-Y., 1990, 'Machine Learning Approaches to Knowledge Synthesis and Integration Tasks for Advanced Engineering Automation' in *Computers in Industry*, Vol. 15, No. 1–2, p.105–120.

van Luttervelt, C.A., Childs, T.H.C., Jawahir, I.S., Klocke, F., 1998, 'Present Situation and Future Trends in Modelling of Machining Operations' in *CIRP Annals*, Vol., 47, No. 2, p.587–626.

Maxwell, I. and Pigram, D., 2012, 'In the Cause of Architecture: Traversing Design and Making' in *Log*, Vol. 25, p.31–40.

Menges, A. (ed.), 2015, *Material Synthesis: Fusing the Physical and the Computational* (Architectural Design Series), London, Wiley.

Tamke, M., Nicholas, P. and Zwierzycki, M., 2018, 'Machine Learning for Architectural Design: Practices and Infrastructure' in *International Journal of Architectural Computing*, Vol. 16, No. 2, p.123–143.

Tsai, Y.H., Chen, J.C. and Lou, S.J., 1999, 'An In-process Surface Recognition System Based On Neural Networks In End Milling Cutting Operations' in *International Journal of Machine Tools and Manufacture*, Vol. 39, No. 4, p.583–605.

Vaneker, T.H.J. and Van Houten, F.J.A.M., 2006, 'What-if Design as a Synthesising Working Method in Product Design' in *CIRP Annals*, Vol. 55, No. 1, p.131–134.

4.5 NOVEL STRATEGIES FOR MATERIALISATION

Making Timberdome

Christopher Robeller and Valentin Viezens
Digital Timber Construction DTC, Technische Universität Kaiserslautern

State of the Art

Double-curved shells are efficient and elegant designs, which allow large distances to be spanned with little material. Many of these surface-active structure systems are situated in Latin American countries, such as the famous buildings designed by Félix Candela and Eladio Dieste. These impressive constructions are, however, costly and time-consuming to build, as they are largely realised in concrete, stone and brick, and involve complicated support structures. The possibility of constructing large shells with wood-based panels was impressively demonstrated in 2014 in the Elefantenhaus Zoo Zürich project, which features a roof structure spanning up to 85m, column-free (Bagger, 2010). Several current research studies are investigating complex surface structures made of planar, polygonal plate elements, using CAD-programming interfaces and 5-axis CNC technology (Krieg, et al., 2015; Li and Knippers, 2015; Manahl and Wiltsche, 2012; Robeller, et al., 2017).

The First Cross-Laminated Timber (CLT) Shell with Self-Tensioning Wood Connections

The connections between the plates play a decisive role, considering the number of differently-shaped elements with a variety of obtuse dihedral angles in such structures. Not only do they help to achieve the required rigidity of the structure, but they also contribute to its simple, fast and precise assembly. Form-fitting connections provide a solution, in which forces are transmitted by the shape of the components, and the form also serves as an alignment and assembly guide (following the LEGO principle). Form-fitting fasteners made of hardwood laminated veneer lumber (LVL) have been used in recent years, for example in the 2010 Centre Pompidou Metz (Scheurer, 2008) and the 2015 Tamedia building in Zurich. One challenge with such connections, however, is to achieve a perfect fit: due to material and production tolerances, this is practically impossible. Gaps and additional metal fasteners may, therefore, be added in practice, but these can negatively affect the structural performance.

One solution to this problem is provided by wedge-shaped joints, which are widely used in traditional carpentry. For instance, in the bridge–wedge connection, a slot-and-tenon joint is secured with an additional wedge and, due to the diagonal shape, tolerances can be compensated; a similar principle has been used in the robotic integral attachment research paper (Robeller, et al., 2017). A modern interpretation of the wedge-joining principle is offered by the X-fix C connectors, which we are using for the first time in a shell structure. We mill the cut-outs for the connectors using 5-axis CNC technology at precisely the angle of the slightly-inclined side surfaces of the components. Compared to an alternative connection with screws, this technique offers an integrated alignment guide, or joining aid, and thus a considerable time saving. Particularly in the construction of wood plate shells, the very obtuse dihedral angles between the adjacent plates present a particular challenge. In the constructions we studied, the average angle was 173°.

For the Innovation Area of the International Wood Fair Klagenfurt 2018, we designed a shell measuring 16m^2, consisting of 59 components made of 100mm-thick five-layer CLT. The 149 internal edges between the components, with an average dihedral of 173.4° and

1. Construction of the first Timberdome prototype, Innovation Area, International Wood Fair, Klagenfurt, Austria 2018.

an average edge length of 346mm, were each joined with one X-fix C connector. The high number of components and connectors (ten connectors per m^2 of shell) was due to the small footprint of the construction, and was a compromise between a model and a full-scale building construction. It was calculated that for a dome with a 15m span, only two connectors per m2 of roof area were needed. The connectors were inserted 90mm into the 100mm-thick plates, and are invisible on their underside.

Automated Generation of Geometry

The CAD plug-in, developed with the software development kit Rhino Commons, calculates the component geometries based on a 3D-polygon mesh and the CLT plate thickness. The polygon mesh defines the underside of the CLT plate elements, allowing for differently shaped facets, such as three-, four- or six-edged plates (fig.2); hybrid shapes known as 'hybrid meshes' are also possible. The various shapes of the facets have different properties, which must be taken into account for specific applications. A general requirement is that the facets must be planar. While this is always the case with three-edged facets, plates with four or more corners are only planar in rare cases. With the help of algorithms, such planar special cases of quad (PQ) and hexagon (P-Hex) meshes can be created, where the algorithm must always be given a certain freedom to deviate slightly from the initial surface shape. Deviations from the structurally optimal shape are typically required to obtain a PQ/P-Hex polygon mesh with planar facets.

Another basic property of the mesh is the valence, which describes how many edges meet at the nodes. This is relevant to the fabrication and the details. Fig.2

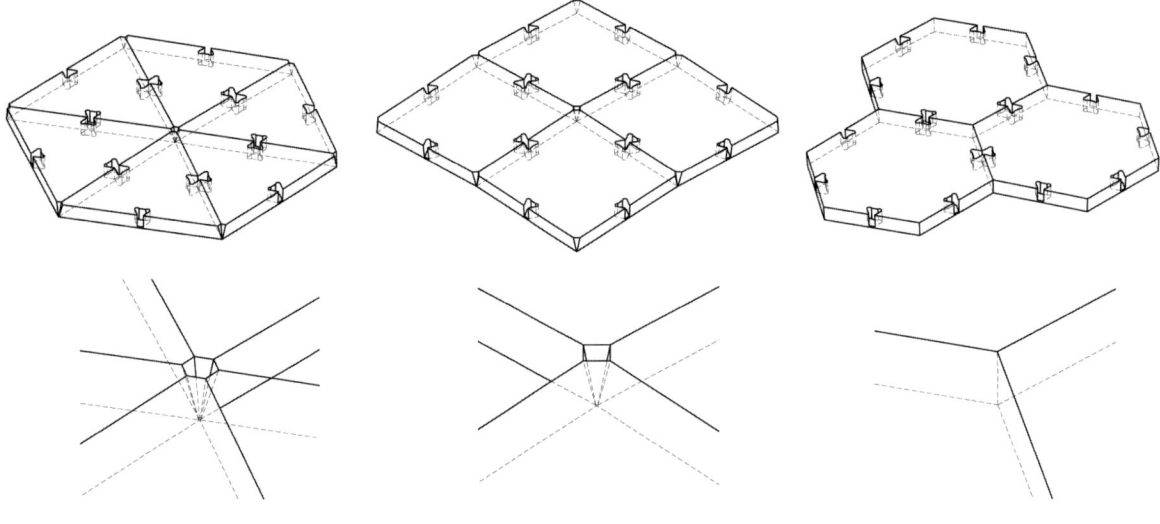

2

shows a comparison of three-, four- and six-edged plates. In this case, the number of edges meeting at the node is indirectly proportional to the number of sides of the components. From a manufacturing point of view, meshes in which a maximum of three edges meet at each node (so-called 'trivalent networks') present advantageous properties. In addition to the favourable structural properties of trivalent networks (Kübler, 2014), it is always possible to construct a mesh offset by the thickness of the CLT plate without errors (fig.2, bottom right). For other meshes, this is only possible in special cases (parallel networks). Nevertheless, even in meshes that are neither trivalent nor parallel, it is still possible to construct a mesh offset by the thickness of the plate. The diagram shows how, in these cases, cone-shaped cut-outs are added at the nodes. On the underside, the surface always remains closed, but, from a building physics point of view, the completely closed knot of the trivalent mesh is ideal. In the case of the cone-shaped cut-outs, the resulting cavity should be filled to avoid condensation.

Apart from design considerations, another aspect in the choice of the facet-shape is its influence on the total edge length. With a constant plate size of 1m², a comparison of the three different facet shapes shows that the total edge length is the lowest for the hexagonal facet-shape. For the four-edged panels, the edges are about 5% longer, while for the three-edged panels they are about 15% longer. This determines the number of connectors required and therefore impacts on production time.

Fabrication and Assembly

The 59 components for the Klagenfurt exhibition stand were cut on a five-axis CNC system with a 9kw spindle. The convex outer shape of all of the components offers a major advantage in production, in that the entire cut of the slightly sloping edges can be made with a saw blade. This is not feasible for components with concave corners on the outer contour, which must instead be cut with the end mill, significantly increasing the time required. The cut-outs for the X-fix connectors were made with a milling cutter in five passes. To prevent the plates from moving as they normally would (vertically to the shell) during assembly of the elements, two recesses for Lamello connectors were milled, per edge, using a hand machine. For this first prototype, the total production time per component was 20 minutes. With a higher spindle power, the number of in-feeds during milling could be reduced, significantly shortening the total production time.

The construction confirmed the main advantage of the Timberdome system principle: within just a few hours, the exhibition stand's 59 components were assembled simply, quickly and precisely. It is particularly important that no costly and time-consuming substructure, which is normally required for freeform panel structures, was required here. The assembly comprised two steps. First, the two prefabricated halves of the shell were assembled using 131 connectors, taking into account the size of the vehicle which would be used to transport them to the site. Then, onsite, the two parts were assembled using 17 additional connectors. Another advantage was the simple and quick disassembly of the construction after the test setup.

2. Comparison of three-edged, four-edged and six-edged plates. Enlargement of the node detail.

3. 59 components fully assembled.

4. Assembly of components during test setup and interior view of construction with birch excellence surface.

Structural Performance

The aim of our structural analysis was to show which spans could be realised with the X-fix Timberdome construction system, considering particularly unfavourable loads under snowy or windy conditions. First, the load assumptions, as well as the static systems used for the calculation, were discussed. The calculations for the spherical shell were carried out on trusses as well as systems with orthotropic plates, taking into account the mechanical compliance of the connections. For our structural analysis with the Finite Elements Software RFEM, we used a dome geometry with a span of 15m, a height of 3m and a surface area of 187m^2. The rise-to-span ratio was 1:5. The uniform curvature of the dome lent itself to homogenous division into regular hexagonal elements. This is important, because the 384 inner edges were each joined with one X-fix C connector. Increasing the number of connectors per edge is only possible in relatively large steps. To avoid weak points in the overall system, we kept the variance of the edge lengths low (Ø 715mm).

For the subdivision of the surface, first we used an algorithm that evenly filled the doubly-curved surface with circles. We chose 1,300mm as the diameter of these circles in order to optimally use the working space of the CNC cutting machine. We then created a polygon mesh based on the centre points of these circles, using the Delaunay triangulation method. This resulted in a network with equilateral triangles. Next, we generated a dual network, in which the centres of the areas in the triangle mesh formed the nodes of the dual network. This created a hybrid, trivalent polygon mesh, with 141 facets and five-, six- and seven-sided shapes.

The most unfavourable load case and the resulting deformations were calculated on the basis of the aforementioned characteristic values. Due to the load applied, the shell indented on the left and bulged out on the right. The small deformations (maximum 4.7mm) suggested there was a high overall stability of the construction system. Long-term deformations, which can arise due to the creep behaviour of wood, as well as yielding in the supports, were not taken into account in this model and require further tests. Likewise, the accuracy of the pressure transmission was limited by the local application of force in the coupling model.

Decisive for the load-bearing capacity of the entire system, however, are primarily the tensile and bending forces on the connectors, which were investigated with the help of the static replacement system. Load-bearing joints between the side faces of CLT plate elements are generally challenging, and due to the many different angles metal plate connectors were not an option either.

Conclusion

The Timberdome system is a new assembly technique for segmental shells, made from CLT. The greatest advantage of the system is its very simple, fast and precise assembly. When constructing the first prototype, two larger components were prefabricated, each with an area of 8m^2, so only a few connectors needed to be joined onsite. No substructure or formwork was needed for the construction. From a design perspective, the system allows for a variety of applications. Openings for lighting and ventilation are easy to implement in the planar plates, in contrast to concrete and brick shells. The desired shell geometry can be subdivided with different facet shapes, e.g. with three-, four- or six-edged plates. Trivalent meshes offer advantages from a structural, manufacturing and building physics perspective. The total edge length is the lowest for six-sided plates, which influences the required number of connectors and the manufacturing cost. Our structural investigations show that, based on the construction system described here and using 100mm-thick spruce wood CLT plates, a self-supporting shell structure with a span of 15m can be realised. CLT is the ideal material with which to produce the structure, which is primarily subjected to pressure. The load capacity of the pressure surfaces is high, and a positive effect on the load-carrying behaviour is that each plate element is connected to adjacent panels on all sides. As a result, the concentric pressures and tension take-up and deformations are reduced. The system's redundancy – such as for the failure of connectors and diverted force transfer – is a topic ripe for future research. Furthermore, based on the test report data, even larger spans than that attained in this project could be achieved through an optimisation of the shell geometry, thicker plates and different plate materials.

5. Geometry of the FEM test dome: span 15m; height 3m; rise-to-span ratio 1: 5; total area 187m^2. Number of plates: 141; Ø plate size: 1.33m^2; inner edges/X-fix connectors: 384; Ø edge length: 715mm.

6. Bending moments at the couplings around the y-axis (kNm).

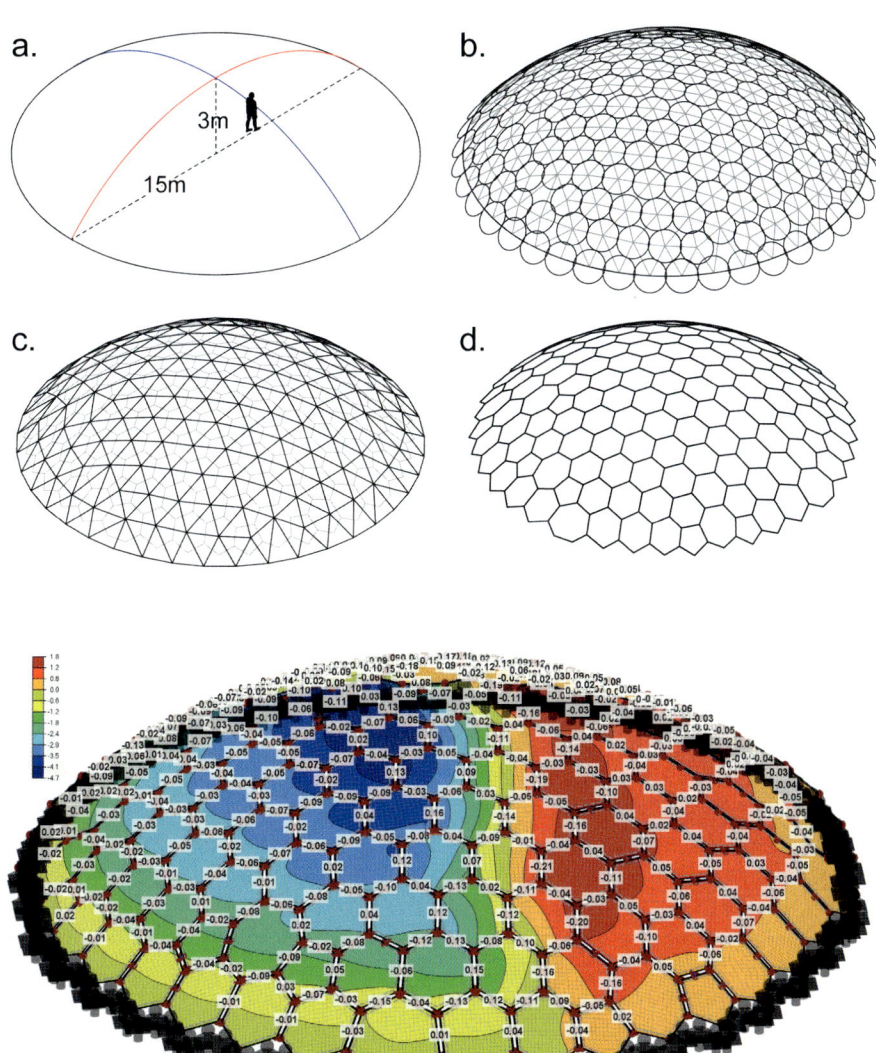

5

6

Acknowledgements

This research was supported by X-Fix GmbH, HOKU OG CNC Fertigung and Hasslacher Norica Timber GmbH.

Bibliography

Bagger, A., 2010, 'Plate Shell Structures of Glass: Studies Leading to Guidelines for Structural Design', Ph.D. Thesis, Technical University of Denmark.

Krieg, O.D., Schwinn, T., Menges, A., Jian-Min, L. and Knippers, J., 2015 'Biomimetic Lightweight Timber Plate Shells' in *Advances in Architectural Geometry 2014* (conference paper), p.109–125. Springer, Cham.

Kübler, W., 2014, 'Das Neue Elefantenhaus im Zoo Zürich' in *Bautechnik*, Vol. 91, No. 1, p.51–57.

Li, J.M. and Knippers, J., 2015, 'Segmental Timber Plate Shell for the Landesgartenschau Exhibition Hall in Schwäbisch Gmünd', in *International Journal of Space Structures*, Vol. 30, No. 2, p.123–139.

Manahl, M. and Wiltsche, A., 2012, '"Kobra" aus Brettsperrholz: Neue Methoden zur Realisierung von Freiformflächen aus ebenen Elementen an Prototyp erprobt', in *Konstruktiv*, Vol. 286, p.26–27.

Robeller, C., Helm, V., Thoma, A., Gramazio, F., Kohler, M. and Weinand, Y., 2017, 'Robotic Integral Attachment', in Menges, A., Sheil, R., Glynn, R., Skavara, M., *FABRICATE: Rethinking Design and Construction*, 2017, London, UCL Press, p.92–97.

Robeller, C., Konaković, M., Dedijer, M., Pauly, M. and Weinand, Y., 2017, 'Double-Layered Timber Plate Shell', in *International Journal of Space Structures*, Vol. 32, No. 3–4, p.160–175.

Scheurer, F., 2008, 'Digitaler Holzbau: Komplexe Geometrien effizient realisiert', in 14 *Internationales Holzbau-Forum*. www.forum-holzbau.com/pdf/ihf08_forum_scheurer_f.pdf (accessed 9 February 2020).

4.6 NOVEL STRATEGIES FOR MATERIALISATION

Robots for Skill Digitisation

Johannes Braumann
Creative Robotics UfG Linz, Robots in Architecture

Robots in Architecture

In the past decade, robotic fabrication has rapidly become a relevant field of research within architecture, and is now increasingly investigated for commercial applications by both innovative startups and established companies. A key step toward that development has been the evolving mindset that logic and algorithms can also constitute design. While high-end architects have been using these strategies for many years, accessible visual programming tools like Generative Components, Explicit History and Grasshopper have opened up parametric and generative design to a much wider range of users. The resulting ecosystem in which developers create plugins and add-ons for these environments has extended the software's scope beyond architecture, e.g. the combination of generative design with robot simulation and code generation has enabled the automated and efficient fabrication of elements with small lot sizes.

Innovation for the Skilled Crafts and Trades

This area of small-scale fabrication with a high degree of customisation was the exclusive domain of the skilled crafts and trades for centuries, but has been increasingly outsourced to low-wage countries in recent years. Robotics are considered a promising industry through which we can bring fabrication back into Europe. This does not necessarily have to mean that architects need to take charge of fabrication, but that crafts and trades have the possibility to innovate and modernise by adapting the architect's computational tools, combining them with their deep knowledge of processes and materials.

However, automation and digitisation have mostly been limited to medium- and large-scale companies, and have been much less relevant to the skilled crafts and trades. Some professions have already entirely disappeared, and traditional knowledge is being lost. The reason for the lack of digitisation is not primarily the cost of hardware, but the need for specialised software to control specified tasks. Cross-disciplinary efforts have also been hindered by the lack of clear task definitions, as skills are mostly passed down orally. We therefore consider digitisation and robotics in combination with accessible software not just as an efficiency-enhancing tool for craftspersons, but also as a way to capture and preserve craft knowledge and cultural heritage.

Previous Research

As part of the AROSU (Artistic Robotic Surface Processing of Stone) research project funded by the European Union – in collaboration with several partner institutions – we have investigated the manual process of stone structuring. As there is hardly any pertinent literature with usable metrics, consortium partner TU Dortmund had to carefully measure the process forces, as well as the spatial movement of the robot (Steinhagen et al., 2016), with high-end measurement equipment. This analysis data was then used to inform the design of customised robotic tools, as well as the robot's parametric toolpath layout, providing a live visualisation of the predicted groove made by the tool, the process time and approximate wear. Grasshopper was chosen as the interface for that project due to its immediate feedback and usability, with our in-house developed software KUKAlprc providing the link to the robot simulation and fabrication, ensuring

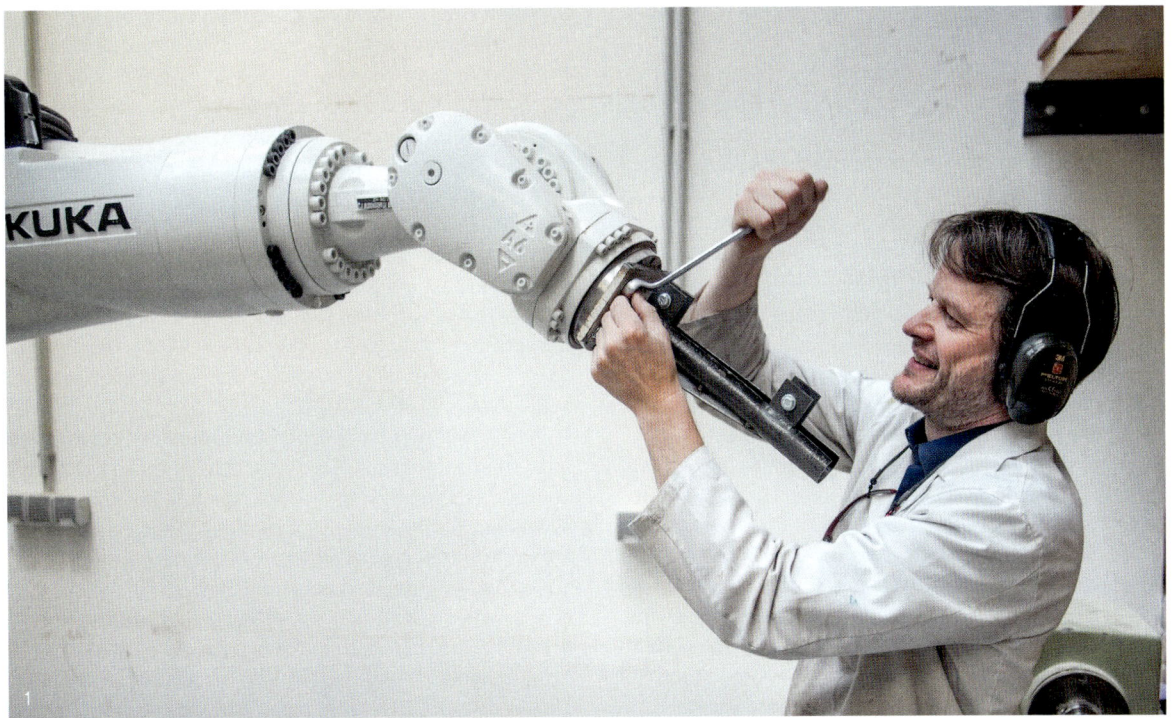

1. Research into robotic craft processes.
Robotic woodcraft.

2. Research into robotic craft processes.
Stone chiselling process analysis.

that the developed process can actually be performed on the physical robot.

Through the Robotic Woodcraft research project (Hornung and Braumann, 2015), we introduced a robotic arm into the previous (mostly manual) carpentry workshop at the University of Applied Arts Vienna. During the three-year project runtime, the robot was used for numerous high-profile projects, both artistic and commercial in scope (figs 1 & 2), educating numerous students in robotic fabrication and enabling them to realise elaborate designs. While the established makers provided crucial feedback, and by the end of the project could advise on reachability and other machinic constraints in robotics projects, the availability of highly skilled computational designers prevented them from actually taking charge of developing their own processes and they remained in project management roles instead.

While both projects achieved their goals and realised a significant knowledge transfer between makers and roboticists, there was still a strong division between the disciplines, with the latter professionals providing tools and interfaces to the makers, which they could then utilise for their own purposes. This process will not change in the immediate future, as it makes sense that people specialising in certain fields can gain a deeper understanding than generalists. It is important, therefore, to provide interfaces with more flexibility and openness, so that the craftspeople cannot only adjust specific parameters but can turn their craft knowledge into code and robotic processes.

An important step in that direction has been the development of accessible parametric programming software over the past ten years, which built upon the Grasshopper visual programming environment, while most other robotics software at the time was either standalone or integrated into Computer Aided Manufacturing (CAM) software. This made it largely application-independent, enabling the user to create toolpaths for milling, 3D printing, weaving, etc. with the same software tool. Today, our software KUKAlprc (Braumann et al., 2011) is used at over a hundred universities as well as by innovative, industry-leading companies internationally, and forms the basis of our research.

We believe that having accessible tools and interfaces is crucial in fostering innovation, and that innovation can best happen from within. In architecture, we are now seeing companies that automate manual technologies, such as ROB Technologies with bricklaying (Bonwetsch et al., 2016); Odico with fabricating formwork (Søndergaard and Feringa, 2016); and mx3D with turning regular welding into an additive construction process. These companies demonstrate that there is demand for such processes, and that smaller companies can have an impact on large fields, such as the construction industry.

While smaller fields like the skilled crafts may not turn over a total volume approaching the trillions of Euros of the construction industry, there is also significantly less competition and small companies can completely revolutionise a field with innovative processes.

Research Environment

The global goal of making robots accessible to the creative industry is pursued by the Association for Robots in Architecture. The goal of the research department Creative Robotics (CR) at UfG Linz in Austria, however, is to have an impact on a regional scale (Braumann et al., 2017).

A key challenge for collaborations between universities and small companies or workshops is to make the initial contact, as only a few small companies actively approach academic institutions with research proposals. The reasons for that are manifold, from concerns regarding costs to preconceptions regarding the actual usability of academic research. Most importantly, they may not even be aware of the potential of technologies such as robotics within their field. For that reason, we are working closely with two local partners. Firstly, the Ars Electronica Center in Linz, Austria, is one of the leading institutions in the field of digital arts, and as the 'museum of the future' is one of the city's main attractions with nearly 200,000 visitors every year. One focus of their work is to make technology and science attractive to young people, while also engaging their parents. There is a CR exhibition every year on the ground floor of the AEC, inviting internationally renowned institutions such as the Institute for Computational Design (ICD) of the University of Stuttgart, the Centre for Information Technology and Architecture (CITA), Individualised Production at RWTH Aachen University, the Institute for Advanced Architecture of Catalonia (IAAC) and others to showcase their work. These exhibitions have often inspired visitors to share their ideas with us on how robots may be used within their own fields.

The second local partner is the Grand Garage – a 3,000m2 'innovation workshop' – funded by the non-profit Future Wings Foundation, recently set up at Tabakfabrik, a creative hub in Linz for startups and creative companies. The Grand Garage is equipped with high-end machinery – including metal and SLS 3D printers, five-axis CNC machines, measuring devices, etc. – for companies that want to perform research and product development without having to purchase those machines, as well as private enthusiasts. As part of a public–private partnership, CR was provided with a large lab-space within the Grand Garage, in exchange for knowledge transfer and inspiration for its robotics lab that is equipped with several KUKA robots.

Through these and other efforts, we have been able to start talks with companies and individuals who would otherwise not have approached a research institution and have realised a number of prototypical projects, described in the following case studies. These range from small but innovative craft businesses that create high-end products for end-customers, to a small enterprise that is among just a few companies worldwide capable of performing high-accuracy polishing for the automotive industry. Finally, we explore an experimental, non-commercial project that 1:1 matches motion-captured movement to a robot.

Case Study: Saddle Building

Niedersüß is one of the last saddle-making companies in Austria. A small company of around 25 employees, it ships most of its high-quality products to international customers, but also supplies well-known national institutions like the Spanish Riding School in Vienna. Niedersüß approached us with the idea of investigating the potential for digitalisation and automation, as qualified staff were increasingly hard to find, especially when their tasks included repetitive and injury-prone work. As part of a preliminary study, we analysed their internal production workflows regarding the potential of digitisation and robotics (fig.3).

After collecting data onsite, we came to the conclusion that machines could be used for several purposes, from the CNC fabrication of the saddle core to the trimming of foam and leather-cutting. While machines can increase productivity, customers do, however, prefer a handmade leather finish on their saddles; machine-made products are perceived to have less worth and would consequently be lower in cost. The production would not, however, increase significantly as only so many saddles can be finished by the makers once the cores are milled by a machine. At the same time, automating the entire workflow does not align with the goals and image of the company.

Niedersüß consequently decided to invest in robotic arms rather than a CNC machine, as these provided them with the flexibility to introduce a single new and affordable machine to the saddle-making process that is not limited to a single part of the workflow. Just by changing the robot's tools, it can perform 3D milling with a spindle one day and cut leather with an ultrasonic cutter the next. Introducing such a setup would usually require them to hire a robot integrator for configuring the machine, and possibly a software company to create the software, but they were able to set up a used 150kg

3. Initial workflow analysis for saddle-making (left), customised saddle core, robotically milled out of an offset model to enable individualisation (right).

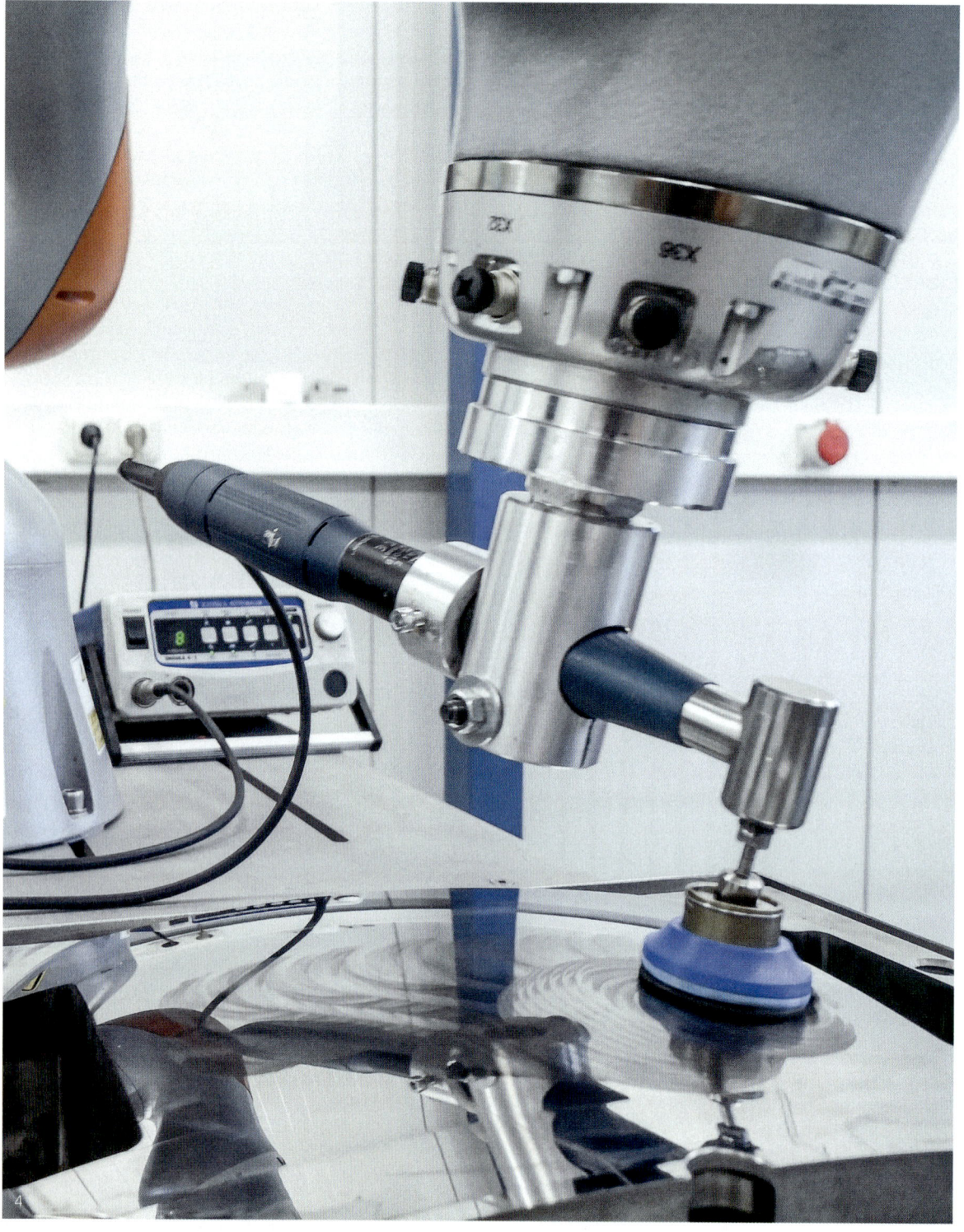

4. Custom-developed metal polishing process using a collaborative robot.

payload robot by themselves and control its processes using Grasshopper and KUKA|prc. By limiting the initial investment, they do not have to decide between machinic and manual labour but can gradually introduce the robot and continually educate their staff so that more repetitive processes may eventually be taken over.

As part of this research project, we developed an initial, parametric model of the saddle-code geometry, making it possible to adjust it according to the individual requirements of the rider and animal. Previously, an aluminium mould had to be fabricated for every saddle, limited to just a few pre-set sizes, similar to the commercial fashion industry. Now, a standard offset model is cast in PU foam using an in-house foaming machine, so that the robot does not need to cut the model out of a single block of foam but instead removes only a few centimetres of material.

Case Study: Metal Polishing Using a Collaborative Robot

A limitation of most current industrial robots is that they do not have a 'soft touch', and instead move to their programmed position without any regard to external forces. While this is a desired behaviour for many robotic applications, it also limits their applicability for processes that involve material tolerances or soft materials. Force-torque sensors can be added to these machines, but they are comparably hard to integrate as their output needs to be calibrated, filtered and processed in order to be usable. With the LBR iiwa, KUKA developed a robot with integrated torque sensors in each axis. These sensors were primarily put there to make the robot safe to work around, as it would feel resistance not just at the flange but at all robotic joints, and be able to react to those stimuli.

We were approached by a surface-finishing company in Upper Austria that polishes CNC-milled metal parts for the automotive industry to micrometre smoothness. To do so, a polishing tool needs to be moved with a constant force in a regular way, so that material is removed evenly. Each polishing extends over many passes, which have to be different from each other so that no discernible polishing pattern emerges. Due to this high degree of complexity that cannot easily be performed by standard CNC machines and CAM software, the company has so far used machines only for measuring, not for the polishing process itself.

While the process of using a robotic arm for polishing is well documented in literature (e.g. Tam et al., 1999) and actively used in industry, existing ready-to-use applications did not fulfil the requirements of the company, as it wanted to directly replicate the existing proven process without having to acquire new tools, workflows and chemicals (fig.4).

A large order by an automotive customer had the company approach us to look into developing a polishing process for a freeformed surface, within a compact timeframe of a few months. As such, we decided that the time would not be sufficient to integrate force sensor in a reliable manner. Instead, we looked to the LBR iiwa as a platform with the necessary force sensitivity already embedded within its software and hardware. Due to this integration, we were able to rapidly deploy a prototype with a robot-mounted manual tool and a constant control force applied in negative Z (vertical) direction. Thanks to the iiwa's ease of use, the main challenge was, therefore, not so much in the hardware as in the software. We had to identify an ideally low number of parameters for the path planning that would change the process in a meaningful way, while ensuring that each part could be fabricated. Ultimately, just the polishing direction and three parameters affecting the layout of the spiralling toolpath were chosen. A particular challenge was the handling of the edge condition, where we had to find a way for the tool to remain on top of the polished surface – as the control force would otherwise cause it to drop – while keeping the spiralling path as even as possible.

Initial testing showed that the LBR iiwa was only able to blend motions with a point distance of 4mm or more, so that very dense toolpaths caused the robot to stutter and move in a non-regular and non-repetitive way. We were able to solve that by splitting the spiral toolpath into a much smaller series of circular movements. Interestingly, the total size of the XML file generated by KUKA|prc did not seem to have a measurable impact on the robot's performance – only local density proved to be problematic.

The company has since integrated the robot into its workflow, having it mostly process regular freeform surfaces, so that its workers can focus on complex surfaces where the effort of programming and testing would exceed the benefit of the machine. As an added benefit, the collaborative LBR iiwa robot also allows the company to reduce the complexity of the safety installation, offsetting its higher price compared to other machines.

Case Study: Direct Skill Transfer

The Direct Skill Transfer project differs from the other case studies in that it is not a commercial research project but constitutes art-based research in collaboration with the Ars Electronica FutureLab. As part of the permanent exhibition at the Ars Electronica Center, the exhibition concept planned for a robot installation playing a marionette (figs 5 & 6). In practice, that proved to be a significant challenge, as robots are usually programmed in relation to geometric space and speed but never to time. A robot may move to a position with a programmed speed, and it may move synchronously to another machine, but we cannot programme it to be at a given position at a given timestamp. As the programme again had a very compact

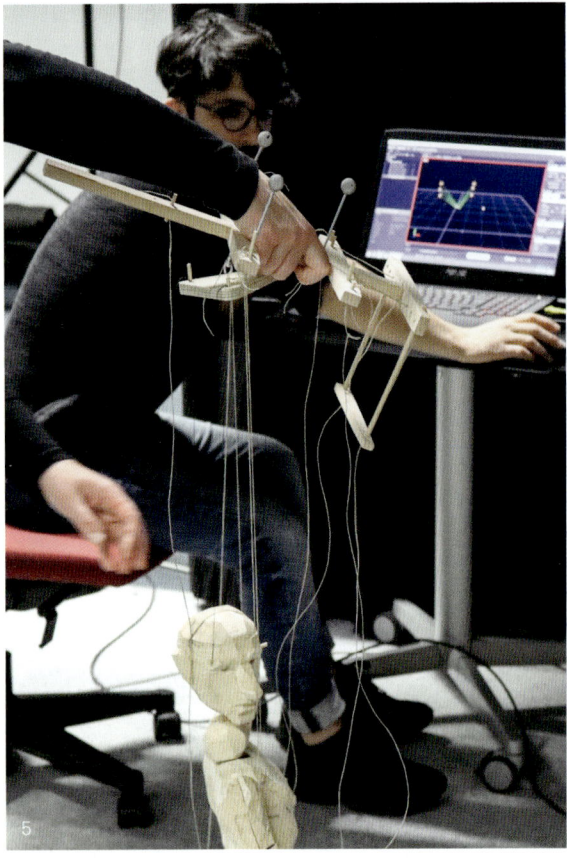

timeframe of two months, we decided to directly capture the performance of a professional puppeteer and transfer it to the robot. Using an in-house OptiTrack motion capture system, three markers were placed on the puppet's cross-bar, generating a text file that consisted of each marker's position in 3D space, as well as the precise timestamp when that position was captured. We then interpolated the data to receive one position every millisecond, rather than at the tracking system's 100Hz. Using KUKAlprc, the robot and toolpath were placed on the virtual stage and, using its inverse kinematics solver, we calculated the axis position for each millisecond and wrote it into a file.

On the robot, we installed the KUKA.RSI (Realtime Sensor Interface) that provides low-level access to the controller, requiring an offset position at the cycle time of four milliseconds. Reliably sending a data package every few milliseconds cannot be achieved with a regular Windows PC, so we programmed a Beckhoff PLC to read the previously-generated file and stream it with perfect timing to the robot, which would then duplicate the puppeteer's movement. As there are few professional puppeteers practising these days, we do not consider this process to be replacing them but rather to be making the craft more readily available to the public.

5 & 6. Direct skill transfer: From motion capture (left), to final installation at Ars Electronica Center (right).

Conclusion: Skill Digitisation

Based on our experience with these and other projects, we see three steps in regards to skill digitisation from human to machine:

- Imitation
- Augmentation
- Autonomy

Industrial applications usually focus on imitation, where we take a given process and try to perform it with a robot rather than a person. While some processes are easy to imitate, other crafts such as puppeteering are much more difficult.

Our main interest lies in the second step, augmentation, where we look into the value that a machine can contribute to a process that goes beyond what is possible on a human scale. For example, with the AROSU project we were able to generate non-regular chiselling patterns, while for the saddle project we enabled highly customisable saddle cores at nearly the same efficiency as identical cores.

The third step, autonomy, is significantly harder to achieve as it requires the machine to learn and improve by itself. While machine learning is making huge strides at the moment, the main challenge is the quality of data required by the machine, e.g. the exact force of the chiselling movement or the 3D data of the impact, and processing that large amount of data in a meaningful way. As such, the greatest potential in developing 'augmentation' processes is to not just duplicate manual labour but find alternative ways to offer new products through machinic processes. To enable even better customisation, we are working on new software solutions that enable a direct and safe streaming of complex toolpaths to the robot, as well as porting to new platforms, from Autodesk Dynamo to The Cloud, where it can be integrated into innovative workflows that directly link the customer's input parameters with robotic fabrication.

It is hoped that robots combined with accessible software interfaces can have a similar impact within the skilled crafts and trades as it has had within architecture, leading to innovations that benefit the entire community of users, from architects to craftspeople and beyond.

Acknowledgements

The research was conducted in collaboration with multiple partners and institutions. The AROSU consortium consisted of Bamberger Natursteinwerke, Klero Automation, TU Dortmund, Labor, Gibson Tools, and Robots in Architecture. Contributors to the saddle project were Sander Hofstee and Benjamin Greimel, with Maria Smigielska contributing to the metal polishing case study. The DST project team consisted of Amir Bastan and the author from Creative Robotics, Peter Freudling, Stefan Mittelböck, and Erwin Reitböck from the FutureLab, and Katharina Halus as puppeteer. We are grateful for the support of KUKA Robotics and Beckhoff Automation.

Bibliography

Bonwetsch, T., Willmann, J., Gramazio, F. and Kohler, M., 2016, 'Robotic Brickwork: Towards a New Paradigm of the Automatic', in Worre Foged, I. (ed.) 2016, *Bricks / Systems*, Aalborg, Aalborg University Press.

Braumann, J. and Brell-Cokcan, S., 2011, 'Parametric Robot Control: Integrated CAD/CAM for Architectural Design', *Proceedings of ACADIA 2011 Conference*, Banff.

Braumann, J., Brell-Cokcan, S. and Stumm, S., 2017, 'Accessible Robotics', in Daas, M and Witt, A (eds.) 2017, *Towards a Robotic Architecture*, Novato CA, ORO Editions.

Hornung, P. and Braumann, J., 2015, 'Robotic Woodcraft', *Proceedings of eCAADe 2015*, Vienna.

Steinhagen, G., Braumann, J., Brüninghaus, J., Neuhaus, M., Brell-Cokcan, S. and Kuhlenkötter, B., 2016, 'Path Planning for Robotic Artistic Stone Surface Production', RobIArch 2016: *Robotic Fabrication in Architecture, Art and Design*, Sydney. doi: 10.1007/978-3-319-26378-6_9

Søndergaard, A. and Feringa, J., 2016, 'Robotic Hot-Blade Cutting', RobIArch 2016: *Hobotic Fabrication in Architecture, Art and Design*, Sydney. doi: 10.1007/978-3-319-26378-6_11

Tam, H., Chi-hang Lui, O. and C.K. Mok, A., 1999, 'Robotic Polishing of Free-form Surfaces using Scanning Paths', *Journal of Materials Processing Technology*, 95, p.191–200.

NOVEL STRATEGIES FOR MATERIALISATION

Research Summary
Building with Earth and Drones

Stephanie Chaltiel
Industrial Partners: Cloud 9, Rippmann Oesterle Knauss GmbH
Academic Institution: Institute for Advanced Architecture of Catalonia (IAAC),
Universitat Politècnica de Catalunya

Bioshotcrete is a new technology based on drone-spraying clay mixes onto light formworks, enabling the development of onsite fabrication protocols at large scale. Bioshotcrete is being developed through the Innochain network by Stephanie Chaltiel and a multidisciplinary team of architects, engineers and drone experts to offer highly sustainable and affordable architectural envelopes at the intersection between shotcrete, wattle and daub. The drone spray eases the deposition of mortars in high or difficult-to-coat areas – including extreme geographies such as cliffs – without the need for labour-intensive, bespoke scaffoldings. An embedded Artificial Intelligence system – already being developed by machine learning experts – controls crack recognition, temperature mapping, variable thickness and, also, automated flights. It is predicted that such techniques will, in the future, support the development of affordable, bespoke architectural possibilities. Furthermore, the unique ergonomics of the custom-made Bioshotcrete drone fitted with an adjusted Euromair pump and nozzles enable carefully formulated raw material mixes to be sprayed, following a precise sequence of deposition whereby each mortar and drying time needs to be respected to achieve viable structures.

Several projects were designed and constructed as prototypes at pavilion scale, investigating, in great detail, 'mud shells' or freeform, self-standing, compression-only vault structures and the techniques required to implement drone-spraying construction protocols. As a continuation of the initial prototypes, research and physical tests are being undertaken to help improve existing façade refurbishments, providing drone-spraying of both wet and dry matter, and using local raw materials to provide high-inertia insulation and affordable finishings.

Key developments in Bioshotcrete were made through

1. Jute bags filled with straw are arranged in a geodesic dome to be drone-sprayed with sustainable mortars at a later stage. Mud Shell project, London Design Festival 2018.

2. 'Future Earthen Dwellers' workshop (2019) at Domeaine du Boisbuchet, where the drone spray technique was first implemented in a built project.

the construction of five built prototypes, ranging from 2 to 5m high. An initial test was undertaken at the Barcelona Drone Center, where a large inflatable dome was coated and cured until sufficient compression strength had been reached for the temporary inflatable to be removed. A DIY sprayer was fabricated for this incipient test, in which the drone performed various trips.

The mud shells – built in France, Denmark and the UK – were subsequently shaped according to the Drone Center's findings. The technique started to be viable when the drone was adapted to be fitted with a Euromair spraying pump-hose that allowed a strong and constant flow of material to be projected onto the light formworks. Furthermore, the 2018 mud shell projects (Domaine de Boisbuchet, London Design Festival and KADK interior 5m wall) featured prefabricated, light, dry modules arranged and fitted onto a prefabricated geodesic frame, to be drone sprayed with a smooth mortar at a later stage.

Such manufacturing strategies were designed to achieve very high inertia and indoor comfort using light straw modules – jute bags of 15cm x 20cm, filled with straw cut at 3cm long – that can be carried and fitted by one person. Blockage in the spraying phase was avoided by formulating mixes that contained only fine grains of clay and sand and thin linen fibres, which break in the spraying pump after five minutes of stirring time. The mud shells perform very well in terms of sound and wind protection. Precise numbers in such performances are being mapped and archived for future improvements, with potential for the drone spray to achieve constant uniform coatings without blockages.

These positive emergent aspects have shaped recent developments in the construction of large housing prototypes of 8m high – designed and engineered with CanyaViva, AKT II and Summum Engineering (Salone del Mobile Milano, 2019) – and also refurbishments of existing façades, where dry matter can be drone-sprayed onto wet coatings for good adhesion. This approach lends itself to fabrication of envelope insulation that does not rely on labour-intensive prefabricated panels. Tested at a height of up to 30m in the drone-spray phase, such protocols mark a turning point in the shotcrete industry and its use of sustainable, unbaked materials in dense urban centres.

NOVEL STRATEGIES FOR MATERIALISATION

Research Summary
Information Modelling for Assembly Planning, Sequencing and Optimisation

Ayoub Lharchi

Industrial Partners: Blumer Lehmann AG, Design-to-Production GmbH
Academic Institution: Centre for Information Technology and Architecture (CITA), the Royal Danish Academy of Fine Arts, Schools of Architecture, Design and Conservation

While digital tools support architects, engineers and constructors in almost all aspects of design and manufacturing, their role in planning and design for the assembly of buildings remains an unexplored area. This ongoing research aims to bridge this gap by developing a general framework for the design and planning of assembly sequences within the architectural realm. Specifically, the project focuses on timber construction and aims to lay the foundations of a novel computational approach to Design for Assembly (DfA). The approach would facilitate assembly decisions in the early design phases using integrated digital assembly models.

As a first step, this project analysed existing DfA principles in other disciplines, such as mechanical engineering and product design, and speculated on their translation to an architectural scale. By combining computer-science techniques and design practices from other disciplines, it proposed scheme through which professionals can describe, analyse and communicate assembly information. A set of computational methods and tools then provided a complete simulation of the assembly procedure and Assisted Assembly Planning (AAP) workflows, which detect any problems or clashes.

The project was carried out in close collaboration with two industrial partners with significant expertise in architectural practice, structural engineering and industrial timber manufacturing: Design-to-Production (D2P) – a design consulting firm with extensive experience in complex timber projects, which was able to contextualise the research methods and identify real-case challenges within the timber industry – and Blumer Lehmann, a manufacturer specialised in timber construction, which brought in-depth material and fabrication insights to the project and is embedding the outputs into existing real-world projects.

The expected outcomes of this work are already beginning to bear fruit. For example, it will make a contribution to considerations of assembly in architectural design and how it can be enabled in the early phases and translated into a set of recommendations and guidelines for DfA in an architectural context. Furthermore, it presents a novel approach to information modelling, in which assembly takes a central role along with other traditional embedded data. This approach has led to the development of a general framework and digital model specifications. The framework, entitled 'Assembly Information Modelling', is implemented as a central digital model containing the architectural design of the structure, construction details, 3D representations, assembly sequences, issues management and other necessary data for a seamless procedure.

The research is investigating several applications, in various fields, to demonstrate the potential of the proposed approach: first, augmented assembly – leveraging augmented reality devices to assist the user during the assembly procedure; second, automatic robotic assembly, whereby the assembly model is stretched to expand its capacity to new applications, such as industrial robots for digital fabrication; third, collaborative assembly design, whereby cloud-AEC platforms are used to provide a common working platform; and, finally, machine learning for assembly sequence optimisation.

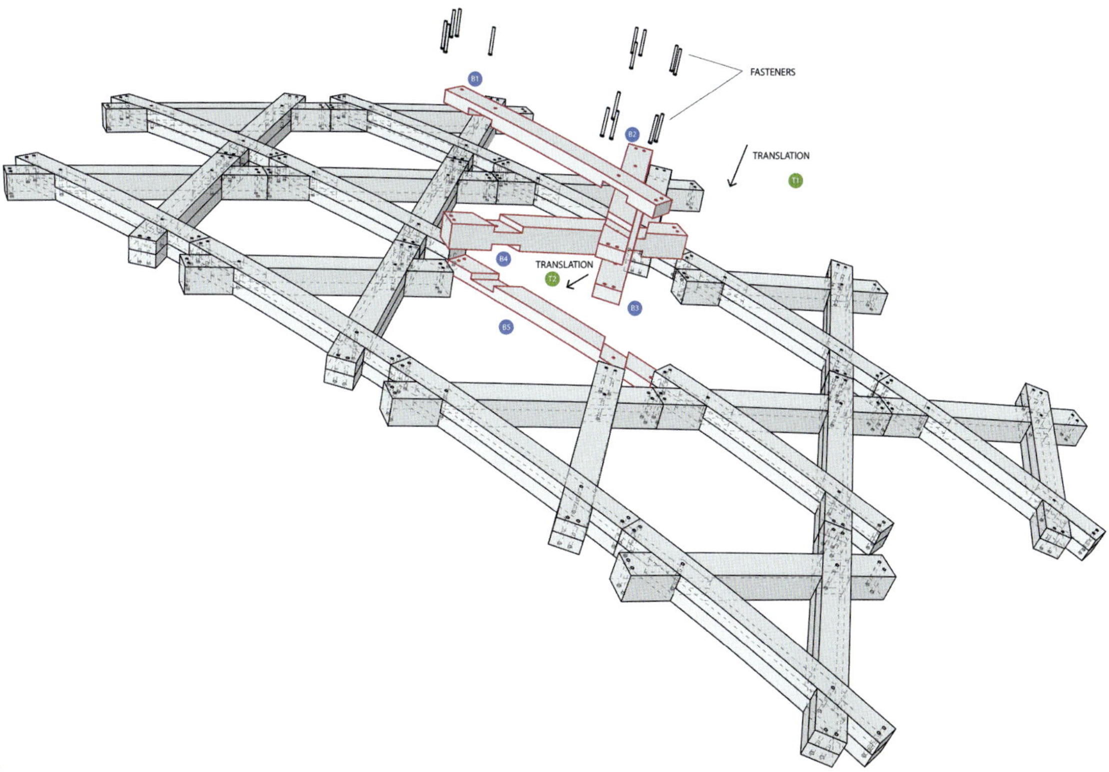

1. The model is enriched with assembly instructions and sequencing.

2. Assembly Information Modelling (AIM) enables the assisted assembly of complex structures without previous training.

NOVEL STRATEGIES FOR MATERIALISATION

Research Summary
Digital Clay: Hybrid Manufacturing for Automotive Design

Arthur Prior
Industrial Partner: Foster + Partners
Academic Institution: The Bartlett School of Architecture, UCL

Clay modelling plays a crucial role in automotive design. It is widely acknowledged that physical sculpting results in high-quality surfaces that the end-user can see and touch. Horizontal arm-milling machines are standard throughout the industry for transferring CAD data onto clay models. To date, however, clay application remains an entirely manual process.

- During model preparation, 750–900l of heated clay is applied manually to a Styrofoam armature.
- This physically demanding and repetitive process takes up to 120 hours, during which employers must balance productivity with Occupational Safety and Health (OSH) compliance, such as assessment of repetitive tasks, manual-handling operation regulations, and so on.
- Overcompensation occurs when trying to judge the correct thickness of clay to apply, resulting in 15% material waste after models are milled-out. Ford is the only automaker known to recycle clay (10% annually).
- Model production hinders time to market. Vehicle styling takes a minimum of 12 months before 'design freeze' is reached – for example, designers spent 20,000 hours modelling the Ford F-150 Raptor.

There are over 200 design studios internationally: 48% in Europe, 34% in Asia, 15% in North America and 2% in South America. Studios are particularly concentrated in areas such as Bavaria, Baden-Württemberg, California, Coventry, Turin and Shanghai. These studios consume a lot of clay: 90,700kg per year at the Ford Product Development Center in Dearborn (United States) and 80,000kg per year at the Mercedes Benz Advanced Design Studio in Sindelfingen (Germany). Collectively, the industry uses 3,000 tonnes of clay per year, which is enough to create 2,400 models.

In this context, the potential for efficiency gains is significant. Seeking alternatives, automakers began investing in CGI and VR/AR/MR technologies from the 1990s.[1] Despite major advances, car designers have remained faithful to clay. Life-sized models are considered the most direct way of communicating design information. However, while automakers are increasingly incorporating Additive Manufacturing (AM) into design workflows, conventional additive materials (e.g. photopolymers) cannot be reshaped retrospectively, making design changes less direct and spontaneous compared to clay. The use of AM is generally limited to small-scale interior components (such as air-conditioning vents and door handles). Modelling clays have not been considered in the context of AM before.

There are currently no solutions in the marketplace for applying clay automatically. This three-year project responded to this need by developing a solution that allows modelling clays to be used for additive manufacturing. Liquid Deposition Modelling (LDM) technology exploits the phase-change properties of modelling clays, allowing complex freeform surfaces to be printed quickly and efficiently, layer by layer. This offers a pragmatic way for designers to both utilise AM and retain the time-proven benefits of clay modelling. This approach:

- Provides a solution for automatically applying clay quickly and accurately.
- Makes 'lights-out' (overnight) production possible by reducing time to market.
- Provides a way for employers to avoid manual-handling operations that involve a risk of injury.

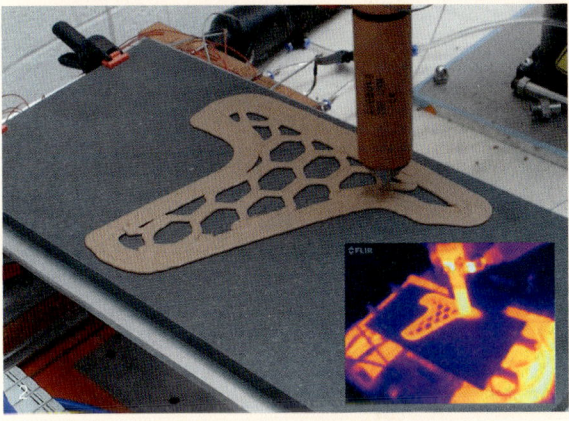

- Reduces material waste from >15% to 5%.
- Promotes the continued role of physical sculpting in automotive design.
- Interfaces with existing downstream workflows and studio equipment (e.g. milling).
- Enables design studios to further extend their engagement with digital manufacturing.

This innovation has so far been demonstrated via a small-scale proof-of-concept machine (Technology Readiness Level 3, as per European Commission definition). A new project is currently under way in Germany to develop this technology for full-sized vehicle prototyping in a studio environment.

Note

1. CGI: computer-generated imagery
VR: virtual reality
AR: augmented reality
MR: mixed reality

1. Liquid deposition modelling.

2. Thermal imaging study.

3. 3D printed clay prototype: automotive interior part.

NOVEL STRATEGIES FOR MATERIALISATION

Research Summary
Flectofold: From Academic Research to Architectural Application

Saman Saffarian
Industrial Partners: str.ucture GmbH, S-Form GmbH
Academic Institution: Institute of Building Structures and Structural Design (ITKE) at the University of Stuttgart

The aim of this project was to devise a lightweight, energy-conscious, materially intelligent and economically feasible solution for climate-adaptive building envelopes. These aspirations materialised in the form of a bionic (bio-inspired) product called Flectofold, which is a modular shading system capable of controlling the penetration rate of solar radiation through the building envelope. Each Flectofold module covers an area of approximately 1m^2 and has an integrated pneumatic cushion. Once pressurised, the cushion induces elastic bending onto the body of the materially-graduated Fibre-Reinforced-Polymer (FRP) laminate and, as a result, generates movement and transformation. Flectofold is economical in terms of fabrication and transportation, thanks to its modularity and its capability to be flat-packed. It is also lightweight and materially intelligent, thanks to its tailored and graduated FRP composition, and is efficient in terms of maintenance, due to its reliance on material compliance rather than mechanical hinges. In terms of operation, it is energy-efficient, thanks to the low air pressure (approximately 0.04–0.06 bar) required, and due to its capacity to store the potential elastic energy during actuation (opening) and harvest it during deflation (closing).

Research Methods

The initial concept of the Flectofold module was created by a large collaborative team of researchers, and resulted in a proof-of-concept prototype (Körner et al., 2018). The Flectofold module was further developed into two consecutive full-scale demonstrators that integrated all technologies into an architecturally detailed solution (Saffarian et al., 2019). This was crucial, not only for scientific assessment of the system in research contexts, but also for eventual implementation in the building and construction industry.

Three parallel strands of development were needed to move from the successful concept to a credible building-scale demonstrator piece: 1. Development of the Flectofold laminates through a precise investigation of fibre deployment (lay-up) strategies, and constant monitoring of the resulting kinetic performance. This strand aimed to increase scale and movement efficiency, optimise cyclic performance and reduce material fatigue; 2. Development of a suitable support system to secure the correct alignment of Flectofold modules with the underlying guiding geometry, incorporating a tilting mechanism to adjust the axial rotation of individual modules for optimal and symmetrical surface coverage, and to implement a pneumatic tubing-management system to enhance the clarity of systematic assembly and maintenance; 3. Development of a fully controllable pneumatic actuation system, capable of driving each module in an individual or synchronised fashion, based on active user input or pre-programmed responses to sensory data. This strand required careful design and implementation of both hardware (pneumatic and electronic circuits) and software (web-based user-interface and autonomous mediation of sensory data).

Research Partners

A large group of industry and academic partners contributed to the development of this project. Most notably, the successful implementation of the materially-graduated lamination process was achieved through an active collaboration with the Institute for Textile and Fiber Technologies (ITFT) at the University of Stuttgart

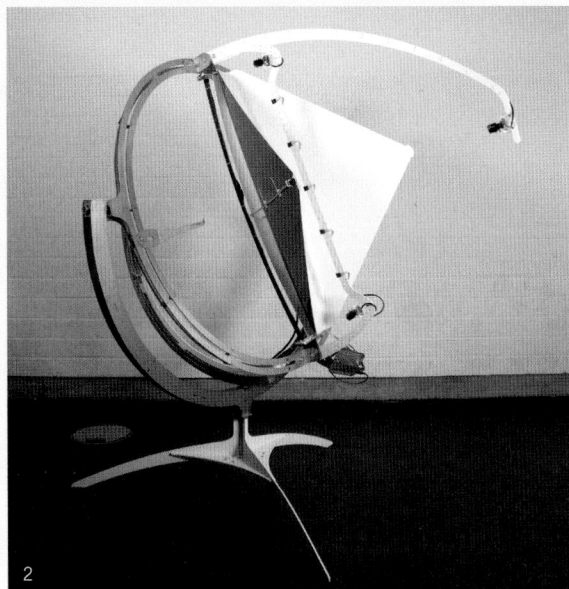

1. Flectofold Demonstrator I at *Baubionik: biologie beflügelt architektur* exhibition, Natural History Museum, Stuttgart, 2017.

2. Flectofold kinetic performance monitoring device at *Practice Futures: Building Design for a New Material Age* exhibition, KADK, Copenhagen, 2018.

and a mutually beneficial partnership with C-Con. The pneumatic actuation and control system evolved over the course of the project into an advanced solution through an iterative prototyping process, in close collaboration with the Institute for Control Engineering of Machine Tools and Manufacturing Units (ISW) of the University of Stuttgart. The development of the substructure required the active engagement of local steel manufacturers Roleff GmbH and Grözinger GmbH, alongside engineering colleagues at the Institute of Building Structures and Structural Design (ITKE).

Research Outcomes and Applications

During the course of the project, many proof-of-concept prototypes, probes and assemblies were designed and manufactured. Most of these were produced to inform consequent development steps and to propel the research forward. Interim (milestone) results were showcased at various events, among which the following two exhibitions stand out: *Baubionik – Biologie Beflügelt Architektur* at the Natural History Museum, Stuttgart – which presented the technology to the public, using the demonstrator as a testing ground for monitoring and assessment of the long-term kinetic performance of individual modules – and *Practice Futures: Building Design for a New Material Age* at The Royal Danish Academy of Fine Arts, Copenhagen. This latter event exhibited a revised version of the Flectofold demonstrator as a full-scale architectural mockup, together with an enhanced kinetic performance-monitoring device that collected in-depth motion-tracking data, using multiple sensors and cameras, on the kinetic performance of a single Flectofold module over the course of the exhibition. The collected data will be utilised to enhance the design and inform the materialisation strategy of the next generation of materially-graduated FRP laminates for elastic-kinetic modules on climate-adaptive building envelopes in the near future.

Bibliography

Körner, A., Born, L., Mader, A., Sachse, R., Saffarian, S., Westermeier, A., Poppinga, S., Bischoff, M., Gresser, G.T., Milwich, M., Speck, T. and Knippers, J., 2017, 'Flectofold: A Biomimetic Compliant Shading Device for Complex Free Form Facades' in *Smart Materials and Structures*, Vol. 27, No. 1, p.42–51.

Saffarian, S., Born, L., Korner, A., Mader, A., Westermeier, A., Poppinga, S., Milwich, M., Gresser, G.T., Speck, T. and Knippers, J., 2019, 'From Pure Research to Biomimetic Products: The Flectofold Facade Shading Device', in Knippers, J., Schmid, U. and Speck, T. (eds.), 2019, *Biomimetics for Architecture: Learning from Nature* (first edition), Basel, Birkhauser Verlag GmbH, p.42–51.

NOVEL STRATEGIES FOR MATERIALISATION

Research Summary
Concrete Deposition: Choreographing Flow

Helena Westerlind
Industrial Partner: White Arkitekter AB
Academic Institution: Royal Institute of Technology (KTH), Stockholm

This project investigates how additive manufacturing, supported by digital workflows, can inform new material strategies for concrete in architecture. The additive process is explored to develop concrete as a medium that *performs*, as opposed to merely reproducing form. For this purpose, concrete deposition signifies a fundamental departure from formwork-based techniques. The formal articulation of concrete-flow is no longer shaped by the constraint and control imposed by a static mould, but by the programmable motion performed by a numerically-controlled machine, turning lines into material traces. Similar to weaving, lines come together to form a surface, and, in the notation of architecture, the role of the line shifts from representing the perimeter of form to constituting the path along which the material preforms. Beyond the mere stacking of material, this project asks how the controlled interweaving of lines can be programmed to introduce structure and variation into a previously uniform and monolithic material.

In extrusion-based additive manufacturing, an object is typically materialised through the incremental stacking of contour lines in which the notion of 'resolution' serves as a quantitative measure of the level of detail to which the physical object corresponds to its digital counterpart. When the additive process is scaled up, the layered structure becomes an increasingly visible feature of the surface quality of the finished object as the level of resolution typically associated with so-called 3D printing is not achievable within a realistic timeframe. Therefore, instead of the simple stacking of contour lines, this project set out to expand the tectonic potential of the additive process by investigating the relationship between the local geometry of the line itself and the effects of aggregation.

The project began with studying the correlation between robotic motion and material behaviour. Formal features, such as overhang and bridging, were tested in relation to the rheological properties of various concrete mixes. The project then focused on incorporating these findings into the numerical control of continuous depositions of material. By exploring variable stacked configurations of selected line types (oscillating, looped, alternating loop), motion patterns were developed that presented new means of controlling the density, porosity and surface articulation of the material. The ability to further control the parameters of the line in terms of frequency and amplitude made it possible to locally adapt patterns according to specific requirements. After having shown the feasibility of the approach, the project moved on to expand the selection of possible line types by weaving new lines from control points. In addition to the standard subdivision of a surface geometry into contour lines, a further discretisation of the line introduced a finite set of derivatives defined for each constituent control point. From this set of points, a numerical sequence was used to reconfigure the line in an automated process that generated 6561 new line types from the same set of points.

The approach developed within this project demonstrates the need to re-evaluate the norms and conceptions that so far have defined concrete as a primarily monolithic material. By choreographing the path of deposition, variable material structures can be achieved, combining architectural qualities with advanced material performance.

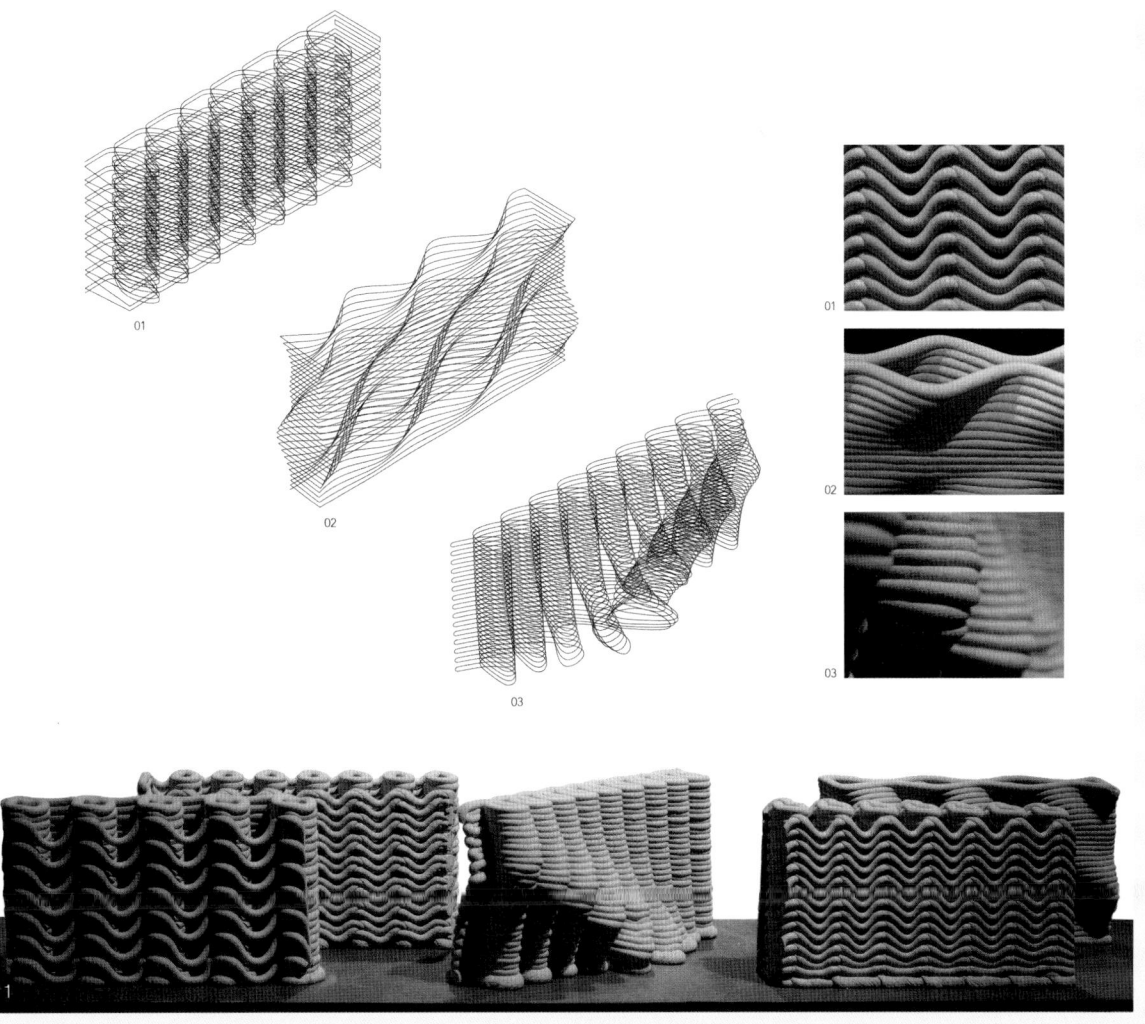

1. Generated toolpaths and resulting surface qualities. Made in collaboration with José Hernández and prototypes manufactured by XtreeE, Paris.

NOVEL STRATEGIES FOR MATERIALISATION

Further Perspectives
Performative Materials and Systems, and Additive Manufacturing Futures

Johannes Braumann
Creative Robotics UfG Linz, Robots in Architecture
Isak Worre Foged
Aalborg University

Materials

All materials perform. The level of performance is tied to objectives, processing systems and context. Water can be a fluid thermal reservoir at 15°C; a gas-like cooler at 40°C; or a solid casting block at -5°C. When subjected to environmental changes, the material undergoes a transformation of properties, which fundamentally alters its capacity to perform.

Clay, meanwhile, is a natural material found a few metres below ground. As a raw material it costs little to extract and, therefore, is economically performative. Clay is formed into bricks, fired at around 1,000°C to create a structural element with high compressive strength, thermal capacity, ability to sustain weathering and an articulated colouration. The firing process has a high-energy cost that, from a material-processing perspective, renders clay bricks a low performance material. Bricks are transported to a construction site and there they find their final position in the brickwork. The heavy weight of bricks – at 2,100kg/m³ – produces a high transport-energy cost, which equates to poor material performance compared to lighter materials. This aspect is, of course, related to the distance between raw-clay site, brickyard and construction site, which then adds a material's origin into the equation of its performance. Following construction, fired-clay brick buildings stand for centuries, if not millennia, significantly reducing the embodied annual energy cost of firing and transport, and alleviating the total material energy performance of such buildings. Depending on the brickwork design and constellation with other materials, clay bricks embody thermal and humidity-regulating capacities, visual and tactile qualities and extraordinary possibilities for design articulation, creating

1. Computer-generated map of historic brickyards in Denmark. Each dot represents a registered brickyard. Thin lines represent distances between brickyards of less than 50km, while thick lines represent distances of less than 25km. Material sourcing and processing possibilities lead to embodied material performances and, therefore, support a high diversity and local articulation of clay bricks in buildings. Map by IW Foged (2014).

2. Robotically additive-manufactured bricks for the Thermal Tower Project (2018), based on developing thermally-designed concrete composite made through additive manufacturing processes. Photo: MB Jensen (2018).

3. Robotically additive-manufactured Thermal Tower Project (2018) in the Utzon Center Courtyard, Aalborg, based on thermally-designed concrete composite. Photo: IW Foged.

environmental and compositional advantages that, in turn, support the design and making of architectures that are treasured and maintained.

Concrete is an ancient material invented by the Romans, then forgotten, and later re-engineered in modern society. It is a composite of cement (as binder), an aggregate and water, with the ability to perform state-transition from fluid to solid through the chemical reaction of hydration. Similar to clay, cement is developed by heat processing or calcination, where the kiln is heated to 1,450°C. Hence, from a performance metric of embodied energy, concrete shares the same problems as clay bricks. An engineered composite, concrete's structural and thermal performances can be designed and configured by inducing air to create internal pockets, which alter its density, thermal conductivity and structural capacities. Air, therefore, becomes a performative ingredient of the composite. Similarly, when a few grams of colour are added to 1,000g of concrete, the composite changes its thermal properties, depending on the absorption of solar radiation, while structural properties are maintained. When water is added and mixed with the dry components, the composite design of cement, aggregate, water, air and colour forms a temporary fluid condition.

For robot-based layered additive manufacturing, the specific cement type and water content enabling the fluid state must be precisely designed to pass easily through pumps and tubes. Aggregates must be small and must not cluster if the speed of material flow changes, and the fluid material must be solid enough to allow additive layers to be added successively before the final hydration process solidifies the material. When all dynamic processes of the material composite interactions have taken place, the final material and form enter a combined articulated material performance. This material-form state is designed through a series of integrated processes between molecular material properties, processing techniques from kiln to robot, and the developed making hardware.

Systems

Turning a material into a product demands different types of processing, ranging from traditional craft methods such as chiselling, sawing or casting to highly automated cyber–physical systems, where production processes stretch from the digital realm into the physical space. These machinic systems enable higher productivity and efficiency at a potentially lower total cost compared to manual craftsmanship, but also greatly increase the complexity. Processes that were previously handled by a single maker may now require a team of professionals, from programmers who work with Computer-Aided Manufacturing software to application engineers, machine operators and quality assurance staff. The main costs therefore no longer relate so much to the manufacturing time, but rather to the preparation costs, as well as the required infrastructure.

For a long time, this move toward cyber–physical systems formed a significant gap between the individual makers who relied on their own mastery of tools and materials, and industrialised fabrication, which depends on highly accurate and expensive machinery. We can observe a change, however, as machines become increasingly accessible, in both a technical and a financial sense. That process is driven by expiring fundamental patents (such as in the case of 3D printing), greater demand, growing digital literacy among potential users, and a resulting interest in technology and innovation.

Machines are commonplace in industry, such as in the timber industry, where Computer-Numeric Control (CNC) machines can even be found in smaller

workshops. At the same time, we can observe the increasing proliferation of industrial robots, not only in experimentation-friendly environments, such as architecture or startups, but also within traditional fields that previously relied on manual making. The advantage of robotic arms, compared to regular CNC machines, is that they can be equipped with a wide variety of tools to perform myriad tasks. While the timber industry's requirements are mostly fulfilled by subtractive processes that are readily available in industry, the crafts are looking for ways to transfer their manual knowledge to machines, requiring the development of new hardware and software. So-called 'cobots' (collaborative robots) offer entirely new approaches to skill digitisation, combining a robot's accuracy and speed with safety and control over the applied forces.

New machinic possibilities previously reserved for large-scale businesses and research institutions are now opening up new fields of investigation for smaller companies. Within additive manufacturing, many startups are developing potentially disruptive innovations in their respective fields, such as 3D-printed concrete in architecture, as demonstrated by XtreeE in France and Mobbot in Switzerland. While the technologies underlying these evolving processes have been around for many years, it took until recently for them to enter the market and provide services. What is particularly interesting about these developments is that they are coming from within the architectural design community, rather than from engineering. The significant challenges that these innovators are facing are not just technological but also regulatory, as the standards differentiate between regular and 3D-printed concrete. To solve these problems, the community will need to collectively engage with regulatory bodies.

Futures

While the aforementioned materials may be considered somewhat old-fashioned, especially compared to more exotic material composites, they represent a significant part of the primary building fabric and are studied in numerous ongoing architectural research projects for additive manufacturing. The design and control of the material phase-state condition (being solid, liquid or gaseous) is central to the making process, which means that architects must understand and compose not only a material's end-state, but also its transformation processes and changing properties. Both concrete and clay are becoming favoured material substrates for additive manufacturing, precisely because they embed material performances from fluid to solid states. As familiar and tangible materials, they point to how we might describe and develop material performances for future manufacturing processes in architecture, and how these are tied to our abilities to understand complex dynamic material systems across time domains.

This future-orientated endeavour is helped by current technological developments, where machinic systems are no longer exclusive to high-end industry, but are also available to small enterprises, which account for the bulk of GDP in most countries. Innovations in making these machines accessible and affordable are, in turn, enabling startups to develop disruptive technologies, especially in the crafts field, where there is a constant demand for skilled labour. These technologies allow users to combine their in-depth knowledge of materials and manual processes with the advantages of machines – thus, not replacing labour but creating entirely new products and services. Most importantly, this innovation can happen within high-wage countries, keeping manufacturing within the region, minimising brain drain and reducing emissions from long-range transport.

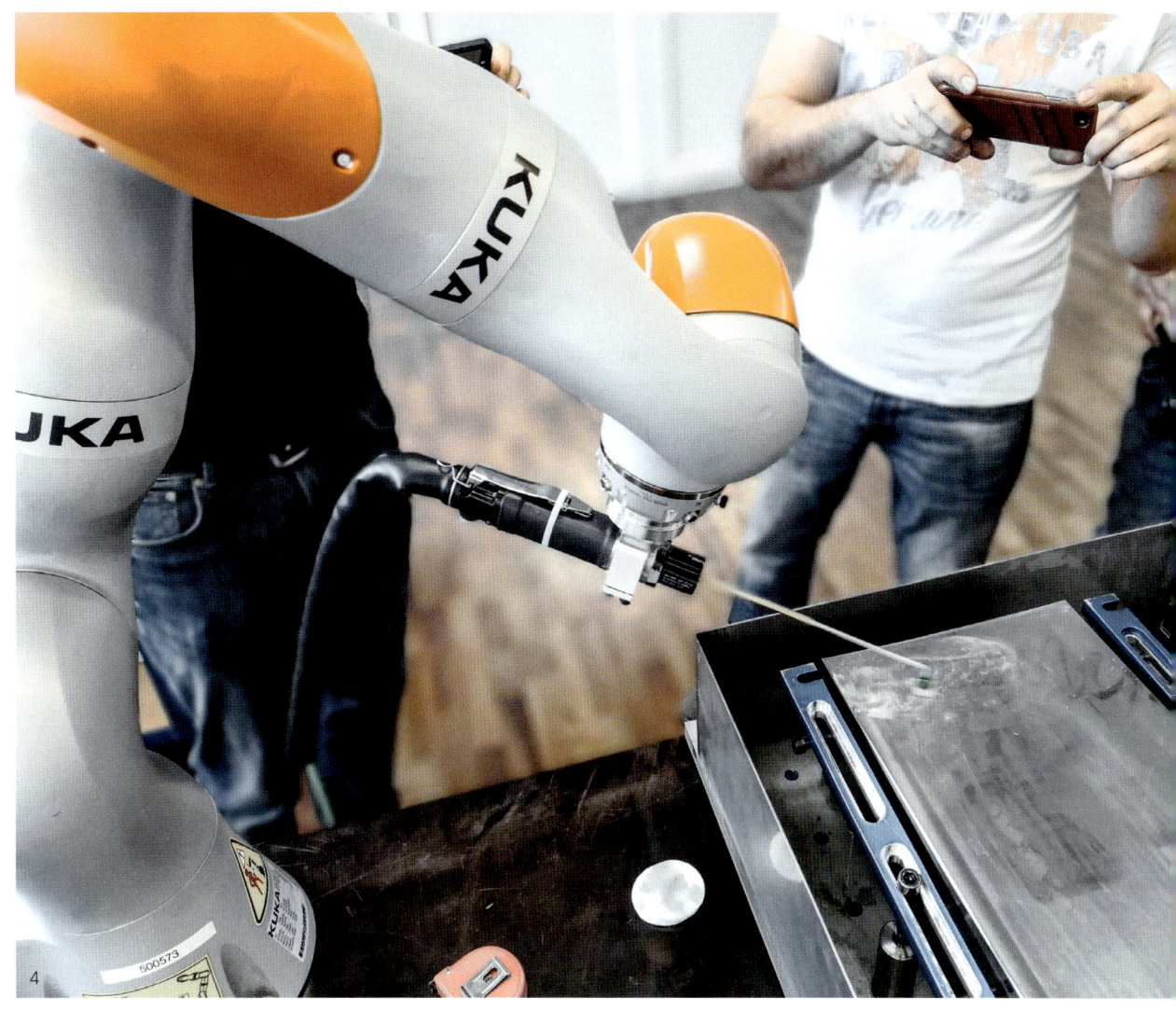

4. Machinic processes previously performed by hand are now transferred to 'cobots': automotive metal-polishing prototype. Photo: J. Braumann.

Reflections

5.1 REFLECTIONS

Innochain: External Perspectives

Visiting Scientists:
Mark Burry
Swinburne University of Technology, Australia
Christoph Gengnagel
Berlin University of the Arts
In dialogue with:
Anja Jonkhans
Institute of Architecture, University of Applied Arts, Vienna

Anja Jonkhans (AJ): I would like to start by asking what is the role of the Visiting Scientists and how were you engaged in Innochain?

Mark Burry (MB): To respond to presentations with our reflections on how new enquiries correlate to established research in the field, how emerging and emergent papers, presentations, exhibitions, conferences, etc. span both the science and art of the work.

AJ: You attended two Innochain colloquia some months apart, which gave you the opportunity to observe and measure rates of progress, varying approaches, and different combinations of academic and industry partner.

MB: Yes, there seemed to be a variety. Some candidates were embedded within ongoing group research projects, others were operating with greater levels of freedom, and some seemed to be seeking more constraint. Likewise, commitment from industry varied, where typically engagement relied on a key contact with a deep personal interest. So one of the key challenges for Innochain, and for future similar collaborations, is to seek some kind of normalisation in terms of expectations of how a candidate should be supervised. Located across five EU countries, this was inevitably a steep and complex challenge.

Christoph Gengnagel (CG): I can support this comment, because if I'm comparing the Innochain constellation with a PhD programme that we are running at the same time at the University of the Arts in Berlin, then I think there are several additional challenges. One of the specific issues in Innochain was the very different approach of the international academic environments to executing a PhD in the UK, Austria, Spain, Germany or Denmark. For me these differences became, at a certain point, a greater challenge than the expected frictions between industry and academia. Here, the completely different ideas about time and speed in academic and professional practices were an issue, although, on the other hand, the importance of a project like Innochain lies in precisely this difference between scientific or design exploration

1. Centre Pompidou Metz. Architects: Shingeru Ban. Modelling and Fabrication: Design-to-Production and Blumer Lehmann. Photo: SJB Kempter Fitze.

and professional developments. I took part in three colloquia, one in Copenhagen, one in Vienna, and one in Berlin. In all colloquia these aspects arose.

AJ: Industrial cooperation with academia is always crucial, and I think mostly depends on personal relationships as well. How would you define the relevance of the academic–industry partnership?

MB: The ideal scenario for me is one we've created in Australia called the 'embedded practice' model, and it has received Australian Research Council funding. The participating architectural and engineering practices had to cover one-third of the costs and the government two-thirds, which meant that the practices were paying a significant amount of money so they couldn't take the opportunity lightly.

The second thing that we did, which I think is really important for us, was to seek candidates who had already been working within practice for at least five years, and in a situation where they had reached a plateau, a situation from where they could see a massive loss of opportunity in the practice that they were in and an opportunity to make a difference. In other words, candidates who saw their PhD as a means to experiment on new ways of working within the practice.

Practice experience engenders knowledge on constraints that are different to someone coming straight out of university. So, I think the answer to that question is: how well did you get those things to happen? Industry or practice partners are mentors. Academics are supervisors. Each role must be easy to explain and not be hindered by the process.

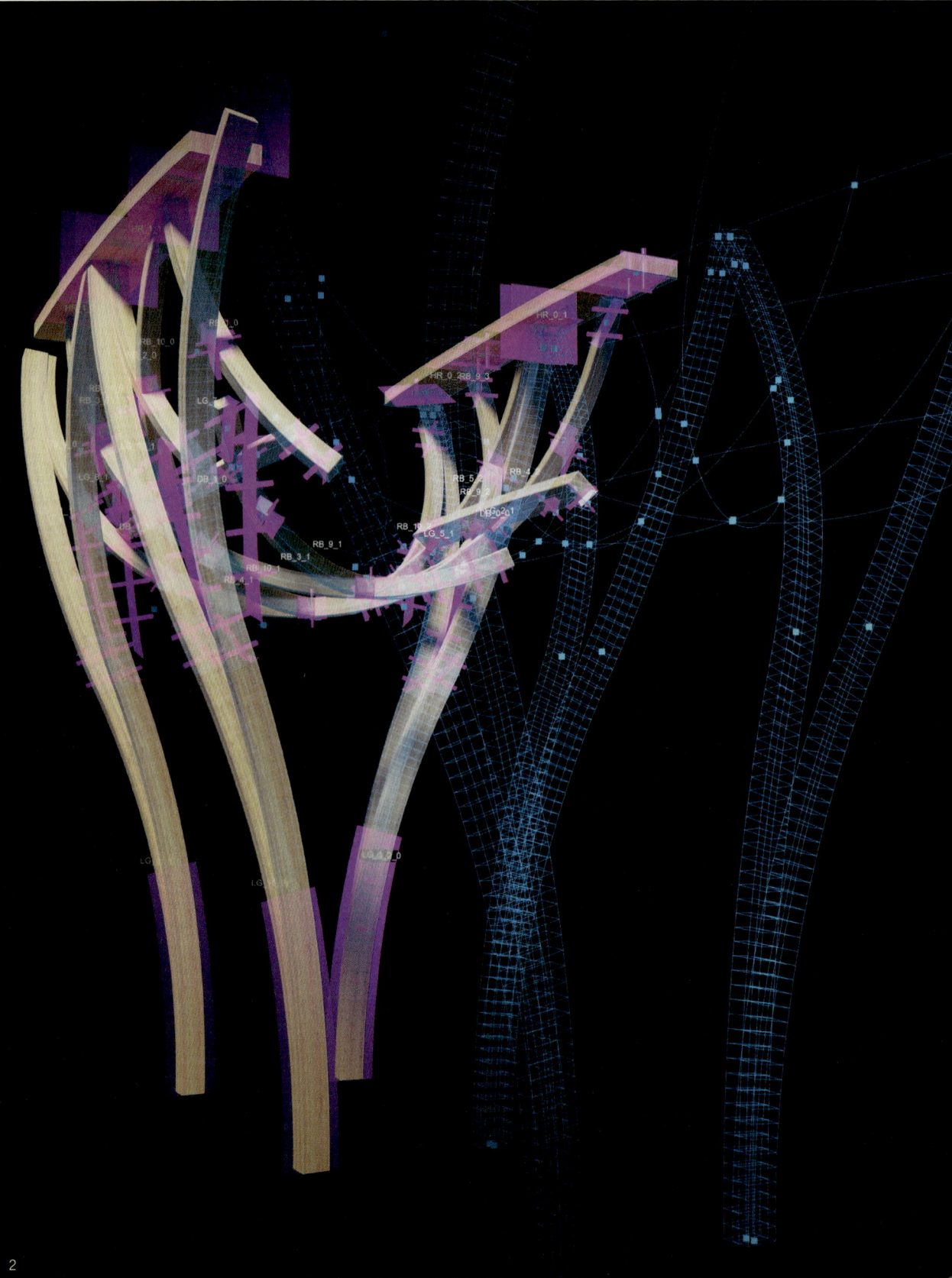

CG: Innochain has this configuration. The supervisors are from the academic side and the mentors from the side of the industry partners. But I see it as you expressed it: the commitment of the industrial partner and their agenda must be clear. Looking back, I would say that smaller companies, with very short communication channels, seem to be more agile and able to react well to unexpected situations in the research praxis. In addition, they are highly motivated to use and support the opportunity of in-house research and development, because normally they can't afford any investment in this kind of project on this scale. So, my recommendation would be to make such programmes more open and more attractive to small enterprises. This could be one of the findings of Innochain.

AJ: How would you define the urgency for collaborative design research with industry in the field of digital fabrication?

CG: For small-to-medium enterprises (SMEs) there's urgency because for them it's, as I said, very difficult to do or afford in-house research. Huge companies have better equipment and resources – sometimes better than small universities have, to be honest. Many large companies are also very focused on selling established products. We don't have enough huge companies that invest in research for building processes. Too many are focused on selling materials and products. What we call the building industry today is mainly an industry of material production. There's only a very small amount of innovation going on at a large scale.

MB: We've had probably 30 years of insignificant productivity gains in the building industry compared with manufacturing, which is why it's a difficult sector to find external funding from unless there's a climate of fear to milk, such as the digital isolation of practice at the turn of this century, when practices became aware that there were things they could be doing better, software that they could be accessing to give them competitive advantage, but they couldn't afford to take the risk to buy a full license. In this context, Innochain was perfect, because candidates, embedded in practice as researchers, had access to cutting-edge technology and a network of peers in the same boat.

AJ: Do you think we can already identify the potential consequences of Innochain research?

MB: You'd have to do a matrix that charts what were the differences they were seeking to make, what they set out to do and what they achieved, once the PhDs are finished.

CG: Some industry partners are already quite happy. The Speckle project, for example, developed at UCL with Henn in Berlin, is a successful case that got a tangible result, where the partner got a lot of interesting new ideas to improve their own work.

MB: So, what they would claim is that their moral high ground is that they facilitated a game-changing software environment?

AJ: Yes. They had influence in how the project developed, and without Innochain it wouldn't have happened.

CG: Yes, and the other point is, for the industry partners, I think they're using this because it was developed in dialogue with them. In Germany, I think we

2. Tom Svilans, digital production model of the MBridge prototype. Material performance and fabrication data are overlaid onto the design model, demonstrating the multi-scalar and integrative modelling approach to freeform glue-laminated timber structures.

have a slightly different situation from other countries, especially English-speaking ones. Architecture still has a super-conservative culture, which means there's only a very small number of architectural practices that are really trying to use computational tools processes, and so on, in the creative process.

MB: It's universal.

CG: So for the partners it was a real boost for internal discussion: is this really productive, is this helpful? So, I think for them it's positive, and they wouldn't have had this level of access to the tool and to discussions around the tool if they hadn't been part of the development team.

MB: That's a very good point, when the researcher becomes an agent of change in the office in terms of their work and practice, it's a great outcome.

AJ: Innochain is aiming to establish a new paradigm for design research for construction, can this be achieved?

CG: I was struggling with this question because, in some contexts, we still have a huge discussion about what design research means. We have yet to understand the term.

MB: My answer is that design research is tautology, because if design doesn't have any research in it then you're not innovating, you're repeating or you're copying or you're mimicking. So you can't possibly design something as a response to an idea or question unless you do the research. What I would say from Innochain is that it was yet another fantastic opportunity to prove that design *is* research. There's three ways of looking at it as far as I'm aware.

You can do research about design and that's the stuff I find incredibly tedious – the researchers who sort of look at designers and seek to explain to everybody else what designers do, and they come up with terms like 'design thinking'. For me it's like 'music thinking' or 'surgery thinking'. Then there's design for research, which is like 'I'm going to design a new cup, so I'm going to look at cups in history and see what I need to know about cups and why we need new cups. But then there's design *through* research, which is 'I'm designing a cup and I'm treating that process as research. As I design the cup, I'm going to reflect on what I'm doing, and I'm going to use that reflection to improve not only the design of the cup that I'm undertaking but all my design processes and therefore my designs in the future'.

In this sense, PhDs are excellent opportunities for designers because they are formalising the research aspect of design. Innochain really succeeded in that, and the good thing is it doesn't really matter what happens at the end, as long as the narrative of the candidate is one of investigation and a new understanding is articulated in their thesis that wouldn't otherwise have been achieved if they hadn't done that work.

AJ: Last question: If there's an Innochain 2, what should it address?

CG: There's a real urgency for the building industry to reduce its CO^2 emissions and consumption of resources. We are far too late with all this and we're part of a very conservative discipline. So for Innochain 2 or 2.0, whatever you would call this, it should have a strong focus on the crucial contemporary challenges in the production of the built environment. One aim, for me, would be to focus on increasing diversity in construction methodologies and in architectural design for specific local and regional contexts.

MB: I endorse that completely and would add that governments should lead this agenda by funding affordable housing and using this as a platform for innovation, because then you get everybody – engineers, architects, economists, builders and sociologists – all working together investigating how we transform fundamental operations. Such vital shifts in thinking and practice are not going to come from the market, that's for sure.

CG: I agree. We have to create new aims and conditions, because the market itself never will change the current situation fast enough or radically enough. The market needs pushing in the right direction.

MB: Innochain broke the ice, you've managed to get five EU universities from quite diverse communities to pool their intellectual resources, and it's always better to build a second bid based on the success of the first one. Personally, I think it would be good to do a matrix, and seek to establish the things that didn't work out and why (as well as capturing the successes). I'm sure all sorts of mechanisms will emerge to make sure the next iteration has even greater success.

Biographies

Zeynep Aksöz is a partner in the Vienna-based design research studio OpenFields. In her ongoing research, teaching and practice, Aksöz explores generative design processes in the collaboration between human and machine intelligence, in particular, design as an emergent process, co-authored by human and non-human agents. Aksöz was a Marie Curie fellow and Early Stage Researcher (ESR) in the Innochain European Training Network. As a result of this fellowship she has a technical doctorate from University of Applied Arts Vienna, that focuses on applications of AI and Machine Learning in the Early Design Phase.

Efilena Baseta is an architect and engineer whose interests lie in exploring material behaviours, both physically and digitally, in order to create innovative structures and optimise construction processes. She studied at the National Technical University of Athens the Institute for Advanced Architecture of Catalonia (IAAC) in Barcelona. In 2019, as an Innochain ESR, she received her technical doctorate with distinction from the University of Applied Arts Vienna. Baseta is an architect at Coop Himmelb(l)au; she is also a co-founding partner of Noumena – a multidisciplinary practice that focuses on digitalising designs and production methods, and merging computational strategies with advanced manufacturing techniques. Baseta has designed and coordinated advanced-construction exhibitions and has led various educational programmes internationally. In 2014 she received the 'Innovative Structure' award from IAAC and in 2018, she was awarded the Emerging Research Paper award by Autodesk. In 2019 she received a scholarship for the Young Academy from the Academy of Arts in Berlin.

Klaus Bollinger studied Civil Engineering at the Technical University Darmstadt and taught at Dortmund University. Since 1994 he has been Professor for Structural Engineering at the School of Architecture, University of Applied Arts Vienna; since 2000 he has been guest professor at the Städelschule in Frankfurt. In 1983 Klaus Bollinger and Manfred Grohmann established the practice Bollinger + Grohmann, now located in Frankfurt am Main, Vienna, Paris, Oslo and Melbourne, with around 100 employees. The office provides a complete range of structural design services for clients and projects worldwide, and have collaborated successfully with numerous internationally recognised architects. The scope of their work includes building structures, façade design and building performance for commercial, retail and exhibition facilities as well as classic civil engineering structures such as bridges, roofs and towers.

Charles Bouyssou is an architect and graduate of ENSA Paris – Malaquais (2015). He has worked for several years on architectural robotics and holds a strong IT background. Within XtreeE, Bouyssou focuses on the design, testing and commissioning of large-scale robotic systems for architectural applications.

Mads Brath Jensen is a PhD fellow at the Department of Architecture, Design and Media Technology at Aalborg University. Brath Jensen's research focus is on design methods and procedures, and how they can establish a direct link between architecture and interactive robotic fabrication, with an emphasis on interactive, real-time, human–material–robot processes. Brath Jensen teaches computational architecture, parametric design and rapid-prototyping technologies. His research-based teaching has resulted in a series of pavilions showcasing the interconnection between computational form-finding, material behaviour, thermal and acoustic simulation, and fabrication techniques.

Johannes Braumann is professor for Creative Robotics at UfG Linz, leading an interdisciplinary team of researchers exploring robots as an interface between the digital and physical world. As co-founder of the Association for Robots in Architecture, Braumann is tightly linked with both the robotics and design communities. He is the main developer of the accessible robot simulation and programming tool KUKAlprc, which is today used by more than 100 universities and 50 companies worldwide.

Maite Bravo is an architect, educator and researcher, studying concepts and design methodologies emerging from the use of digital design and its immersion into architectural praxis, with emphasis on robotic fabrication techniques and built shell-structures. She holds degrees from the University of Chile, IAAC, Universitat Politècnica de Catalunya, including a PhD with a 'Cum Laude' distinction from the latter. Her academic experience includes several universities including IAAC, LCI, and UIC in Barcelona; Strathclyde; and ETH Zurich, among many others. She is currently senior faculty at the British Columbia Institute of Technology, Canada. Her professional experience includes several architectural firms in Chile, GBL Architects in Canada, Barcelona Municipality and Barcelona Regional Agency, B3 architects, and MuDD Architects. She has received several awards for her built and research work (including the prestigious MIT ACADIA 2017 research award, and a Dezeen Awards 'highly commended' mention), for ongoing collaborations with Stephanie Chaltiel on Robotic Fabrication for Monolithic Earthen Shells.

Giulio Brugnaro is an architect, designer and researcher working in the field of robotic fabrication for architectural production. He is currently a PhD candidate and Marie Curie Fellow at The Bartlett School of Architecture, UCL, as part of Innochain. His research focuses on developing adaptive robotic fabrication processes and sensing methods that allow designers to engage with material behaviours and tool affordances to explore novel design opportunities. Brugnaro is also a Design Research Tutor on The Bartlett's Design for Manufacture MArch programme.

Stephanie Chaltiel is a French architect working with digital fabrication and natural materials. She began her career in Mexico and French Guyana, building houses by hand and promoting local cultures. After working for Bernard Tschumi in New York on the International Center for the Americas, OMA for the Monaco Hotel and Zaha Hadid for the construction phase of Les Pierres Vives in Montpellier, she started her own practice, MuDD Architects, in 2019. Her award-winning projects include Mud Shell in London and Terramia in Milan. They marry cutting-edge technology with raw materials and have been presented and exhibited worldwide, receiving the MIT ACADIA 2017 research award, a Dezeen Award 'highly commended' mention and being listed in the ICON Design 100 in 2019. Chaltiel has taught at SUTD Singapore, University of Westminster in London, The Architectural Association in London, Ravensbourne College in London, at the University of Brighton and more recently at Elisava Barcelona. As an Innochain Marie Curie ESR, she developed drone-spray technology for sustainable architectures.

Angelos Chronis is head of the City Intelligence Lab at the Austrian Institute of Technology (AIT) in Vienna and an Innochain Marie Curie Fellow at IAAC in Barcelona. In addition, he has taught at IAAC, UCL, TU Graz and IUAV University of Venice. Chronis is the general chair of Symposium on Simulation for Architecture and Urban Design (SimAUD) and a member of its steering committee; he is actively involved in scientific committees internationally. He has worked across many fields including generative design, artificial intelligence, virtual and augmented reality and interactive installations. His main research interest lies in the integration of simulation, optimisation and performance drive in the design and fabrication process, with a focus on computational fluid dynamics.

Kenn Clausen is an architect and computational designer at GXN, the research and innovation unit at 3XN Architects. His research and interests range from parametric modelling and robotic fabrication to workflow strategies and geometry development. Clausen is part of the team leading the digital design group, working to fuse architecture and innovation by utilising a data-driven approach at all stages of projects. He works with applied research across scales, from large-scale building projects to experimental prototypes. His current architectural work includes the design and development of parametric models, geometry optimisation and workflow strategies for the Olympic House in Lausanne, the New Fish Market in Sydney and the SAP Garden sports arena in Munich. Before joining GXN he worked at Electrotexture LAB in Denmark and UNStudio in Amsterdam.

Justin Dirrenberger is Associate Professor of Materials Science & Engineering at Conservatoire National des Arts et Métiers in Paris. He holds a PhD in materials engineering from Ecole Nationale Supérieure des Mines de Paris. His research is focused on architectural materials, additive manufacturing and multi-scale modelling. Dirrenberger contributes to various research and development programmes at XtreeE.

Moritz Dörstelmann is a registered architect and managing partner of FibR GmbH, a specialist company for computational design and robotic fabrication of bespoke fibre-composite structures, which enables the exploration of a novel design and construction repertoire for expressive high-performance lightweight structures. His work on digital fabrication technology provides socially relevant solutions for resource-efficient manufacturing and architectural construction, and explores integrative computational design methods as interface and catalyst for interdisciplinary collaboration. Dörstelmann developed the digital design and robotic fabrication strategies that underpin his work over seven years of research at the University of Stuttgart, Harvard University and as visiting professor for Emerging Technologies at the Technical University of Munich.

Romain Duballet is a structural engineer, graduate of the Ecole Nationale des Ponts et Chaussees and ENSA Paris – Malaquais. He has been working for several years on the topological optimisation of concrete structures. Alongside his work at XtreeE, Duballet is currently pursuing a PhD in the field of additive manufacturing of concrete structures at Ecole Nationale des Ponts et Chaussées and Ecole Nationale Supérieure des Arts et Métiers.

Al Fisher is a technical director and Head of Computational Development at BuroHappold. Based in London, he helps orchestrate code development across a decentralised global network of contributors. Encouraging a diversity of skills and experience – across engineering, computer science, architecture, construction and design – the aim is to empower mass-participation in tool creation through a globally accessible open coding framework. Fisher's background is in structural design computation, with a Master's and PhD in Civil and Architectural Engineering from the University of Bath. He has focused on performance-driven design and optimisation, applying these principles to projects such as the Louvre Abu Dhabi and the London Olympic Stadium Transformation. Most recently his research has focused on solving wider wicked-type problems and the subjective performance of co-authored distributed systems. He has a particular interest in the cultural and technological challenges of networked human–to–human and human–to–machine collaboration.

Nadja Gaudillière is an architect and a graduate of ENSA Paris – Malaquais (2016). She has been studying the environmental impact of additive manufacturing and its conditions of implementation in the contemporary construction context. She currently contributes to the supervision of XtreeE's prospective architectural and design projects.

Christoph Gengnagel studied structural engineering at the Bauhausuniversität Weimar and architecture at the Technical University of Munich; he has been working as a structural engineer since 1993. He was a founding partner of the engineering office a.k.a.ingenieure in Munich, and since 2013 has been a consulting partner with Bollinger + Grohmann Ingenieure. In 2005 he completed his PhD in Mobile Membrane Structures at the TU Munich. He was appointed as professor in the department for structural design and engineering at the Berlin University of the Arts in 2006; from 2012 to 2014 he held a guest professorship at the Royal Academy of the Arts, Copenhagen. Gengnagel's research focuses on computer-aided structural design and the development of novel material systems. His work has been published internationally.

Sean Hanna is Reader in Space and Adaptive Architectures at The Bartlett School of Architecture, and a member of the UCL Space Syntax Laboratory, recognised as one of the UK's highest-performing research groups in the field of architecture and the built environment in consecutive UK Research Assessment

BIOGRAPHIES

Exercises. His research is primarily in developing computational methods for dealing with complexity in design and the built environment, including the comparative modelling of space, and the use of machine learning and optimisation techniques for the design and fabrication of structures. It is often conducted in close collaboration with leading architects, engineers, artists, and technology producers. He has contributed to more than 100 academic publications addressing the fields of spatial modelling, machine intelligence, collaborative creativity, among others, and his work has been featured in the non-academic press, including *The Architects' Journal* and *The Economist*.

Anja Jonkhans is an architect working and teaching at the University of Applied Arts in Vienna. She received her Part 2 diploma and Master's degree in architecture from The Bartlett School of Architecture, UCL. Having worked for, amongst others, Alsop Architects and Grimshaw Architects in London, she was founding partner of Spacelab with Peter Cook, Colin Fournier and Niels Jonkhans for the Kunsthaus Graz Museum. Before teaching at the Angewandte she held a position as an assistant professor at the TU Graz between 2001 and 2004. Her teaching and research subjects are in the field of building construction and drafting techniques.

Ulrika Karlsson is an architect and founding member of the practices Brrum and Servo in Stockholm. She has a specific interest in the role of architectural representations and their translations, where we sometimes encounter the conflation of material and information. Karlsson is Professor of Architecture at KTH School of Architecture, Stockholm and a guest professor at Städelschule SAC, Frankfurt. She has taught at Konstfack, Stockholm; The Bartlett, UCL; and UCLA, Los Angeles. She received her Architecture degree from Columbia University, New York, and her Landscape Architecture degree from the Swedish University of Agricultural Sciences. She has contributed to numerous journals, curated exhibitions and exhibited internationally. KTH School of Architecture, through Karlsson, was an academic partner for Innochain. In 2018 she received a three-year artistic research grant for the project Interiors Matter: A Live Interior, from the Swedish Research Council.

Jan Knippers is a structural engineer and since 2000 has been Head of the Institute for Building Structures and Structural Design (ITKE) at the University of Stuttgart. His interest is in innovative and resource-efficient structures at the intersection of research and development and practice. In 2001 Knippers co-founded Knippers Helbig Advanced Engineering, with offices in Stuttgart, Berlin and New York. Key projects are the EXPO Axis for Shanghai in 2010, the Thematic Pavilion at EXPO 2012 in Yeosu, South Korea, and the Gallery at the Staatsoper Berlin, in 2017. In 2018 he founded Jan Knippers Ingenieure, to give personal attention to innovative projects, from concept to completion. From 2014 to 2019, Jan Knippers was coordinator of the collaborative research centre TRR141 Biological Design and Integrative Structures between the Universities of Stuttgart, Tübingen and Freiburg. Since 2019 he has been Deputy Director of the Cluster of Excellence in Integrative Computational Design and Construction, and Vice-Rector for Research of the University of Stuttgart.

Ayoub Lharchi is an architect and computational designer, interested in complex geometries and advanced digital-fabrication techniques. Lharchi has worked internationally, from Germany to the USA, and is currently a PhD candidate and research associate, as part of Innochain, at the Centre for Information Technology and Architecture (CITA), at the Royal Danish Academy of Fine Arts, Schools of Architecture, Design and Conservation in Copenhagen. His research focuses on assembly planning, sequencing and optimisation in complex timber structures.

Sean Lineham is a structural engineer at Arup's Copenhagen office. Lineham's research focus is the implementation of technologies, tools and processes that will aid design and foster creativity. He has worked on projects internationally with Arup, from stadiums to art installations. Lineham's recent work includes Camp Adventure Tower in Denmark and the Japan Pavilion for Expo 2020 Dubai.

Alban Mallet is an architect and graduate of ENSA Paris – Malaquais (2015). He has been working for several years on additive manufacturing processes and bio-sourced materials. At XtreeE, Mallet develops 3D printing processes for concrete, clay and polymers. He also contributes to the design of innovative large-scale additive manufacturing systems.

Mathilde Marengo is an Australian–French–Italian architect whose research focuses on the contemporary urban phenomenon, its integration with technology, and its implications on the future of our planet. Within today's critical environmental, social and economic framework, she investigates the responsibility of designers in answering these challenges through circular and metabolic design. She holds a PhD in Urbanism and is Head of Studies, faculty and PhD Supervisor in IAAC's Advanced Architecture Group, an interdisciplinary research group investigating emerging technologies of information, interaction and manufacturing for the design and transformation of the cities, buildings and public spaces. Working within the group's agenda of redefining the paradigm of design education in the information and experience age, Marengo carries out research, design and experimentation with innovative educational formats based on holistic, multidisciplinary and multi-scalar design approaches, oriented toward materialisation, as well as through EU-funded projects including Innochain.

Areti Markopoulou is a Greek architect, researcher and urban technologist working at the intersection of architecture and digital technologies. She is the Academic Director at IAAC, where she also leads the Advanced Architecture Group. Her research and practice seek to redefine architecture as a performative 'body' beyond traditional notions of static materiality, approximate data, or standardised manufacturing. Markopoulou is co-founder of StudioP52 and co-editor of Urban Next, a global network focused on rethinking architecture through the contemporary urban milieu. She is the project coordinator of a number of funded European Research Projects on topics including urban regeneration though data science, circular design and construction and multidisciplinary educational models in the digital age. Markopoulou has also curated international exhibitions such as *Future Arena* and *On Site Robotics* (Building Barcelona Construmat 2019 and 2017), *Print Matter* (In3dustry 2016), *HyperCity* (Shenzhen Bi-city Biennale, 2015) and *MyVeryOwnCity* (World Bank, BR Barcelona, 2011), while her work has been featured in exhibitions worldwide.

Morten Norman Lund has worked as a computational designer, architect and project manager at GXN since 2011, mainly working on research that focuses on material, sustainability and digital technology, as well as architectural projects. Norman Lund has been a part of GXN's digital fabrication project, Digital Factory, and is currently part of 3XN's work to integrate computational design research into the company's practice and workflows. Current architecture projects include the Cube, Berlin; Schüco Headquarters, Bielefeld; and Duale Hochschule Stuttgart.

Silvan Oesterle is an architect and researcher with special expertise in the field of computational design and digital fabrication. In 2010 he co-founded ROK, an architectural office in Zurich. ROK's work focuses on the development of integrated design processes at the intersection of design computation, engineering and digital fabrication. After graduating from ETH Zurich in 2007, he joined the Faculty of Architecture at ETH and conducted research with Professors Gramazio & Kohler. In 2013 he was a guest lecturer at the Academy of Fine Arts in Stuttgart. Since 2014 he has been a lecturer at the Accademia di Architettura di Mendrisio. Oesterle presents regularly at schools and conferences including the Architectural Association, CITA and SmartGeometry. Whilst at ETH Zurich, he received the Global Holcim Inovation Award for the research project TailorCrete.

Anke Pasold is an associate professor at the Material Design Lab, Copenhagen School of Design and Technology, where she is developing the technological side of the lab and structuring new educational programmes. Pasold's academic and research focus is on material practice, in particular advanced design methodologies and fabrication processes by means of experimental prototypes. Educated as both an architect and a cross-disciplinary designer, Pasold is co-founder of the research-based architectural studio, AREA, in Copenhagen, with Isak Worre Foged. The studio explores academic activities, material properties, design methods, generative systems and fabrication techniques.

Paul Poinet is currently a Research Fellow in web-based collaboration at The Bartlett School of Construction and Project Management, and Design Tutor at The Bartlett School of Architecture, UCL. Poinet is working within a consortium of partners – Arup, Speckle Works, BuroHappold Engineering, 3D Repo, Rhomberg Sersa Rail Group, HOK and Atkins – on the Innovate-UK funded project AEC Delta Mobility, which aims to increase productivity, performance and quality in the construction industry by streamlining data exchange, in an open-source manner, early on in the design process. Previously, Poinet was an Innochain ESR and PhD Fellow at CITA, collaborating with Design-to-Production and BuroHappold Engineering.

Arthur Prior is a specialist in digital manufacturing. He received a Marie Skłodowska-Curie scholarship for research in additive manufacturing at UCL as part of Innochain. Currently, Arthur works as a research and development engineer for Staedtler Mars GmbH in Germany and also as a senior teaching fellow on The Bartlett's Design for Manufacture MArch programme. Previously, Arthur worked as a 3D-scanning technician for the Madrid-based company Factum Arte, renowned for their ambitious public projects within the cultural heritage sector and collaborations with high-profile international contemporary artists.

Line Rahbek is a senior architect at Dorte Mandrup Architects in Copenhagen. Rahbek specialises in complex modelling and works on the studio's geometrically advanced and large projects, implementing Building Information Modelling (BIM) strategies and Information and Communications Technology (ICT) management. Over the past 14 years Rahbek has worked in international practices, including Zaha Hadid Architects, London; Gottlieb Paludan Architects, Copenhagen; and Cox Architecture, Melbourne, on projects including mixed-use high-rise buildings and rail transit. Rahbek has also taught at The Royal Danish Academy of Fine Arts, Copenhagen, and at RMIT University, Melbourne; and has been an invited guest critic at the Architectural Association and Central Saint Martins in London.

Mette Ramsgaard Thomsen is Professor of Digital Technologies at CITA, which she founded in 2005 at the Royal Danish Academy of Fine Arts, Schools of Architecture, Design and Conservation. Her research examines how computation is changing the material cultures of architecture. By investigating advanced computer modelling, digital fabrication and material specification in projects including Predicitve Response, Complex Modelling and Innochain, she has been central in the forming of an international research field examining advanced modelling method that integrate simulation and predict material behaviour. In 2016 she was awarded the Elite Research Prize for outstanding researchers under 45 years of international excellence by the Danish Ministry for Higher Education and Science. In 2018 she was appointed General Reporter for the UIA2023 world congress 'Sustainable Futures'.

Christopher Robeller leads the Digital Timber Construction group (DTC) at the University of Kaiserslautern. Robeller previously worked at the National Centre of Competence in Research Digital Fabrication, Zurich; IBOIS Laboratory for Timber Constructions EPFL, Lausanne; and the Institute of Computational Design (ICD) at the University of Stuttgart. Robeller's award-winning research on innovative timber structures, design for assembly and digital fabrication is widely published and has been implemented in experimental structures, including the X-fix Timberdome pavilion in 2018. Recent buildings include the timber-folded plate structure for the Théâtre *Vidy-Lausanne* in 2017 and the Multihalle Manternach in 2018.

Philippe Roux is an engineer and graduate of Ecole Nationale Supérieure des Arts et Métiers in mechanical and industrial engineering, as well as graduate of the University of New South Wales (Australia) in structural engineering, as well as ENSA Paris – Malaquais (2016). Roux focuses on the optimisation of 3D printed concrete structures and on helping XtreeE clients to operate large-scale 3D printing systems.

Jonas Runberger is an architect, research and educator, focusing on emergent technologies applied in practice. He heads Dsearch, and development team for computational design at White Arkitekter, where his team has been involved in over 80 Swedish and international architectural projects, as well as research projects. He is also Artistic Professor of Digital Design at Chalmers Department of Architecture and Civil Engineering in Gothenburg, heading the Architecture and Computation research group, and will be a research leader for architectural and structural design in the forthcoming Digital Twin Cities Research Center. Runberger was an industry representative in the Innochain project, with the role of integrating the research of PhD candidates into architectural projects. Previous academic positions include the Royal Institute of Technology from which he also holds a PhD (2012), the Architectural Association School of Architecture and the ETH Zurich.

Saman Saffarian is an architectural designer, technologist and researcher, and is currently the Associate Dean of Science and Research at the Faculty of Arts and Architecture at the Technical University of Liberec. As part of the Innochain network, Saffarian is pursuing a PhD in digitally and materially-informed design at the Institute for Building Structures and Structural Design (ITKE), University of Stuttgart. His research focuses on design development and manufacturing of climate-adaptive building envelopes and the potential of material gradient fibre-reinforced polymer (FRP) for kinetic architectural applications. Previously, Saffarian worked as a lead designer for Zaha Hadid Architects in London, delivering concept designs for projects and competitions of various scales and complexities. In collaboration with Zaha Hadid Architects Computation and Design group (ZHAICODE), Saffarian contributed to the development and fabrication of a number of experimental and research-based installations and exhibitions.

Gavin Sayers is a structural engineer specialising in lightweight and tensile structures. He studied Civil Engineering at City University in London and subsequently gained an MBA from the University of Bath. He started his professional career with Tensys Ltd, developing in-house software and providing form-finding and patterning consulting services to the tensile industry. Upon leaving Tensys he continued as a specialist engineer at David Dexter Associates, helping to realise a portfolio of projects including stadia, tensile structures, aviaries and extensive ETFE projects worldwide. Sayers has recently joined AKTII as a Director within their parametric applied research (p.Art) team where he continues to be fortunate enough to work alongside talented individuals in an exciting sector of the engineering field.

Fabian Scheurer is co-founder of Design-to-Production and leads the company's office in Zurich. He graduated from the Technical University of Munich with a diploma in computer science and architecture and gathered professional experience as a CAD trainer, software developer and new media consultant. In 2002 he joined Ludger Hovestadt's Computer-Aided Architectural Design (CAAD) group at the ETH Zurich, where he co-founded Design-to-Production as a research group to explore the connections between digital design and fabrication. At the end of 2006, Design-to-Production teamed up with architect Arnold Walz and became a commercial consulting practice, supporting architects, engineers, and fabricators in the digital production of complex design.

Peter Scully is Technical Director of B-made, The Bartlett Manufacturing and Design Exchange. He has worked in bespoke manufacturing for 25 years, developing a special focus on design at the interface between the disciplines, and has run companies that play a key role in the realisation of bespoke architectural and artistic works. Scully has worked with architects, engineers and artists, deploying holistic project stakeholder understanding throughout the full process to curate workflows toward buildable outcomes. He has contributed to a range of built projects internationally, deploying procedural and tacit knowledge within design.

Bob Sheil is Professor in Architecture and Design through Production at The Bartlett School of Architecture, UCL, and has been Director of School since 2014. He is the author of multiple book chapters, refereed papers, and articles on design, making and technology. He has co-designed and built six artefacts/built works, and his work has been exhibited internationally on eleven occasions. He has edited seven books, including three issues of *Architectural Design*: *Design through Making* (2005), *Protoarchitecture* (2008), and *High Definition: Negotiating Zero Tolerance* (2014), an AD Reader, *Manufacturing the Bespoke* published in 2012, and *55/02: A sixteen*(makers) Monograph* (also 2012). He is a Co-Founder of the FABRICATE conference and book for which he was Co-Chair and Co-Editor in 2011 (London) and 2017 (Stuttgart) and Co-Editor in 2020 (London).

Vasily Sitnikov is an architect and Innochain PhD researcher at KTH School of Architecture, Stockholm. Sitnikov's research concerns architectural technology, specifically the advancement of precast concrete design and production in consideration of contemporary environmental concerns and the development of digital fabrication. Sitnikov previously worked in a material science laboratory in Moscow, where he honed his knowledge of high-performance concrete, before pursuing a postgraduate degree in art and architecture at Städelschule, Frankfurt am Main. He then worked with Berlin-based artist and architect, Tomas Saraceno, on the design and development of large-scale installations.

Evy L. M. Slabbinck is a freelancer focusing on project development for Design-to-Production in Zurich. Until recently, she was a research associate and tutor at the Institute of Building Structures and Structural Design at the University of Stuttgart. Slabbinck gained her professional experience in various international practices, including Bollinger + Grohmann and Teuffel Engineering Consultancy, where she worked as a membrane engineer and computational specialist on several international projects. Her interests lie in structural and parametric design, form-finding and bending-active tensile structures. She has published and presented her work at international conferences and in journals, including the International Association for Shell and Spatial Structures (IASS) and the International Association for Bridge and Structural Engineering (IABSE). Slabbinck's PhD research, as part of Innochain, focuses on multiple states of equilibrium for bending-active (tensile) structures, in collaboration with Foster + Partners.

James Solly is a Director at Format Engineers and a teaching fellow at The Bartlett School of Architecture on the Design for Manufacture MArch and Engineering and Architectural Design MEng programmes. James previously worked at Ramboll UK and BuroHappold Engineering before taking an academic role at the University of Stuttgart between 2015 and 2018. At the ITKE, under Professor Jan Knippers, he was a member of the Innochain network: his research focused on the development of structural design methods for additively-fabricated glass and carbon fibre lattice structures. He returned to London in late 2018 where he continues this work toward a PhD, alongside his current professional roles.

Dimitrie Stefanescu is the founder of Speckle. He works as a senior software developer at Arup, where he develops open source and proprietary tools for digital design automation, data collection and computation globally across the firm and for the broader AEC industry, based on the open Speckle core. Previously, he was a Marie Curie Fellow at The Bartlett School of Architecture, as part of the Innochain network, where he initiated Speckle during his research into digital design communication.

Hanno Stehling is partner and head of software development at the digital building process consultancy Design-to-Production in Zurich, where he leads a team of architects and programmers developing digital tools for CAD-CAM workflows and general data management for both in-house and external use. He graduated with a diploma in architecture from University of Kassel, Germany. He has a background in computer programming and gradually focused his studies onto the intersection between architecture and computer science, joining a research group about parametric design led by Prof. Manfred Grohmann of Bollinger + Grohmann and Oliver Tessmann (now Professor of Digital Design at TU Darmstadt). After graduating, he worked as a freelance programmer and as computational designer for renowned architects including Bernhard Franken, before joining Design-to-Production in 2009.

Kåre Stokholm Poulsgaard works with applied design research in architecture and is Head of Innovation at GXN. He is interested in research and innovation in the built environment, specifically the way that digital technology impacts human wellbeing, work and learning, and what this means for design strategy. Alongside this, he is studying for a DPhil at the University of Oxford on how digital technologies impact human cognition and creativity, and what this means for creative practice and the organisation of work.

Kai Strehlke is working on the interface between digital data and CNC manufacturing of large-scale timber structures at Blumer Lehmann AG. Since 2016 he has been teaching digital manufacturing at the Bern University of Applied Sciences. In 2015 he was invited by the Technical University Graz in Austria as a Guest Professor at the Institute of Architecture and Media. Between 2005 and 2015 he built up and led the Department of Digital Technologies at the architectural office Herzog & de Meuron in Basel. He integrated a digital workshop in the office with different CNC technologies and with his team supported various projects on geometric issues as well as on parametric design. From 1997 to 2004 Strehlke researched and lectured at the chair of CAAD at the Swiss Federal School of Technology in Zurich and submitted his PhD with the theme of 'The Digital Ornament in Architecture, its Generation, Production and Application with Computer-Controlled Technologies'.

Tom Svilans is an architectural designer and researcher based at CITA. His research as part of the Innochain network focuses on the use of emerging technologies to reveal new design potentials in freeform timber structures, and how this can lead to new practices formed around a deeper engagement with material behaviours. As part of this research, Svilans collaborates with Swiss timber contractor Blumer Lehmann AG and multidisciplinary architectural practice White Arkitekter AB. This research has been presented and published internationally in a variety of forums and peer-reviewed publications. As an educator, Svilans is a Senior Teaching Fellow on the Design for Manufacture MArch programme at The Bartlett School of Architecture, UCL, and runs fabrication-based student workshops at other institutes in the EU.

Martin Tamke is Associate Professor at CITA. He is pursuing design-led research into the interface and implications of computational design and its materialisation. He joined the newly-founded CITA in 2006 and shaped its design-based research practice. Projects on new design and fabrication tools for wood and composite production led to a series of digitally fabricated demonstrators that explore an architectural practice engaged with bespoke materials and behaviour. His current work is characterised by strong interdisciplinary links to computer science, with a focus on Machine Learning and 3D sensing; structural engineering, with a focus on simulation and ultralight hybrid structures; and material science, with a focus on bespoke computational knit. Currently he is involved in the European research projects Innochain and Exskallerate, the Danish project Predictive Response and the industrial collaboration Precision Partners.

BIOGRAPHIES

Diederik Veenendaal is a structural engineer and parametric designer, working on lightweight structures and sustainable construction. He studied Civil Engineering at the University of Technology in Delft, and was a visiting student at the Louisiana State University (LSU) Hurricane Center, working on floating structures and buoyant foundations. He completed his Master's thesis on the topic of evolutionary optimisation of fabric-formed beams. He started his professional career at Witteveen+Bos engineering consultants in the Netherlands, working on the groundfreezing of the downtown stations of the North/South subway line in Amsterdam and the structural design for the largest tensioned-membrane roof in the Netherlands, De Scheg. He then joined the Block Research Group at the Institute of Technology in Architecture at ETH Zurich, Switzerland. While carrying out his doctoral research on flexibly formed concrete shell structures, he also co-edited the book *Shell Structures for Architecture* (Routledge, 2014), and coordinated the NEST HiLo project. He successfully defended his doctoral thesis in 2017 while also founding Summum Engineering in Rotterdam.

Valentin Viezens is a structural engineer. During and after his bachelor's degree, he worked in several engineering offices and was responsible for the planning of structures and construction details. He also worked as a teaching assistant for structural analysis and e-learning at the TH Nuremberg. In the laboratory for structural engineering and building informatics, he gained initial experience with experimental tests, 3D printing processes and measurement technology. His passion is to find solutions for constructive and architectural problems in wood and steel construction. He likes to code in Python, C / C ++, C #, Swift and Java to develop applications for Windows, iOS and Android. He is currently working as a research assistant on the development of plugins for computationally generated wooden structures in the DTC research group at TU Kaiserslautern.

Helena Westerlind is an architect and PhD candidate in the technology research division at KTH School of Architecture, Stockholm. Her work explores material strategies in additive manufacturing where she specifically addresses the relationship between robotic motion and material structures by applying principles of knitting in concrete deposition. As part of her interest in the history and prehistory of concrete, she is the initiator of the research project The Liquid Stone Cookbook, which traces entanglements between the human and the lithic from geological beginnings through historical recipes of artificial stone. She holds a degree in architecture from the Architectural Association, London and previously worked with Factum Arte in Madrid.

Isak Worre Foged is an Associate Professor at Aalborg University, where he leads research on adaptive architecture. Worre Foged's primary research objective is the ongoing formulation of a theoretical, methodological and operational framework for environmental tectonics, approached through environmental morphogenetic design methods and models, and adaptive, environmentally-sensitive physical systems. Worre Foged is co-founder, with Anke Pasold, of AREA, Copenhagen.

Philip F. Yuan is Professor at the College of Architecture and Urban Planning (CAUP), Tongji University; Visiting Professor 2019 at Massachusetts Institute of Technology (MIT); and Thomas Jefferson Visiting Professor 2019 at University of Virginia. His research mainly focuses on the field of performance-based tectonics in architecture as well as robotic fabrication. Yuan has published more than 10 books on this work and related fields in both English and Chinese. His research and projects have received many international awards, have been published and exhibited worldwide and have formed parts of several renowned museum collections, including the permanent collection of the Museum of Modern Art (MoMA) in New York.

Mahriz Zakeri is an architect and graduate of ENSA Paris – Malaquais (2015). She also holds a bachelor of science degree in surveying from Teheran University, College of Engineering. At XtreeE, Zakeri focuses on the development of large-scale additive manufacturing systems and on corresponding material science issues.

Additional images

Cover image: Digital production model of the MBridge prototype by Tom Svilans, Innochain Early-Stage Researcher and PhD Candidate, CITA.

p.2: Prototyping canopy components for the Elytra Filament Pavilion, developed in collaboration with James Solly. © ICD/ITKE, University of Stuttgart.
p.8: Stephanie Chaltiel presenting at the Innochain Project Mid-Review, at IAAC Valldaura Labs, 2017. Photo: Clara Orozco.
p.40: Innochain researchers Tom Svilans, Zeynep Aksöz and Dimitrie Stefanescu at Innochain 'Future Wood' workshop, Copenhagen, 2017.
p.90: Efilena Baseta presenting at the Innochain Mid-Review, at IAAC valldaura Labs, 2017. Photo: Clara Orozco.
p.142: Drone spraying by Stephanie Chaltiel. Photo captured by drone camera at *Practice Futures – Building Design for a new Material Age* exhibition, KADK, 2018.
p.202: Hanif Kara of AKT II presenting at the Innochain Conference 2018, 'Expanding Information Modelling for a New Material Age'. Photo: Philip Ørneborg.

Acknowledgements

There are many people to thank for their help in putting this book together: from the EU commissioners who supported the Innochain grant application, to staff at each of the academic institutions and industry partner organisations who assisted in administering research development, events, content, communications, travel and accommodation. The complexities of this task were handled with unerring elegance, efficiency, cooperation, partnership and friendship by all. We are grateful to Lara Speicher and the team at UCL Press for their support and guidance. Finally, the editors wish to thank Laura Cherry, our project editor, for her immense dedication, patience, and care – qualities that have made this book all the more valuable and enjoyable to read and share.

Design Transactions

Editors
Bob Sheil, Mette Ramsgaard Thomsen,
Martin Tamke and Sean Hanna

Project Editor
Laura Cherry

Design
Patrick Morrissey / Unlimited

Printing
Albe De Coker, Antwerp, Belgium

Copyeditors
Phoebe Adler and Amanda Dale

First published in 2020 by
UCL Press
University College London
Gower Street
London WC1E 6BT

Available to download free: www.uclpress.co.uk

Text © The Bartlett School of Architecture and the authors
Images © The Bartlett School of Architecture and the authors

A CIP catalogue record for this book is available from
The British Library.

This book is published under a Creative Commons 4.0 International license (CC BY 4.0). This license allows you to share, copy, distribute and transmit the work; to adapt the work and to make commercial use of the work providing attribution is made to the authors (but not in any way that suggests that they endorse you or your use of the work). Attribution should include the following information:

Sheil, R., Thomsen, M.R., Tamke, M., Hanna, S., (eds.). 2020.
Design Transactions. London: UCL Press.
https://doi.org/10.14324/111.9781787355026

Further details about CC BY licenses are available at
http://creativecommons.org/licenses/

Any third-party material in this book is published under the book's Creative Commons license unless indicated otherwise in the credit line to the material. If you would like to reuse any third-party material not covered by the book's Creative Commons license, you will need to obtain permission directly from the copyright holder.

ISBN: 978-1-78735-489-0 (Hbk.)
ISBN: 978-1-78735-502-6 (PDF)
DOI: https://doi.org/10.14324/111.9781787355026

The Innochain project received funding from the European Union's Horizon 2020 research and innovation programme under the Marie Skłodowska-Curie grant agreement No. 642877